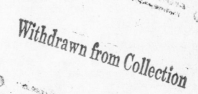
Acclaim for Michael Zielenziger's

SHUTTING OUT THE SUN

"Vivid. . . . Inspired. . . . Frequently disturbing but most often enlightening."
—*San Jose Mercury News*

"Michael Zielenziger's focus on the real people who make up modern Japan is what makes his book so fascinating. He shows what the change in Japan's overall fortunes has done to its citizenry, and how their response affects their country's future prospects—and its effects on the world. This is an important look at a limitlessly intriguing culture."
—James Fallows

"A pioneering effort. . . . Certain to gain deserved attention."
—*The Far Eastern Economic Review*

"An incisive, well-written account of Japan's recent social and economic malaise."
—*Kirkus Reviews*, starred review

"Consistently engaging and written with a good reporter's eye for colorful detail, *Shutting Out the Sun* is both fascinating and informative."
—*The Wichita Eagle*

"Michael Zielenziger offers us a classic, and a warning."
—Studs Terkel

Michael Zielenziger

SHUTTING OUT THE SUN

Michael Zielenziger is a visiting scholar at the Institute of East Asian Studies, UC Berkeley, and was the Tokyo-based bureau chief for Knight Ridder Newspapers for seven years. Before moving to Tokyo, he served as the Pacific Rim correspondent for *San Jose Mercury News*, and was a finalist for a 1995 Pulitzer Prize in International Reporting for a series on China.

Vintage Departures
Vintage Books
A Division of Random House, Inc.
New York

SHUTTING OUT THE SUN

How Japan Created Its Own

Lost Generation

Michael Zielenziger

FIRST VINTAGE DEPARTURES EDITION, SEPTEMBER 2007

The Library of Congress has cataloged the Nan A. Talese/Doubleday edition as follows:
Zielenziger, Michael.
Shutting out the sun : how Japan created its own lost generation / Michael Zielenziger. —1st ed.
p. cm.
1. Ethnology—Japan. 2. National characteristics—Japan. 3. Ethnopsychology—Japan.
4. Social values—Japan. 5. Japan—Economic conditions. 6. Japan—Politics and government.
7. Japan—Social life and customs. I. Title.
GN635.J2Z54 2006
305.800952—dc22
2005055940

Vintage ISBN: 978-1-4000-7779-3

Author photograph © Paula Bronstein/Getty Images
Book design by Song Hee Kim

www.vintagebooks.com

Printed in the United States of America
10 9 8 7 6 5 4 3 2 1

For Kenji

Contents

A Note to Readers

To outsiders, Japan often appears as a murky, mysterious, and insular society that, over its many centuries, has proven exceptionally difficult to pierce. One of the missions of this book is to make Japan's contemporary plight more accessible to those who were not born and raised there. To that end, I have adopted certain conventions to ease the foreign reader's path along the journey.

First, I have reversed the order of Japanese names to make them less confounding to Western readers, with given names preceding surnames. Thus, the prime minister is referred to as Junichiro Koizumi, the psychiatrist as Hayao Kawai—not the reverse as they normally would be rendered in Japanese. Both names are used on first reference whenever an individual is being properly identified.

However, I have also felt compelled to use pseudonyms to identify many of the individuals whose psychological conditions are addressed here, in order to protect them from the extreme social pressure Japanese can exert on those who refuse to conform to group standards and on those who choose to seek some form of psychological treatment. Hence, when a person is referred to by only a first name, i.e., Jun, or Hiro, this indicates that the person's name has been altered to protect his or her privacy.

It is important for readers to recognize, however, that the use of such pseudonyms does not alter the essential nature of the research and reporting this book contains. This is a work of nonfiction, a book composed entirely from real accounts. Though I have chosen to protect the identity of many people quoted herein, there are no composite characters or fictional descriptions contained within these pages. Though at times I have chosen to make the Japanese conversations a bit more colloquial, they represent complete and accurate descriptions of my interactions with these Japanese.

Without being able to assure many of my Japanese contacts that their true identities would be concealed and protected, I had little hope of being able to accurately convey their stories, or, in turn, their nation's fragile state.

Introduction

On a rainy June morning in 1993, Masako Owada, a twenty-nine-year-old Harvard graduate, trade negotiator, and diplomat's daughter, awoke at 4 A.M. in her parents' suburban Tokyo home to be trundled off by secretive emissaries from the Imperial Household Agency and purified with sacred waters. She then was bound inside a multihued, seven-layered silk kimono dominated by greens and oranges and that weighed nearly thirty pounds and, under the exacting direction of a phalanx of assistants, shuffled noiselessly into an austere cedar-wood temple within the shrouded grounds of Tokyo's Imperial Palace to take part in a mystical Shinto ritual.

As millions of her countrymen and women watched on their high-definition televisions, Masako and Japan's Crown Prince Naruhito sipped saké from separate cups, bowed to the Sun Goddess and then to each other, and left the shrine separately with their respective retainers, their wedding now officially sealed. Not once during the austere fifteen-minute ceremony did the newlyweds touch or kiss. The stillness was broken only when the prince offered a brief prayer in an archaic form of Japanese few of his countrymen could understand. Later, the newlyweds were paraded through the streets in a white Rolls-Royce convertible to accept the cheers of a nation brimming with joy.[1]

Eleven years later, in the spring of 2004, the Imperial Household Agency acknowledged that the crown princess—now forty, the mother of a young daughter, and mysteriously absent from public view—was suffering from an "adjustment disorder" whose symptoms included sleeplessness and anxiety. She would, the agency advised, be kept out of sight indefinitely while undergoing unspecified medical treatment.

*   *   *

The disclosure that the pressures of palace confinement had seriously unnerved the princess staggered her nation, and not simply because of the personal tragedy weighing on such a sympathetic and widely venerated figure. Masako was considered one of Japan's very best and brightest. A former top diplomat in the Foreign Ministry, she offered—with her cosmopolitan bearing and extraordinary international experience—the promise that her charisma and influence, as well as her striking good looks, might transform Japan's insular and hidebound government and soften the distant, forbidding image of the Imperial Family. She held the potential, many felt, to shake up the entire Japanese system from above.

Her setbacks, however, also signify something deeper and more widely tragic. Sixty years after the end of World War Two, contemporary Japan is at peace, but everyone who lives there knows something is wrong.[2] During three exhilarating decades of economic triumph Japan exercised its own unique brand of government-guided capitalism and seemed destined to outmuscle the United States, redraw the map of global influence, and take its place as the world's next superpower. Yet today its people remain afflicted with a habit of gloom, disappointment, and chronic underachievement. Like its crown princess, the nation and its young people seem to be teetering on the edge of a nervous breakdown.

*   *   *

Japan is a complex and enigmatic nation, dignified by a culture far more ancient than our own. It is a place where the traffic on the streets and the type in the newspapers flow from right to left; the opposite of white is not black, but red; and a can of hot coffee comes from a vending machine that bows graciously as it delivers it. Japan also embodies a unique civilization, one that rocketed into the modern world without acquiring the same values, norms, and modes of thinking most inhabitants of advanced and prosperous nations today associate with modernity.

For two hundred and fifty years, until pried open by U.S. Commander Matthew Calbraith Perry and his four heavily armed "black ships of evil" in 1853, Japan had existed as a *sakoku*, or closed country, which burned the vessels of any merchants who mistakenly sailed into its waters and killed any countrymen who strayed offshore.[3] Perry sought to open Japan for trade and commerce, but the Japanese were astonished, frightened, and ultimately impressed by the wondrous machines these uninvited gatecrashers brought to their shores: a sewing machine, a telegraph, and a steam-powered quarter-gauge model railroad the intruders set up to run along the beach, a contraption that so beguiled the samurai warriors, they were soon clambering aboard for a spin.

Japan rushed to modernize quickly, determined that its people would never be forced to grovel before Western invaders, and set out to guide the modernization of greater Asia, a path that would ultimately lead to colonization and war. In its rapid transition from rice field to factory, Japan's leaders sought to maintain a strong government at the center of its economic life to restrain unbridled competition and to control scarce resources, including capital. By maintaining its tribal uniqueness and asserting group-enforced social harmony, Japan also hoped to avert the invidious consequences of industrialization—especially the gap between rich and poor of which Karl Marx had warned, a gulf starkly evident in most Western capitalist societies.

After the horror of the atomic bombings that ended World War Two, Japan's economy and infrastructure were a shambles, and this small island nation found itself starting up anew. Yet, under the sheltering umbrella of the United States, which furnished military protection and opened its consumer markets to Japanese imports, the nation staged a remarkable recovery, one in which the corporate world, the government bureaucracy, and the nation's political leaders evenly meshed their communal goals to focus on a single goal—national prosperity. Never in modern times had a society so successfully achieved such an aim. The government determined which industries to encourage and which technologies to invest in, and manipulated finances to keep corporate borrowing costs low. Hierarchy, consensus, and obedience ruled the corporate world, together forging an ideal of "group harmony." With skillful planning, high savings, and hard labor, Japan soon became a leading steelmaker, car producer, and shipbuilder in its quest to "catch up." In the process, children were swept along from grade school to high school and then placed into jobs they kept for life. In so many important respects, Japan's seemed the ideal system for the industrial age.

By 1990, when I arrived in Silicon Valley to study international business on a fellowship at Stanford University, the Japanese challenge was very much a fixation of the American mind. The U.S. semiconductor industry reeled from the Japanese onslaught; American carmakers watched anxiously as companies such as Toyota and Honda sliced off fat hunks of market share with their fuel-efficient, durable models. The Pebble Beach golf resort was now in Japanese hands—as were most of the skyscrapers in downtown Los Angeles and the towers of Rockefeller Center, the symbolic heart of Manhattan. Japan had become America's major creditor, while America's trade deficit and unemployment soared. Whatever you called this contest, Japan seemed to be winning. It wowed us with its work ethic and impressed us with its relentless obsession for getting details right.

It wasn't just Japan's success that worried Americans; it was that Japan prospered by doing so many things differently. Business and government worked arm in arm, often limiting financial returns to enhance social stability. Industries invested for the long term, received steady infusions of capital, and guaranteed their workers a job for life, unlike U.S. firms obsessed with measuring their profits each quarter. So committed to constant, continuous improvements were factory workers that the consistently high quality of their output humiliated their average American counterparts, and there was seldom conflict visible on the Japanese factory floor. Japan's opaque political system, in turn, seemed to bleach out contention. Citizens believed their leaders to be competent and hardworking, dedicated to furthering national goals. Unlike Americans, who saw their officials as incompetent, lazy, or corrupt, Japanese wished that their children might grow up to be bureaucrats. Not only did Japan's burgeoning prosperity fail to drive a chasm between rich and poor, but selfless corporate leaders moderated their salaries in the interest of group harmony, and nobody went to court to settle their differences. Japan had achieved an ideal: a vast middle-class culture.

The Japanese challenge extended from the workplace to the classroom: its schools turned out a higher percentage of graduates better trained for the industrial age than their American counterparts. Nearly everyone who wanted a job found one. The poverty rate was exceedingly low. The trains ran on time, the platforms were antiseptically clean. Japan had entered the club of the world's wealthiest without the social baggage—the urban ghettos, the disaffected underclass, the plague of drugs and violence—that tormented Western society.[4]

At cocktail parties and academic conferences, terms like "competitiveness" and "patient capital" and "targeted investment" in technology reverberated in the halls and filtered into the national political debate. A slew of books were published examining the elusive elements and secret management schemes that had shot Japan skyward. Forecasters predicted the emergence of a new region, now dubbed the "Pacific Rim," with Japan at its hub, as the world's next growth arena. When you buttonholed Silicon Valley chief executives and asked them what skill they wanted their top managers to acquire urgently within the next five years, most said, without skipping a beat, "Learning Japanese."

*   *   *

Then in 1989, Japan's speculative bubble collapsed.

At nearly the same time, the world outside Japan was being turned upside down. The collapse of the Berlin Wall ended the fifty-year battle between communism and capitalism. The demise of the Cold War redrew the world's political map, creating new competitors and new markets. Economic paradigms shifted, too. A new, mobile, global "knowledge economy" not only spawned whole new industries, but radically altered the definitions of economic value, relegating "metal bending" and basic industrial manufacturing to a lower tier than innovative design, supply-chain management, and systems integration. Mental labor supplanted physical exertion, software trumped hardware, and financial engineering and services flourished. As the world stepped boldly into this novel, global information age, an Internet era of digital commerce subverted old models. Modern technology compressed time and space. It emphasized flexibility and risk-taking and dispersed innovation in ways that challenged the core strengths upon which Japan's vertically integrated conglomerates had traditionally relied.

Innovation tends to flourish in a complex habitat like the variegated ecosystem of a rainforest, where a diverse selection of birds, grasses, insects, and animals randomly rub up against one another and cross-pollinate, adapting to one another's spontaneous behaviors. The new world powered by information technology placed a premium on the transformative power of innovation. It seemed to promise individuals better access to knowledge, more power to influence others, and greater means for self-expression. It rewarded critical thinking, customization and agility in serving a market more than repetition and unity.

Yet in its remarkable sprint for industrial growth, Japan had never created such a diverse and forgiving microclimate. Instead, it had contrived the monoculture of a rubber plantation, where ruler-straight rows of identical trees are planted equidistantly, tended uniformly, and allowed to grow only to a prescribed height so they can be tapped most efficiently. Japan had prospered in a relatively closed and regimented world, where business and government worked hand in hand to lash together collective values, where foreign innovators or investors were systematically kept at bay, and where group-oriented discipline, hierarchy, and gradual consensus-making guided almost all behavior and had for generations restrained individual initiative. Some observers have suggested that the nation was never able to work through the psychic consequences of the atomic bombings that ended World War Two, and so instead focused narrowly on bulking up its economic biceps and pectorals. When a wholly new system of global commerce appeared, however—one involving innovation, adaptability, and creativity—it proved especially unnerving to this

Japanese regimen. As the fleet and flexible began gaining traction in other parts of the globe, Japan seem to slip farther behind. It had become muscle-bound, locked into an inflexible system that deadened any demands for change and seemed unable to bend without breaking.[5]

When I moved to Japan in 1996 to cover the country and run a newspaper bureau in Tokyo, I expected to witness the resurgence of the world's economic dynamo. Japan was the future, the builder of bullet trains and video games, and I was eager to see how Asia's leader in high technology, manufacturing, and finance would reassert its global dominance in semiconductors, automobiles, and consumer electronics. Though a few years of shuddering stock market declines and financial uncertainty had taken its toll, the world felt as certain as I did that Japan was readying itself for reinvention and rebirth.

Yet the world and I were wrong.

The Japan I encountered was unable to rejuvenate itself after a mysterious "lost decade" of financial failure and slowing growth. It seemed without the power or will to overhaul an ossified political system. Indeed, Japan systematically stifled change and resisted innovation rather than allow itself to be swept into this fluid and more global era, and I had trouble understanding why.

Many nations experience periods of economic turmoil and painful adjustment—America's "Internet bubble" crashed, too—but no nation has lagged so persistently as Japan since the collapse of its speculative "bubble economy" in 1989. Exhausted, traipsing through a wilderness without a compass, the nation suffers rising joblessness, especially among young adults, crushing national debt, and an unprecedented deflation that hammers prices, wages, and self-confidence. It also lacks the innovation and leadership to guide its revival. A nation that had grown wealthy through its unstinting focus on exports and on its manufacturing prowess, and relied on top-down planning to guide national policies of industrial investment, suddenly found these old formulas counterproductive.

Now in 2007, more than fifteen years after first stumbling into recession, Japan is viewed around the globe more with hesitation than with adulation, with indifference instead of fear. Over the past decade, the nation's average growth has barely nudged 1 percent, making it the worst performer among the world's wealthy countries belonging to the "rich man's club" of the Organization of Economic Cooperation and Development. By the last quarter of 2004, Japan had once again plunged into recession only to rebound modestly by the second half of 2005. Where political leaders and business executives had once worried about an economically dominant Japan becoming too assertive, they now worried that a frail and faltering Japan could destabilize the global economy or be elbowed aside by fast-rising China. After this "lost decade" of economic stasis, retrograde politics, and promises unfulfilled, many business executives and political leaders have all but given up hope for Japan's rapid and sustained revival. It is a remarkable reversal: few American parents today want their child's school to emulate a Japanese classroom.

Americans still buy Toyota automobiles and Sony DVD players, but these products are now manufactured in Kentucky and Malaysia. To those who still follow the process of economic integration within Asia, Japan—once viewed as a potential region leader—is now viewed more as a spent force, a marginal also-ran among the global field of economic competitors. Although some Westerners remain interested in Japanese *anime* and aesthetics, its architecture and artifacts, or are charmed by cultural icons like sushi and ikebana, they no longer believe that they need to emulate or cultivate the peculiar customs and codes that govern Japanese business and social practices. For those focused on commercial opportunities in Asia, the emergence of China and its feeder network of entrepreneurs and investors based in Hong Kong and Taiwan have gained primacy, while on the horizon India beckons. Japan's moment seems to have passed, its sun eclipsed.

The most ominous aspect of Japan's long stagnation—far beyond the obvious symptoms that regularly crowd the business pages—is the plight of its people. Young Japanese today face their own forms of adjustment disorder and concoct disturbing new ways to escape a society that annihilates their hopes and washes out any promise of self-realization in a torrent of rootless materialism. "From social mores, to art and culture, everything is two-dimensional," writes the *anime* artist Takashi Murakami of his seething, uneasy nation. "[Japan is] a place for people unable to comprehend the moral coordinates of right and wrong as anything other than a rebus for 'I feel good.' Those who inhabit this vacant crucible spin in endless, inarticulate circles."[6]

This pervasive distress is reflected in Japan's plummeting birthrate—which now ranks among the lowest in the world—and in the nation's diminishing population, which began to shrink, in absolute terms, in 2005, when the number of deaths surpassed annual births by some ten thousand.[7] This sharp decline can be attributed to women who marry later, if at all, because they don't want to give up their independence to raise children in an unhappy environment; or who, if married, decide that having children is a poor investment of their time and energies, and so refuse to bear them. Radical dissent is also reflected in the proliferation of suicide—Japan has the world's highest rate among wealthy industrial nations—as well as in the growing number of group suicides committed by complete strangers who meet on the Internet in order to die together. Alcoholism and depression are rampant, if seldom discussed, manifestations of adjustment disorder, while exhaustion and overwork claim thousands of casualties each year.

Frustrated and disaffected, many young Japanese just abandon their homeland. Hundreds of thousands of others wander like nomads outside the rigid traditional system, refusing to work, go to school, or accept job training. Even more disturbing—perhaps most disturbing—is the cadre of more than one million young adults, the majority of them men, who literally shut themselves away from the sun, closing their blinds, taping shut their windows, and refusing to leave the bedroom in their homes for months or years at a time. Thus, the anguish the Imperial Family discreetly confronts behind stone palace walls reflects a crisis now being visited on the wider family of Japan.

* * *

What happened to Japan? How did a nation poised to dominate this dawning Asian century, as well as entire sectors of the global economy—

on its own terms and through its own highly architected patterns of business and social relations—lose its way? Why has Japan been unable to
right itself and regain its old self-confidence? When and how did the
strengths of the Japanese system become weaknesses? And what can this
teach to those of us who live in the United States or in other wealthy
nations?

On a strategic level alone, Japan's future should matter deeply to
Americans. For sixty years, Washington's close bond with Tokyo cemented the peace within a restless, unstable Asia which even today lacks
a common language, a common currency, and deeply rooted institutions
like NATO or the Organization of African Unity. Now that an assertive
new China is emerging to claim its place on the world stage, America's
ability to wield influence throughout the region will be monumentally affected by how Japan adjusts and adapts to meet that rising presence.
America's domestic economy will also be weakened if Japan cannot
reemerge as a dependable engine of growth in an integrated, interdependent world.

On a deeper level, however, the decline of a great power like Japan is
relevant—or cautionary—to citizens of other great nations, who, like
Americans, wonder whether their society, too, might someday lose its vital gift for reinvention and renewal. Like the United States, Japan has for
decades been pampered in material comforts, coddled by its own hubris
and sheltered in its technological sophistication. Like America, it believes that only its unique ways of conducting business and interacting
with the world—methods that were so effective throughout its history—
can continue to sustain a sense of blessed superiority. Like America,
Japan faces the challenges of globalization and of competing in an information age against hungrier rivals without necessarily being willing to
make the drastic sacrifices at home that might be required to overcome
them. And like other great powers in history—and like the United States
in the age of Iraq—its most powerful and entrenched leaders have often
sought to preserve their own interests without regard to the costs such
policies might impose on the nation's innocent and most vulnerable.
Rather than embrace tolerance, compassion, and flexibility as necessary

dimensions of modern life in a complex ecosystem, they have sought refuge in a flat, fundamentalist universe that marginalizes the "strange" and the uncomfortable, and dares not give dissenters their voice.

Also like Americans, Japanese face the paradoxical challenge that wealth creates. For only in societies blessed with unrivaled prosperity do people have the luxury to consider what it is that truly makes them happy. When the pursuit of material extravagance delivers emptiness rather than inner contentment, a people are forced to confront deeper, more existential questions about meaning, value, self-affirmation, and moral purpose that classroom training alone cannot teach. Exploring this inner dimension demands a different vocabulary, one that wealthy nations often deemphasize and deny amid their constant chase for expansion and greater prosperity. To pose such courageous and fundamental questions is, after all, to subvert the underlying mission by challenging its objective.

While wealthy nations share many common challenges, Japan's particular history, social institutions, and economic architecture also set it apart from others. Indeed, no other nation has more stubbornly defied the comprehension of outsiders. Experts in macroeconomics, for example, are frequently stunned that the models they devise for "normal" market economies simply don't work in Japan. Political scientists find it remarkable that in a nation that has endured fifteen years of bad economics, the political structure has not faltered nor have street protests broken out among its increasingly disaffected citizens. Likewise, Western social psychiatrists find it puzzling that inhabitants of a nation as wealthy as Japan score so low on global measurements of subjective well-being, or that the term "self-esteem" does not exist in Japanese.

I, too, often found myself puzzled and distressed, unable to explain Japan's palpable if inarticulate crisis coherently to outsiders, until I began to hear the stories of men like Kenji, thirty-four, who dares not leave his room, or angry Jun, twenty-eight, who bicycles through the darkened streets of Tokyo some nights to work through his frustration and fear. These are two of the more than one million young adults, fearful, isolated, intelligent, and alone, who barricade themselves in their rooms for protection rather than attempt to engage with a society they feel denies them any expression of self. As I entered their mysterious world and got to know some of these extraordinary men, I sensed that understanding Japan through their eyes could offer a whole new perspective on the nation's festering malaise.

In this book, rather than focus primarily on politics or economics, my aim is to unravel the unusual social, cultural, and psychological constraints that have stifled the people of this proud, primordial nation and prevented change from bubbling up from within. First, I examine the plight of the *hikikomori*, the young men who lock themselves in their rooms and find little solace in the larger society. After looking into their lives and those of their parents and caregivers, I explore the history and culture in which their tragic stories are embedded to approach some explanation for Japan's contemporary social deadlock. Then I examine a cluster of behaviors that seem more familiar to Western readers: the fixation on consumerism and brand names in the search for identity; women's painful lives and their reluctance to wed and have babies; and, finally, the high incidence of suicide, depression, and alcoholism. Then, I broaden the view to see how Japan stacks up against its closest neighbor and rival, South Korea. Though these two nations share so much history and culture, I explain the underlying forces which allowed South Korea to rebound smartly from economic crisis while Japan still lags. I also assess how the United States, Japan's protector for the past sixty years, contributes to Japan's profound adjustment disorder, even as Japan permits the United States to prolong its own unsustainable course. Finally, I speculate on how Japan's own survival strategy may come to resemble those of the *hikikomori* who negate themselves and their adulthood, and shut out the sun of vigorous self-affirmation and moral purpose.

In dissecting this very different culture, my goal is to describe and analyze, rather than argue a narrowly focused point of view. I do this deliberately, for when it comes to the nature and pathologies of many of the syndromes I will try to disentangle, there is still a great deal we don't know—a testimony to the relatively shabby state of social science and psychological research within modern Japan as well as to the low status afforded to such inquiry. I also believe that as a Westerner, cast inevitably as an outsider looking inside a very closed world, it is imperative that I use as many Japanese voices as often as possible to elucidate behaviors and describe their own society.

Tragically these are not subjects the Japanese themselves normally choose to discuss. Indeed, they often likened their society to a duck pond, whose tranquil mirror-smooth surface hides the legs churning furiously below the waterline to keep their places in the flock. One day, over a beer at a fireworks-viewing party in a Tokyo suburb, I spoke of my concern about Japan's social dislocation with a journalist recently retired from a powerful Japanese newspaper. He confided that he, too, was deeply anxious about the nation's passive acceptance of failure; its bankrupt banks and corporate malfeasance, rampant political corruption, and the rising pessimism of its people.

"Half the people don't know how bad things are," he told me. "The rest are in denial."

Not just the Japanese live in denial, however. By exploring the deeper inner recesses a people keep hidden, I hope to show that shattering the smooth, glassy surface of a society's appearance represents the first crucial step toward its renewal.

1.

"AN ARROW POINTED DEEP INSIDE OF ME"

He pedaled feverishly down the narrow back streets of Kanda and Asakusa, legs churning, his face—intense dark eyes, a well-trimmed mustache—obscured by his bicycle helmet. He cruised past the silent storefronts selling rice crackers and stationery, past the ancient wooden Senso-ji shrine surrounded by shuttered souvenir stands, and darted through darkened alleys and deserted streets, his mind disengaged from the outside world, the rhythms of J-Wave radio reverberating through his headphones, the beat propelling him forward, no destination in mind.

Manic, angry, indomitable, Jun pumped fast, faster, through these ancient neighborhoods heavy with his history, his legs almost flailing, his knees driving hard. Sweat beading his forehead in the humid night, he sliced through the low-slung neighborhoods of Tokyo's old downtown, the working-class flatlands along the banks of the Sumida River, far removed from the aristocratic, hillier districts to the West, deathly still in the hours after midnight, the road illuminated only by the arc of a few scattered streetlights and the eerie blue fluorescence of the ubiquitous Family Mart and 7-Eleven convenience stores. Later he might stop at one to browse through its huge array of comic books and purchase a polyethylene bottle of orange drink to slake his thirst.

These tranquil few hours before dawn are strangely precious to Jun. Only in this empty calm can this wiry twenty-eight-year-old work off his restless anxiety. Only on these rare dark nights when he can gather the courage to venture out of his tiny room, can Jun be in the world yet be himself, and escape for just a few hours the confinement of a bedroom that has become his citadel. Being alone seems to him his only mode of self-preservation.

"I have an arrow pointed deep inside of me," Jun said to me once, as he sought words to describe his pain. "Listening to music and getting high from the exercise, that's the way I coped. At night you can go out when other people can't see you . . . If I didn't go out at all on those nights," he added darkly, "I'd probably have done something violent to my parents."

*   *   *

Jun is not alone in his pain and anxiety. Nor is he uncommon in his solitude. There is also gangly, nineteen-year-old Hiro, whose long hair nearly obscures his face, who dropped out of junior high when he was thirteen and lives at home uneasily with his bickering parents, seldom stepping outside. Hiro has no idea what he's going to do with himself as he emerges into adulthood. And there is thirty-four-year-old Kenji, who almost never leaves his tiny room in his mother's modest apartment on Tokyo's western fringe. He is a pale, quiet child-man, his smile wan, his hair thinning. For most of the past twenty years, his daily rituals have seldom varied. He reads the newspapers each morning and watches Tokyo Giants baseball games on television every summer evening. He passes long afternoons with magazines and daydreams. Sometimes he speaks to his mother. Other days he sits silent, deep in thought. Anxious, trembling, and alone, Kenji is scared—too scared and too scarred to venture into the world beyond his front door.

Across Japan, more than one million men and boys like Jun and Hiro and Kenji have chosen to withdraw completely from society. These recluses hide in their homes for months or years at a time, refusing to leave the protective walls of their bedrooms. They are as frightened as small children abandoned in a dark forest. Some spend their days playing video games. A few—an estimated 10 percent—surf the Internet.[1] Many just pace, read books, or drink beer and *shochu*, a Japanese form of vodka.

Others do nothing for weeks at a time. Unable to work, attend school, or interact with outsiders, they cannot latch onto the well-oiled conveyor belt that carries young boys from preschool through college, then deposits them directly into the workplace—a system that makes Japan seem orderly and purposeful to outsiders, even as it has begun to break down.

Men like Kenji, Hiro, and Jun are called *hikikomori*, which translates loosely as one who shuts himself away and becomes socially withdrawn. (The Japanese word joins together the word *hiku* or "pull," with the word *komoru*, or "retire," to render the meaning "pulling in and retiring.") These men—and 80 percent of *hikikomori* are males—cannot be diagnosed as schizophrenics or mental defectives. They are not depressives or psychotics; nor are they classic agoraphobics, who fear public spaces but welcome friends into their own homes. When psychiatrists evaluate these *hikikomori* using the *Diagnostic and Statistical Manual*, or DSM IV, the standard guide used in the West to diagnose mental disorders, their symptoms cannot be attributed to any known psychiatric ailment. Instead, Japanese psychiatrists say that *hikikomori* is a social disorder, only recently observed, that cannot be found within other cultures.[2] These men—as I found during months of conversations with them—are often intelligent, stimulating, highly open and responsive adults full of cogent ideas and fascinating insights into society and themselves.

There is ample mystery attached to this pathology, one that stubbornly pricks at the curiosity of someone hoping to fathom the plight of modern Japan. In Western Europe or the United States, many modern teenagers also resort to antisocial behavior, but exhibit it differently. In rebelling against parents and schools, many "act out" and explode in rage, or wear outrageous styles of dress to make a "statement," or play loud music sure to offend the older generation. Some cut themselves. In the United States, where guns and knives as well as drugs are so readily available, youth violence can seem commonplace, as if representing an unspoken tradeoff for the openness, independence, and self-expression the society demands. Yet a culture that encourages individual freedom from an early age, that instructs young children to "stand on their own two feet" and find their own way through life, actively encourages originality and risk taking and is far more likely than Japanese society to accept certain strains of nonconformist behavior. In a vast and heterogeneous nation like America, a man like Kenji might end up designing computer games, handcrafting furniture, launching a tiny software startup, editing music videos, or writing a Web log.

Yet in the confinement of Japan's neo-Confucian society, which preaches the importance of obedience, discipline, self-inhibition, and group harmony—and where even individual identity is deeply swathed in mutual interdependence—men like Jun and Kenji have imploded like vacuum tubes, closing themselves in, cutting themselves off, and utterly marginalizing themselves. Unable or unwilling to go out, languishing alone in their rooms, they depend on their parents to leave their next meal at the bedroom door.

Is this isolation, I wondered, simply these young adults' peculiar form of rebellion against their prevailing culture? Or are they too sensitive or inquisitive to accept such collective constraints, and flee to their rooms both for protection and self-preservation? Or are they—as Taka, one twenty-four-year-old, suggested—simply and unsettlingly "different" from the society that surrounds them? "I was raised to have a good career and be a good boy," he told me. "My problem is that I can't go to work like other people. I'm different."

I heard another point of view from the sixty-year-old white-haired mother of a *hikikomori*, a gentle and sympathetic woman who accepts and understands her son's plight, much as it grieves her: "*Hikikomori* are kids who value the intangibles," Hiromi told me. I had met her for coffee to talk about the desolate isolation of her son who, now in his thirties, has for five years been living at home, confining himself to his room because he feels he has no other place where he can just be himself. "*Hikikomori* can see the intangibles, but cannot speak out because there is no place in Japanese society that allows them to . . . So," she concluded, "a person who challenges, or makes a mistake, or thinks for himself, either leaves Japan or becomes a *hikikomori*."

And, indeed, leaving Japan has been a partial solution for some like

Shigei, who has been *hikikomori* for the last thirteen of his thirty years. He told me that he was able to relax and meet others only when prompted by a friend to get out of Japan and visit Thailand on a trip his parents paid for. "I felt different in a country where the buses don't always run on time," he told me. Jun found temporary relief from his anxieties during a visit to India.[3] Another *hikikomori*, thirty-five-year-old Yasuo Ogawara, went into hiding in his twenties after being badgered and rejected, often cruelly, by residents of the provincial town where he had relocated with his wife. "In this society, anyone can become a *hikikomori*," he told me, describing how his in-laws had ostracized and bullied him to the point where the couple divorced. "It's the nature of our social system that is really the cause. It's a system operated by factions, and you have to understand the very nature of the social system to understand this problem.

"Today the values of parents and of young people are completely different," he went on. "The post-bubble bills are coming due, and we have just started to pay for our decades of focusing only on the material."

*   *   *

After listening to the tales and predicaments of dozens of these isolated men, I began to better understand the behavior of Jun and other *hikikomori* as their extraordinary but utterly rational indictment of a postindustrial monoculture. It isn't that these adults choose isolation out of indulgence, but that they see no other course. They need some "free space" in which to breathe, without the prying eyes of outsiders constantly judging them, forcing them to join the herd. The only space they can control is their own bedroom.

Hikikomori instinctively know that the world outside Japan—and the way that world works—has changed dramatically in recent years as Japan lags behind. They seem to perceive the nature of Japan's economic and spiritual crisis far more acutely than do the hundreds of bureaucrats and politicians I have met over the years.

Yet if what makes Japan seem so foreign and incomprehensible to most Westerners is its insularity, homogeneity, and lockstep conformity, then it would seem logical that this syndrome—where the young try to escape that singularly compressed and restrictive life—may exist only in Japan. And since every social system is likely to foster its own unique afflictions, investigating this unusual behavior could lead me to deeper truths about Japan and its current malaise. My journalist's intuition was essentially confirmed by Satoru Saito, one of Japan's most prominent psychiatrists, who has practiced psychotherapy and taught psychoanalysis for years. An avuncular, gentle man who wears sweaters and smokes a pipe, Saito counsels dozens of *hikikomori* patients, as well as abusive husbands and troubled families, at the Institute for Family Function, his narrow concrete slab of a clinic in Tokyo's Azabu neighborhood. Saito is one of many specialists who also see Jun's and Kenji's and the other *hikikomoris'* social isolation as reflecting a rational, Japanese style of coping.

"Many Japanese kids don't express themselves. They would rather express themselves in a fantasy world and through passive-aggressive behavior," he told me one afternoon when I visited him and asked him to analyze this syndrome. "They go on behavior strike, they go into emotional shutdown. This is one of the ways of expressing a Japanese way of life. But in acting this way, these children are simply mirroring the behavior they see among adult Japanese, especially those from elite or privileged backgrounds."

Kenji's willful retreat into the bedroom, his unwillingness to fit in, can be sensibly explained, Saito told me. Japan's traditional family structure is splintering, he said. Its educational system, which emphasizes rote learning over critical thinking, is being questioned as never before. Young people now sense that the old rules don't work in a global age.

In the 1980s, when Japan's economy was still humming, no one had ever heard the term *hikikomori*. But after the economy began to sputter and misfire, the pistons began to fail and fluids began to leak, exposing the rigidities and social dysfunction that had finally made the gears seize up.

Saito and I agreed that tracing the roots of *hikikomori* might offer clues not only to Japan's unprecedented breakdown, but could also help explain why the Japanese self seems so ephemeral. Why individual expression remains constrained by bullying, oppressive pressure, and demands for strict conformity even in these modern times. Why Japan—a nation so bold as to build its own Eiffel Tower, learn how to make pizza and play golf, listen to hip-hop, take up aerobics, flock to wine bars, and build a miniature Dutch village as an amusement park—never engaged in the political, sexual, and gender revolutions that once convulsed America and other Western nations. And why the mechanisms that might compel useful political and social change have been short-circuited, keeping gifted young men like Kenji and Jun and Hiro shut in and shut down—an arrow pointed deep inside each, pinning him in place.

2.

BROKEN APART FROM OTHERS

At first the claim that the *hikikomori* syndrome exists only in Japan rubbed me the wrong way. Japanese often pride themselves on their *nihonjinron*, their distinct racial and cultural heritage. This ideology of uniqueness led to the weird misconceptions often espoused by right-wing nationalists: for example, the Japanese cannot digest American beef because their intestines are smaller, or that foreign skis cannot possibly navigate Japanese snow, or that foreigners cannot master the Japanese language because their brains are somehow wired differently. Of course, the Japanese are not biologically different from anyone else any more than the snow that falls on Mount Fuji differs from that atop Mount Rainier. Yet as I got to know the *hikikomori* who showed up at hospital clinics and counseling sessions throughout Tokyo's suburbs, the more I came to understand the nature of their isolated lives. And the more I came to understand how they felt *barra-barra*—or "broken apart from others," as Kiyoko, the mother of one these isolates told me—the more I began to see that their tragic syndrome might indeed reflect something unique about Japan's history and its culture as it collided with the modern world. I felt this particularly about Kenji, Jun, Hiro, and a few others.

*　　*　　*

Kenji materialized at my office one day like a pale emissary from his hidden world. His eyebrows pulsed like the wings of a hummingbird, suggesting how tense and frightened he was. He was so thin that his starched khaki pants, bunched at the waist, stayed up only because of the severe black belt tightly looped around them. I had met other *hikikomori* in clinics and schools and training centers, but Kenji was truly a recluse—a man who literally never left his home. He had exerted himself to emerge from his lair only because Emi, my Japanese assistant, had finally persuaded him to come to us and speak about his extraordinary, anxious life.

When he cracked open the door to my office that morning, I felt as if a rare and delicate white dove had fluttered in. While I wanted to protect Kenji from undue stress or discomfort, I also hoped that by telling me—a foreigner who would not judge him—his own story in his own words, he might unburden himself sufficiently to gather up some inner strength. His happiest memories of school, he now confided to me, were of playing third base in schoolyard games. But he had fled to his room for the first time after being "frozen out" in fifth grade. One day, classmates started giving him the silent treatment. They ignored him in the lunch room, rebuffed him on the playfields, looked through him on the streets, and completely stopped acknowledging his presence in class. He never knew why the hazing started, and never recovered from the trauma. Teenagers can be cruel, and *mushi*—the Japanese word for the conscious decision to ignore another and pretend he does not exist—is just one of the nefarious tactics they might employ to snub a classmate.

After walking out on elementary school, but keeping up with most of his assignments, Kenji attempted to return in seventh grade, only to learn that he could not start out in a new school with his slate wiped clean. Just a few weeks after classes began in his new junior high school, a boy sitting behind him asked if the rumors were true: that Kenji had refused to finish elementary school.

"I honestly thought, 'Oh my God!' I had a feeling everyone in school would soon pick at my dried scab and open up the old wound." This moment, two decades past, was still fresh in his mind, and Kenji narrowed his eyebrows, almost squinting in pain, as he remembered the encounter.

A few days later, Kenji's teacher approached him and confided, "I know all about what happened in your old school."

"I knew," he said to me, "the report she received didn't say that I had been bullied. Here I was going to ask for her help [in adjusting to a new school] but instead she held out her whip."

When he abandoned junior high school a few months later, no teacher genuinely reached out to him; no counselor visited his home. And since no law demanded that fourteen-year-old Kenji return to school, no one forced him from his hideaway. Kenji's father had died when he was four, and Kenji's mother, who had to work as a nurse to support her two children, thought some time outside the classroom might soothe her only son's psychic wounds. Days turned into months and soon into years. Now, two decades later, Kenji rarely wills himself to enter the universe beyond his tiny apartment. He has no friends. He has no counselor or medications to assist him. He once worked briefly delivering medical equipment, but was fired for helping an elderly customer move some boxes—not part of the job, his boss scolded. With no subsequent work experience and few tangible accomplishments to explain away his long seclusion, he has no hope of finding a job. In the elaborate matrix of Japanese society, Kenji simply has no place. However accidental that first rejection may have been, in Kenji's own mind it has taken on a monstrous and overwhelming life of its own.

"I have two personalities," he told me quietly. "One part of me doesn't want to go out and the other does. They are fighting with each other constantly.

"I think more deeply than others," he went on, "but I've lost my ability to communicate with others. Most people just try to hide their own feelings to get along with others, but I'm more pure than that"— untainted and untrammeled by the press of a culture that negates individual spirit. "Regular people have an ability to hide their true feelings just to be able to get along with others in the world"—and Kenji used the word *tatemae* to express the skill of mastering a false face. "I just can't find the value in doing that. Since I want to tell others what I really think, I guess you could say I'm not good at communicating with people. That makes me nervous in front of others."

For Kenji, just opening the front door to fetch the morning papers requires him to muster up superhuman courage. After all, he might accidentally bump into a neighbor or a deliveryman, an encounter that would leave him frightfully embarrassed or profoundly shamed because he does not know how to explain himself. "Maintaining face" serves as a powerful constraint in Japan's close quarters, and Kenji is constantly obsessed with what others might think of him. He uses up his days intending to leave no footprints; yet even on this test he was falling short since he was at my door, reaching out, however tentatively, in his search for help.

*   *   *

Jun and I spoke for hours one afternoon in the day room of a suburban Tokyo clinic where *hikikomori* come to play cards, pick at a guitar, slap around a volleyball on a green swath of fenced lawn, or simply hang out. That day Jun was wearing blue jeans and a brown corduroy shirt, with a gray fleece jacket draped over his shoulders.

In comparison with most isolates—even Kenji—Jun struck me as highly self-aware. He was composed and articulate, talking casually, as if we were meeting at a coffee shop on a college campus. He was able to talk about his condition thoughtfully, almost objectively, as if discussing the problems of a close friend instead of his own. As he described his years of anxiety and isolation, he sometimes rubbed his forehead nervously or rocked his feet back and forth. Like many other *hikikomori*, Jun said he found it easier to speak frankly about his life and trials with someone who was not Japanese, who was not bound up in the same rituals and conformity, who might not be so quick to evaluate or condemn.

For most of the 1990s, Jun had been adrift and alone. At age eighteen, planning to major in philosophy at a prominent national university, he botched an entrance examination. His failing grade destroyed his confidence. It also pulled him off the conveyor belt that would have borne him on to college and then into the workplace. Jun chose not to abandon his dream of attending a prestigious college. Instead he became a *ronin*—a term that traditionally denoted a samurai warrior without a master, but that, in modern Japan, denotes a student who, having flunked his entrance exams, prepares for a full year or longer to try again.

For about half a year, Jun worked hard and concentrated on his remedial studies. Then he lost his resolve. He began questioning himself, wondering what this empty struggle for validation was really about. "I think it was Kant who said, 'I can't teach you philosophy but only how to learn philosophy,' " Jun said. "I often thought of that passage during my studies. Eventually, I wondered, why should I be studying so hard to pass these entrance exams? I didn't want to study for the exam, I just wanted to sit down and read philosophy—you know, sit by myself, pick up a book, and read alone. If that's what I wanted to do . . . I should just do it."

Slowly, imperceptibly at first, he began drifting into his own world. He became increasingly alienated from what he saw as a harsh and controlling universe outside his door. To maintain his individuality, he kept himself apart.

Like a typical young adult in Japan, Jun lived in a small house with his parents, both acupuncturists with busy professional schedules. The cramped quarters and lack of privacy exacerbated tense relations. "When I stayed at home, I just couldn't relax," Jun said. "They were so terribly uptight. I really never got along with my parents. My family was very cruel, and my parents could never express themselves to each other—or to me.

"My house was pretty small, you know, and when we were all living together, I felt the presence of the others. Even though I lived in a second floor bedroom, I could always feel the presence of my parents, I could hear the sounds of them sleeping, coughing, breathing. It felt so suffocating."

Although such close physical circumstances might encourage warmth and emotional indulgence in some families, Jun's parents were simply unable to communicate kindness and love for each other, much less for their only son. "They were living together and eating together, but they barely talked," he said.

"I felt I must have some problem inside of me, but I didn't know what it was. I felt my family had problems, too, but didn't know what the problems were." He paused, scratching his arm nervously. "I felt I had to find the answers to those questions, felt I had to solve my problems with my family and myself. I realize now that my family lacked intimacy, but at the time, I just couldn't understand it. I asked myself questions like, 'Will I learn philosophy, or just *do* philosophy? And if I do philosophy, that's not something I should do in class, is it? It should be something quite different.'"

For three- and four-week intervals, Jun would lock himself up in the family apartment, barricading himself off from his parents, never leaving the house. His dinner was put on a tray and left for him outside his bedroom door. Like many other *hikikomori*, Jun began to transform day into night and night into day, cutting off contact with the unwelcome realities outside his small bedroom. Often, he slept late into the afternoon, then read philosophy books or watched television programs during his waking nighttime. Sometimes he willed himself onto his mountain bike for those solitary rides through the sleeping city.

"Basically, I thought I could go outside anytime, but the reality was that I just didn't," Jun said. "I didn't work. I knew if I stepped outside, the neighbors would see me and wonder how come a kid that age isn't working? Some of the neighbors knew I'd been to visit a counselor, so they must have thought, 'Oh, he has big problems,' like I'm crazy. The cold wind of *sekentei* blowing outside made it very hard for me."

Sekentei—how one appears in the eyes of society, or the need to keep up appearances—can powerfully constrain individual action just as bullying does in the collectivist pressure cooker of contemporary Japan. In Tokyo's crowded old neighborhoods and its vast surrounding suburbs, neighbors live practically on top of one another. They always seem to maintain a high state of alert, always aware of their neighbors' every move. As a foreigner walking the streets, I often felt that cold Japanese stare. They were watching me, but indirectly, through their window shades or peripheral vision, to discern whether I was some "troublemaker." A warm smile did not disarm. If I turned to meet the gaze, the head would quickly turn away. In a community full of stealthy busybodies, neighbors know if you are doing the laundry, what time you fix dinner, and whether husband and wife are getting along.

These prying eyes made Jun resentful. "Sometimes they would ignore me, even when I bowed to them and said good morning in a very polite way when I left the house," he said. "At other times, when I would open the door to our house, they would turn away so they wouldn't even have to look at me. It wasn't like this happened just one or two times . . . but every time I'd try to go out, the neighbors would refuse to look at me. Or they would look at me in some vicious way, like I'm some strange person about to commit a crime." On the other hand, Jun was aware of his parents' feelings. Once, when I brought a photographer with me to take pictures in the clinic, he refused to have his taken. He could not, he told me, shame his parents by letting his real name be used.

Jun once tried to persuade his family to join him in visiting a family therapist. His father adamantly refused. His mother agreed, albeit reluctantly. "Mom could not understand how much I was suffering," Jun said, "even though sometimes I would stay up until three in the morning talking to her. I felt that if I found her a counselor of her own, it might help."

Eventually Jun located a Jungian therapist trained in England and willing to treat his mother, but she quit after one visit. "My mother thought that if she went to the counseling sessions, she might find herself, and that might collapse her world," Jun said. From his perspective, the world his mother had painstakingly constructed for herself was a slender fiction. After years of suppressing her own needs and desires in order to meet the expectations of her husband and the demands of the surrounding community, she was terribly unhappy, but could not summon the energy to find her true identity.

"At that point I realized there was nothing more I could do for my mother," Jun said. "She knew things were wrong, but she couldn't understand or deal with them."

Feeling powerless and inept, Jun soon gave up trying to recast his unhappy family and turned to trying to create alternate escape routes. Since he suffers from asthma in the city, whose air is polluted by the combination of heavy summer humidity and the fumes from diesel trucks, he asked his parents to send him to some quiet rural place outside Tokyo where his health might improve. He landed in the northern city of Sendai, where he briefly held down a part-time job and befriended a Japanese man who operated his own British-style tea shop. Eventually, the man invited Jun to accompany him on a four-month trip to India, where they inspected tea plantations in Darjeeling and toured Calcutta.

"There was such different food and culture, I was shocked," Jun said, recounting his odyssey as a twenty-three-year-old. "You could walk around the busy cities, and the people did not appear to be rich or trendy at all compared to Tokyo, but gosh, they were so energetic! So busy and energetic! Even though they were so poor, they appeared so much healthier and engaged than the *sararimen* pouring out of Tokyo Station each morning.

"I was very surprised. They were enjoying life! The eyes of the kids were shining. They were so different from the dull fish-eyes of kids here. Here in Tokyo, you have to have a nice foreign car or some fancy accessories just to go to class at the university. The people in Calcutta, on the other hand, they don't seem at all bound up in those accessories, and yet they seemed very, very happy.

"After World War Two, maybe Japan was the same way," Jun mused. "Without money, without accessories, people could live happily. So this trip confirmed to me that people can live happily without fancy things . . . But when I came back to Japan, I found the problems inside of me had not gone away."

Throughout the next four years, Jun remained essentially paralyzed at home. "I began to understand how big my problem was. I started to read books. I thought and thought and thought . . . but I couldn't go out."

He remembered reflecting on his childhood and experienced recurring dreams of being abandoned by his mother. "One of the memories I could vividly recall was being taken to a child-care nursery. I must have been about two. My mom didn't say anything to me; she just talked to the nurse, then left me behind in the room. I tried to chase after her, but the staff grabbed me and held me down, pulling me back inside the room.

I'm screaming 'Mom! Mom!' but she doesn't respond. Then I look out the window, and she has already left.

"I still remember that. I see that moment, over and over again."

Jun recounted another episode of traumatic rejection, which occurred when he was brought to his grandmother's house at age five or six while suffering from a severe asthma attack. It was during the festive New Year's period of O-shogatsu, when Japanese extended families tradition- ally gather together to eat ceremonial foods, drink saké, and ring ceremo- nial bells at temples to hope for good fortune. "I remember my grandma scolding my mother, saying, 'Why did you bring that sick child into my house?'

"These memories kept plaguing me. I blamed myself for my unhappi- ness. I pummeled myself. I said to myself, 'Am I worthy to be alive with these problems inside of me?' On top of that, there were the prying eyes of the neighbors looking at me. That accelerated my depression."

His long spiral downward was finally broken by another impulsive trip abroad, this time to Thailand. Once again outside the constraining walls of Japan, where the eyes of others seemed to control his every move, Jun felt less anxious. He stayed at an inexpensive backpackers' inn in Bangkok and befriended the owner of a small handicraft shop, a Japa- nese man who had chosen to emigrate. Their conversations offered him renewed inspiration.

"This man had his own shop, he worked there, and he had found a way to make a living," Jun said. "After a while of getting to know him, I real- ized that I wanted to make my own life, too, just as he did in Thailand. I want to be independent! I want to create my own world in Japan. I have an obligation to be myself."

Jun returned from his foreign adventure with renewed resolve. Finally he would move out of his parents' house. A major step on his path toward rehabilitation was to sign up at an outpatient clinic for treatment. The first time we talked, Jun had just returned from a three-week Outward Bound–style camp, where he had lived in a rustic cabin and helped care for horses and livestock on a farm. "The camp was trying to teach me to trust others and experience intimacy and friendship with others," Jun said. "I think it was pretty valuable, since I've been living alone for the past five months."

In a sense, Jun has been lucky. After years of shutting himself inside his room, he is trying slowly to emancipate himself by leaving home to visit a therapist and socialize with others at this clinic. His parents continue to pay rent on the small apartment where Jun is now living in Ibaragi prefecture, about a ninety-minute drive from the clinic. They gave him a car, which allows him to commute back and forth, and send him money for food and gas. Yet Jun again insisted, "I am striving to be independent from them."

Though recognizing that forging a separate, independent life was freighted with difficulties, he wasn't yet ready to abandon his homeland, as others have. "I love Japan, and it's sad to see my country so messed up. But I'm Japanese and I am part of Japanese society, also. I have a feeling that if I change myself, that will eventually change Japan."

Changing Japanese society seems a tall order for an adult who had dropped out of the world for nearly a decade. Freeing himself from the limitations of group identity might prove difficult. What are his prospects? Jun might find work as a part-time clerk in a bookstore or video shop, or even qualify as a part-time salesman, if he could bear it. Occasionally, a place on a construction crew might become available, though the decade-long recession canceled most opportunities for well-paying casual labor. Few Japanese companies even consider hiring full-time workers these days, except as a "class" each April just after they graduate from university or high school. These days, youth unemployment is the highest it has ever been; nearly 10 percent of young graduates have no jobs, and Jun never finished college.

Western cultures—especially America's—routinely encourage independent entrepreneurship, especially among young people like Jun. Entrepreneurial activity in Japan is among the lowest in the developed world, however, below even Russia and Poland.[1] According to some estimates, even if they have an idea for a surefire business and the ambition to run it, adults with résumés far more polished than Jun's find it difficult to attract the financing and support they need. Only a rare banker would risk loaning money to some energetic young dreamer offering a promising vision and a flimsy credit history. Bankers prefer lending to old indebted firms with whom they have relationships stretching back decades.

Nor is escape to another part of the country a real option for someone like Jun. In the small island networks of Japan's "village society," everyone has a family and a history, as enduring and unalterable as one's legal registration papers filed in the ward office. You cannot simply run away— as in mythic America where a man could simply pack up, move to a new city out west, and "reinvent" himself as someone without a past.

Yet many gifted young Japanese like Jun yearn for distinctive careers and grasp for means to articulate their aspirations. Japanese magazines sometimes describe in glowing terms "I-turn" rather than U-turn refugees: that is, disaffected urban workers who return to the countryside of their grandparents to grow organic foods, reclaim traditional papermaking skills or fabric dyeing, or devote themselves to creating Japanese *yakimono*, or ceramics. Surveys among schoolchildren show they are no longer fixated with becoming businessmen or bureaucrats; more kids today say they want to grow up to be cooks, carpenters, or solitary craftsmen.

Jun's problems go deeper than economics. Now that he may want to find a way back into the larger world, how can he gain access to it? What could be his point of entry? The words of Kazuki Ueyama, another *hikikomori* who was eloquent about his years of isolation, echoed in my head. When social isolates "try to protect themselves and their insides, they can't function in economic society," he said. "When they try to adapt themselves [to survive] in economic society, they have to destroy their insides. And in Japan, once you drop out, you can't drop back in."

* * *

Twenty-four-year-old Taka's story was similar to Jun's. He said he had studied so hard for a high school entrance exam that he "burned out" at age fifteen. "I couldn't imagine a picture of myself as an adult," he said. "I looked around at the world and said, 'Why do I have to be like they are?'"

He spent two years alone in his room, refusing to go to school. "I thought to myself, if I don't do anything, nothing will happen . . . I just let time go by."

Taka described his father as being a "very serious man," a successful business executive who refused to speak to him all during his long period of isolation. His mother eventually persuaded him to go to a psychiatric hospital, where he was given drugs and briefly put in a ward with other young adults. But his condition didn't improve. In a bid to please his father, Taka made a brief attempt to attend a night school, but couldn't keep up. Finally, his mother brought him to a clinic operated by Dr. Tamaki Saito (no relation to Satoru Saito), who had made something of a name for himself on television and in popular magazines by exploring the epidemic of *hikikomori*.

Now, free from the stress he had routinely experienced in everyday Japanese life, Taka said his mood was getting better. He was encouraged to "go with the flow" within the protected space of the hospital clinic. "I can get some sympathy here," he explained to me. "There are other people here who feel like I do. We can play sports, and talk to one another, and hang out, so we can feel a little healthier." Taka's aspirations for the future were much like those I heard from many other *hikikomori*: "I want to be a regular person, the person who can go out with friends and be a normal guy." But his words echoed Jun's: "I feel the outside world is very severe, and I don't have the guts to face it."

* * *

Another *hikikomori* whom Thailand opened up was Shigei, whom I met with one day over coffee with his mother at a Denny's restaurant, identical to the American chain, tucked away in a western Tokyo suburb. He was shunned by classmates at age fourteen, after refusing to participate on a basketball team because the coach had a violent temper and a tendency to push his students around or punch them. By age sixteen, Shigei had withdrawn from school for good.

"I couldn't find my own identity," he told me. "I wasn't developing. I couldn't communicate or assert myself, so I stayed in my room." Over a period of two or three years, he visited health clinics and hospitals, "but all they did was give me antidepressant drugs. They didn't analyze me or talk to me. After two or three minutes of superficial conversation, they would hand me some more pills.

"Doctors see only my biological reaction, and the Japanese hospital sees me only as a patient. Neither of them really looked at the environment that was the underlying cause of my distress," he said. "The only thing they could do was give me drugs. That made me very disappointed and distrusting. They didn't have any skills to help."

Shigei said that, after thirteen years as a *hikikomori*, he began to feel better about himself only after traveling to Southeast Asia. "When I go abroad, if I make a mistake or do something which is a bit different from their custom they can accept me because I'm a traveler. I'm a foreigner. That made me realize for the first time that I didn't have to worry about *sekentei* or the invisible rules."

This brief exposure to another culture, the opportunity to see how others live, helped change Shigei's attitude, as it did Jun's. "For example," Shigei marveled, "you'd get on a bus that was supposed to leave at one P.M., and it wouldn't leave until the bus was full, maybe two or two-thirty. People were not so strict about keeping time . . . they were relaxed. And this helped me relax, too, and become more sociable.

"I became *hikikomori* for safety, so I would not dare to go out and take a risk [in meeting other Japanese]," he said. "Now, finally I am starting to understand why and realize that I want to go back among people again."

*   *   *

I got to know Hiro quite well after a year of conversations with him and his mother at their apartment, in a dense neighborhood near Tokyo's Meguro Station. A fidgety half-man with massive, elongated fingers and thick, shoulder-length hair, Hiro spends most of his time in a self-constructed fantasy world of fighter jets, AWACS radar planes, futuristic spaceships, and Rambo-like soldiers he builds from model kits. Among the most fantastic objects in his collection is a pterodactyl outfitted with a giant rocket-launcher.

A tiny model tank and two midget soldiers stand guard in the entranceway to the modest six-tatami-mat apartment where Hiro uneasily coexists with his parents. These statuettes serve as implicit recognition of the boy's true obsessions, if not of his obvious talents. Only recently had Hiro's parents even considered enrolling their son in a design school or computer graphics class to turn his innate interests into career skills. "I love to draw *manga*," or Japanese-style comics, Hiro told me. "But I guess I'd rather make real toys instead of fantasy ones."

Hiro's father works as a travel agent, and his mother, Keiko, admits that the tension in the marriage sometimes spills into her relationship with her only child. Though I rarely got a chance to talk to both a *hikikomori* and his mother about family life, her counseling with Satoru Saito, the clinical psychiatrist, had convinced Keiko that frank conversation might help her confront her own demons. "Looking back now, I realize I had lots of issues with my own family and with my husband. Sometimes I took out my anger on Hiro," and contributed to his isolation, she told me once, as Hiro listened beside her.

A trim, silver-haired woman who tries to play tennis at least once every week, Keiko was thirty-seven when Hiro was born. Even from an early age, she recalled, he seemed very different from other children. "I remember my brother telling me, when the boy was just four or five years old, that Hiro picked up things that he actually liked. My brother's son could never make decisions for himself and always followed others, but Hiro, he had his own ideas all the time."

At age five Hiro was packed off to *juku*, or cram school, like other children, his parents hoping he would win a place in an elite elementary school, a "feeder" program that would ultimately guarantee admission to prestigious Keio University. Hiro had tested very high on intelligence tests, Keiko recalled, but didn't take to the rigors of extra schooling. "The teacher said if there were no entrance exams, Hiro would have really enjoyed the *juku* since he liked being with other children. But other mothers told me that they would sometimes drop off their children at school and see Hiro standing outside, watching the passing cars, instead of going inside with the others." Exhausted from night classes, he was forced to drop out of a science club he enjoyed.

Asked about his childhood, Hiro recalls being constantly fatigued. "I just didn't have the energy, physically," he said. "I'd go to *juku* at four and come home every day around ten at night. I didn't have the physical stamina . . . Maybe you could say I was unlucky."

At six, Hiro flunked the entrance exam and so was trundled off to a normal public elementary school. The battle over his future, however, continued to cloud Keiko's marriage. His father insisted that his only son must set his sights on a top-flight school, while his mother was ambivalent. "I half wanted Hiro to go to an elite school. I knew he was bright. It was my husband who insisted that Hiro study for the entrance exams, but of course he was never around to help since he only came home from work around midnight." That left Keiko the tasks of ensuring that Hiro studied and of punishing him when he misbehaved. "My husband never disciplined the boy, so if I became tough on Hiro and forced him to study, my husband would just praise him and be easy. Then my parents would get involved, criticizing me for not being tough enough. I couldn't win.

"Now when I look back, I see that he did study in his own way, but I kind of abused him. There were times when he broke walls and hit me, telling me in tears, 'I can't go to school!' Last year he screamed at me and said, 'You threw all that stress onto me. What can I do with that now?' "

Hiro, who was sitting at the kitchen table, interjected. "She was always pushing me to hurry up and finish my work and scolded me about irrelevant stuff. So sometimes I would shout at her or tear her blouse, because she made me so angry.

"I remember one time yelling at her and saying, 'I am not going to be your robot anymore.' I remember all this anger welling up inside of me. I threw a cup against the wall. Another time I threw my pencil box out the window. She pushed me so much . . . she ruined my youth."

Keiko began to sob, dabbing at her eyes with a tissue. "I really was at a loss," she said quietly. "I wanted my husband to help me. There was so much pressure. Now, when I look back, I realize that I was trying to use my son to get back at my relatives."

She traced her neediness to her own childhood. In a household where her father returned from the Imperial Army to battle postwar depression, she was forced to put her parents' demands ahead of her own. "As a child, I was always taking care of Dad while my mom worked, so I wasn't allowed to have my own needs. I ended up doing with Hiro what my parents did with me." In pushing Hiro to succeed, she could win the appreciation and recognition as a parent that had eluded her as a child.

After some struggle, Hiro did eventually complete elementary school, but dropped out of a vocational junior high after only six months. His parents wanted him to face less pressure, but he found classes so easy they bored him. "The classrooms were in chaos, and all the kids were in one clique or another. I felt different from everyone else, so it was very hard for me. After a while I just stopped going."

One day a teacher from the school, Yamamoto-sensei, came to the apartment to urge Hiro back to school. "You are not the son of a *zaibatsu*"— that is, the scion of a wealthy corporate conglomerate—Yamamoto warned the thirteen-year-old. "If you don't go to junior high school, you cannot survive." Hiro did return, but after one or two days "my body became too tired. One teacher said I needed ten days' sleep to get what other students got in one normal night." He was weary, he said, from the accumulated stress from years of *juku*, tests every Sunday, and other activities, like swimming and tennis. "I just couldn't face going back to the classroom."

Hiro's decision to drop out gave Keiko a sense of relief and pleasure at first. Any pressure to succeed was now off them both. "Once he stopped going to school, I didn't have to worry anymore about forcing him to take entrance exams," she said. "Instead, I could have him under my control every day."

Keiko's husband, however, accused her of sabotaging Hiro's education to retaliate for his frequent absences and their increasingly bitter domestic quarrels. There may be some truth in his charges, she admitted. "Sometimes, I pulled Hiro's legs out from under him. It's common in Japan, I suppose."

After Keiko's revelation that she might be somehow responsible for her son's isolation, I asked to see Hiro's room, hoping to speak with him privately. A six-by-eight-foot space, it held a Western-style single bed, a baby piano, and a writing desk. Some comic books and a half-built model airplane were scattered on the floor.

The small apartment had recently been renovated, allowing Hiro finally to have a room to himself. "We were so tightly squeezed together before, it was like bondage," Hiro said. "When you face a judge twenty-four hours a day, it's hard to forget things even when you want to. And my parents were always fighting. Now that I have some privacy and can sleep in here, it's a lot easier.

"Lately, like in the past few months, she has calmed down," he said of Keiko. "If my mother had been less emotional and volatile, maybe I wouldn't have ended up in such a bad situation."

As he examined his own state of mind, Hiro's voice grew calm and reflective. "A year ago, I just hated this society," he said, sitting on his bed. "I know it's going to be difficult for me to fit in and I don't feel much value in fitting in. So I'm still thinking, 'How can I live a meaningful life?' "

He told me about the few refuges he had found, including a nearby "drop-in" center that offered computer classes as well as a "free space," where he went sometimes and where he eventually took me. He also takes some medication—antidepressant pills Dr. Saito had given him. As we talked, he began flipping through some of his latest artwork, showing me stark and expressive drawings of colorful spaceships outfitted with laser guns, advanced designs for helicopters and battleships, and blueprints for a space module he was starting to design. Other male fantasies appeared on his walls as comics-like portraits of wide-eyed Japanese females, images culled from the pages of *manga* yet enhanced and reinvented with bold colors and new costumes. Hiro's artistic gift made me wish I knew a comic-book illustrator I might introduce him to.

These days Hiro idles away hours reading hobby magazines, watching TV, drawing cartoons, and building his models. Recently his mother bought him a kitten to play with. Still, he remains lethargic. "Yes, I'm bored, but I'm not starving. I don't have a concrete, original idea about my future, but one day I want to get a job," he said. "Sure, I want to have money. I have vague dreams, but it's hard to move or get motivated.

"It seems like it's hard to recover from a mistake," he said, sighing.

Neither bullying nor acute trauma can really be blamed for Hiro's social withdrawal. In fact, I could find no single trigger for his decision to drop from the world's view. He simply ran out of the energy Japanese youth are expected to have for the obstacle course ahead of them. And now neither his mother nor Hiro can predict how he will navigate his way into adulthood.

"I know now that I went deep enough, so now it's time to step outside, slowly, step by step," Hiro said. Maybe that was why he was beginning to leave the house, occasionally, to go to the free space, and why he was willing to let me spend time alone with him in his apartment.

3.

A LONG TUNNEL

In the lives of all these *hikikomori*, where are their parents? What are they doing to help their suffering sons? Are they protesting to the schools, demanding help from the government, or working with professional therapists, as parents in the United States today seek support for their autistic or learning-disabled children?

The sad fact is that in Japan, this nation of secret hideaways and discreet indirection, nothing seems more hidden from view than the universe the *hikikomori* inhabit. Not only do these isolates take great pains to barricade themselves, pulling down the shutters, closing their curtains, and sometimes taping their windows with black paper and duct tape to deny the world entry, but most parents seem far too ashamed to seek help for their children, or even to be seen venturing into a public health clinic. Repeatedly I learned that relatives dare not inquire about their invisible nephews or cousins for fear of being discourteous or provoking bad feelings within the family. "I couldn't possibly talk to my sister about her *hikikomori* son," a government worker confided to me once, as if uttering a word about this syndrome in her midst would violate a deep and shadowy proscription. Yet invariably, when I brought up the existence of these socially isolated adults, nearly everyone I spoke to acknowledged knowing someone in just such a condition. Everyone knew someone, or so it seemed. Like Japan's repeated unwillingness to face up to its cruel wartime past, such denial is not accidental, but seems rigorously cultivated. In polite company, the subject of *hikikomori* is seldom

brought up, and in any case, in Japan, a form of passive acquiescence—
shikata ga nai, the Japanese say, or "It can't be helped"—often seems the
most common reaction to adversity, enveloping society in a gauzy fabric
of obliviousness.[1]

Therapists sometimes diagnose incomplete attachment between a
child and his parents—an absence of enduring affection—as a key marker
for *hikikomori*. Family counselors believe the inability of adults to express
honest emotions, as well as their helplessness or unwillingness to speak
openly and directly with their children, only exacerbates the pressure the
latter face outside the home. The home is cold and silent, not warm and
nurturing. Nori, a twenty-two-year-old *hikikomori* patient, told me he
could never once recall being cradled or hugged as a child, and said that
when they were together at home, his parents seldom spoke. (As part of
his treatment, Nori's counselor eventually enlisted his own wife to act as
a surrogate mother, and instructed her to hug and caress the patient as
she would her own daughter, while Nori was placed in a semihypnotic
trance. His response to such affection was truly childlike. His eyes grew
wide with delight and he cooed fondly and with joy.) Others routinely describe their parents as "harsh" or "strict," as people who—despite their
high expectations for their children—had difficulty exhibiting affection or
displaying warmth. "Many fathers, especially, are speechless and without
feelings," Satoru Saito, the psychiatrist, had told me.

A self-propagating cycle of silence and shame kept this syndrome
mostly hidden. Finally, in 1999, one man, the sixty-year-old father of a
hikikomori, broke through the taboo against acknowledging how widely
prevalent this problem had become. A slight man with tortoiseshell
glasses, a graying goatee, and a pronounced limp from a long battle with
cancer, Masahisa Okuyama has formed a network of families and therapists to aid the one million or so young adults who suffer from this syndrome. Thus he has become the public face of *hikikomori* parents.

"This is a pathology, not an illness," Okuyama explained the first time
we sat down for lunch to talk about his failing family. "It's not a problem
of one or two years, it's a very long-term problem."

Though not trained as a clinical psychiatrist or counselor, Okuyama had grown convinced that *hikikomori* behavior mirrored a larger array of social ills. "The Japanese system is showing signs of system fatigue," Okuyama told me. "That's why our young people don't want to—or can't—become adult. They are afraid of participating in a society where there is no hope and no ambition. They are only too aware that good old Japan will never come back. When anyone's child can become a *hikikomori*, it's a scary time."

I had arranged to meet Okuyama in the coffee shop of a 1960s-era hotel, complete with white doilies and glass tabletops, in the town of Omiya, a dreary mix of anonymous apartments, narrow two-story houses, and soulless neon signs about an hour's train ride west of downtown Tokyo. This graceless community bears little resemblance to the quaint, rustic Japan of narrow stone streets, verdant rice fields, and slatted wooden temples that foreigners see in their Fujicolor tourist guides. Instead, Saitama, the town's prefecture, is a vast suburban cacophony of corrugated steel factory buildings, squat distribution warehouses, and vacuous strip malls, crisscrossed by crowded highways, railroad tracks, and telephone wires. It is a bleak, hyperindustrial dormitory for hundreds of thousands of Japan's modern working families.

It was not altruism that forced Okuyama to publicly confront the bewildering problem of *hikikomori*, but his own frustration with his family's bitter circumstances. His son, then twenty-six, had not voluntarily left home in almost eight years. No treatment seemed effective in helping him, and now home life itself was under siege. In the past few months, Okuyama and his wife had been forced to abandon their own home after their son repeatedly attacked them.

"I could kill him, or he could kill me, it's just that simple," Okuyama explained quietly over a lunch of curry rice as he chain-smoked. "Until two years ago I lived all the time with a *hikikomori* and did not understand at all what was going on around me. But by then, it was really too late."

Okuyama had spent two decades working as an advertising executive in Tokyo before abruptly resigning in August 1999 to deal with his family's gathering crisis. He and his wife had grown to fear for their lives inside their own home. "We were dissolving as a family," he muttered softly.

Their son often beat them, screaming and threatening more violence. "We were yelling and fighting over even small issues," he said. "He demanded that I sell our apartment and hand over the proceeds to him. Then he would threaten us again."

Though no one talks about it in public, angry, frustrated, reclusive children often beat their elderly parents with anything lying around the house—a baseball bat, a hammer. Attacking a parent has become one of the most common forms of domestic violence in Japan. Although there are no accurate data for it, the consensus among psychiatrists seems to be that at least half of all *hikikomori* treat their parents with some sort of violence.[2] Beating them with an aluminum baseball bat is common; some children just use their fists. In November 2004, a twenty-eight-year-old man, who had been a *hikikomori* for eight years, admitted killing his parents and older sister with a hammer and a kitchen knife. He had committed this crime after his father, a city worker, had demanded that he find a job. "My father and my sister robbed me of my space to live in," Masaru Iijima told police. Unless he got rid of his family, he said, he would have "nowhere to stay . . . I thought I'd kill them before they killed me."[3] So common is the violence that many counselors tend to associate the term "domestic violence" not with wife-beating or child abuse by adult males as Americans do, but with abuse of parents by adolescent children.[4]

Japanese police are often reluctant to get too deeply involved in unpleasant family matters and besides, they have had few legal tools at their disposal. The nation's first child abuse statute was adopted only in May 2000, and "domestic violence" was not formally recognized as a crime until the following summer. Public consciousness has also lagged. It isn't that wife battering and other domestic violence was unknown in Japan. Instead, the denial and shame that permeates much of the culture has made people slow to acknowledge the violence in their midst. Japanese often say that they like to "put a lid on stinky things," rather than bring them out into the open. *Hikikomori*, I would learn, was also deemed a "stinky thing."

Okuyama had once checked his son into a local hospital but found neither the doctors nor Japan's health care bureaucracy able to deal appropriately with his son's mental anguish. In this case, as with Shigei, a child is either locked up in a primitive ward or sedated with powerful drugs and sent home. Because little research has been conducted on *hikikomori* and no data have yet been published in medical or psychiatric journals, doctors have no idea how to treat these unstable adolescents or even what to tell anxious parents. In addition, despite Japan's seemingly constant quest for the "modern" and the "advanced," Western-style psychiatry has never really been embraced within Japan, and by many accounts, treatment is far less sophisticated than what Westerners might take for granted.[5] Parents who dare to seek help from a clinic or a government welfare office often emerge from the experience exhausted and discouraged.

Finding no medical alternatives, Okuyama and his wife had to abandon their own apartment for a small rental unit nearby, leaving their son mostly to fend for himself when he began to carry out his threats of escalating violence. "He was strangling the family so we concluded that we had to move out," Okuyama said. Like most parents, however, Okuyama could not bring himself to completely sever ties with his son. Every ten days or so, he sent him cash by registered mail—11,000 yen, or about $100, enough for the young man to order in soba noodles, pizza, and beer.

The extreme isolation had not changed his son's condition, Okuyama said. "For *hikikomori* like him, going out into ordinary society is more scary than bungee jumping. So I really don't expect him to change."

Convinced his family's dilemma could not be unique, Okuyama nearly single-handedly started organizing a seminar group for parents like him. He thought families might at least feel less isolated if they could talk among themselves.

The organization he founded—dubbed KHJ (an association for parents with troubled children)[6]—sought to raise public awareness, locate untapped medical expertise, and demand more assistance from powerful government agencies, especially the national Health Ministry, which had long sought to deny even the existence of *hikikomori*. Unlike Americans, Japanese don't naturally organize themselves into health-related pressure groups to draw attention to issues like this. (For years, Japan's disabled quietly accepted their third-class status.) In contrast to the nation's dense and intense economic networks, its social networks—its tentacles of charitable and civic organizations—are far less robust and efficacious. Only within the past half decade, since 1998, has Japan enacted new rules permitting nonprofit organizations to incorporate without formal government approval, but contributions to nongovernmental organizations are still not tax deductible.

As he busied himself with organizing seminars and establishing new chapters for parents of *hikikomori* across Japan, Okuyama's family crisis intensified. Now his son was threatening to disrupt KHJ events unless he was paid "hush money."

"He hates me, I know, but the relationship between parent and child is so strong, even stronger than between husband and wife . . . ," Okuyama said. He could not simply abandon his son, he said, even as he feared for his life.

I was impressed by Okuyama's toughness, his stoic demeanor, despite the emotions I felt were clearly churning inside him. Perhaps no one was more surprised than Okuyama himself that the fracture of his family and his son's self-confinement had transformed him into something of a troublemaker. Rather than throw up his hands in frustration, Okuyama had become a gritty and courageous fighter. He was determined to help parents reconstruct the tattered fabric of family life, and resolute in demanding government recognition and support for his cause.

*   *   *

Okuyama knew that neither the Japanese government—the mandarins of Kasumigaseki, the Tokyo neighborhood where all of Japan's public agencies have their offices—nor its health care bureaucracy would willingly acknowledge the scale of this mysterious new social epidemic, set aside funds to help parents, or consider comprehensive plans to treat *hikikomori* patients. Bureaucrats in Japan are never bold, he complained, never willing to take initiative. Like bureaucrats everywhere, they prize order, follow precedent, and usually don't permit new realities to interfere with old formulas; yet in a society so heavily regulated, bureaucrats in Japan hold far more clout than those in most other countries, and usually run rings around the politicians, who tend to lack any background in policy-making and are constantly pressed to raise funds for their next campaign. Until recently, the "best and the brightest" of Japan's elite college gradu-ates sought jobs not in commerce or in universities, but among the ranks of the all-powerful civil service, whose senior officials, rather than those elected by the voters, actually run the country. Japanese often joke bit-terly that they live in a "manual society": that is, if something isn't already written into the bureaucrat's manual of operations and procedures, then he doesn't know how to respond. There is hardly any place for improvi-sation, for compassion, or for common sense.

Japanese had witnessed this failing firsthand during the devastating Kobe earthquake of 1995, to which the bureaucracy responded miser-ably. After the 7.2 magnitude quake destroyed bridges, uprooted homes, fractured whole neighborhoods, and killed more than 6,400 people, nearly two full days passed before adequate numbers of police and res-cue workers were dispatched to the disaster site. The rescue dogs that were specially flown in from Switzerland to paw through rubble in search of survivors were detained for a week at airport quarantine. Officers as-signed to one sector of the city refused to come to the aid of victims trapped under rubble just a few yards away, in a sector outside their juris-diction. Only after the earthquake did it become permissible, perhaps for the first time, for Japanese to openly criticize the rigidity and opaque decision-making of their bureaucrats.

At his first meeting for parents like himself—adults unable to under-stand or deal with the behavior of their hideaway children—Okuyama was surprised that some two hundred and fifty parents from all over Japan had dared to show up. He had spread the word informally, through some clini-cians he had met, through parents similarly plagued, and by visiting the lo-cal bureaus of the three biggest newspapers in the area to ask them to publish small notices about his seminar, yet how heartening to find that he really was not alone in his struggle. Within three years, Okuyama and other volunteers established thirty-two branches around the country. Mainly through his organizing ability and his willingness to encourage public awareness (Okuyama had worked in advertising, after all), the term *hikikomori* soon found its way into the popular lexicon. TV programs and national magazines began writing about children who locked themselves in their rooms. A handful of doctors began arguing causes and treatment for the syndrome. And in 2001, nearly a year after we first met, Okuyama notched his first real victory when the Health Ministry finally acknowledged that at least six thousand families had visited public clinics seeking help for *hikikomori*, and set up a study team to assess the problem. A follow-up survey conducted in 2002 in rural Mie prefecture found that sixteen families out of 1,420—more than one out of every hundred surveyed—reported having a *hikikomori*.[7] Projected across the entire national population of 126 million, the survey indicated that, at a conservative estimate, at least 410,000 families suffered from the syndrome.

Still, Okuyama is convinced that only pressure from the outside—from foreigners, especially—will force Japan to seriously confront its own societal dysfunction. The more outsiders can expose and explain Japan's social ills, Okuyama believes, the more likely Japan's government will be shamed into becoming more responsive and seek help from outside experts. Otherwise, he fears, the mental health system will, like much of the bureaucracy, keep running on automatic pilot. "We need more black ships," Okuyama kept repeating, referring to the *kuro fune* that had brought Commodore Perry to Tokyo Bay in 1853, ending Japan's long isolation and forcing the Tokugawa shogunate to crumble a decade later. Without the attention or interest of the outside world, an insular Japan would be left isolated with its social and psychological maladies allowed to fester, he feared. Japanese are often fixated on what others, especially Westerners, think of them; and just as "keeping up appearances" is a strong constraint in domestic society, they are sometimes ready to bring their nation in line with certain global norms if sufficient pressure is applied. (The Japanese have been among the pioneers working to reduce the emission of greenhouse gases after adoption of the Kyoto protocol, for instance; likewise, in business, there is much conversation, if less concerted action, to improve "corporate governance" and "global standards" for business practices.)

To Americans who often disparage the criticisms of foreigners, the idea that foreign intervention might create momentum for domestic reform seems a peculiar attitude; yet it was an idea I often heard expressed in Japan. People feel powerless to change policy, even when public health or child welfare is at stake. Decisions are made by distant bureaucrats, and there is no way to make them accountable. Citizens in France or Italy don't rely on the condemnation of foreigners to press for reform: they march or go on strike out of their own urge to do so. But in Japan, *gaiatsu*, or foreign pressure—like Commodore Perry's black ships, and the giant cannons mounted on their decks—is considered critical to shattering the thick museum glass that encases airless national institutions and insulates them from the pressure for change. In countless trade disputes, for instance, only foreign pressure, usually wielded by Washington, has opened up Japanese retail markets or its wireless telecommunications industry.

"You foreign journalists are the most important black ships," Okuyama told me. "You are the *kuro fune.*"

This explained Okuyama's eagerness to help me in my research and his invitation for me to attend a community gathering the following weekend.

* * *

On a sultry Sunday afternoon, I joined a muted assembly of more than a hundred and fifty gray-haired parents, most in their fifties and sixties, who were sitting at plastic-laminated tables in a large seminar room. Volunteers brought in extra folding chairs to accommodate the overflow.

Before the meeting started, one troubled mother talked about her thirty-two-year-old son, who had rarely ventured out of the house in ten years, bathed only once a month, and almost never spoke to his family. Sometimes he punched the walls—or his father.

A father complained about his twenty-nine-year-old son, whose only communication over the past five years was through written notes left on the kitchen table with instructions such as, "Get me a video game magazine," or "Do something about the dog that keeps barking."

These parents were confused, anxious, and lonely. Although a scant few had consulted doctors or health clinics, none of the purported experts had adequately explained what was paralyzing their children and tearing their families apart. Nor could anyone recommend effective treatment.

"We are getting more and more requests for help from all over Japan," Okuyama said, as he picked up a microphone and brought the meeting to order. The parents settled uneasily under the fluorescent lights. I noticed that most of the men looked either stern or impatient, as if they had been dragged there against their will, while the mothers were verging on tears. Okuyama looked tired. I wondered whether this was the result of his cancer medications or the trip he had taken the previous evening to Nagano prefecture, site of the 1998 Winter Olympics, to meet with more than seventy-five parents who wanted to form their own local chapter of KHJ.

Gathering support for parents of *hikikomori* in anonymous suburban communities like this one, where neighbors don't easily reach out to one another, was difficult enough. In Japan's nearly vacant rural districts, where nearly everyone in a hamlet seems to know everyone else, neighbors often pry into one another's business, and almost no secret goes undetected. To be seen entering or leaving a public health clinic or doctor's office can trigger shameful rumors and gossip, so many parents refuse to seek help. Groups like Okuyama's are extremely mindful of how much the parents of *hikikomori* fear discovery. When counselors or aid groups conduct home visits, they take care to park a few blocks away from the home, lest the neighbors see them and start to gossip.

"We want specialists, counselors, trauma evaluators," Okuyama said, meaning professionals who would be assigned to clinics around the country to help parents deal with this virulent family disorder. Okuyama outlined the meeting's agenda and reiterated the group's long-term goals, and the need for government funding. Many obstacles lay ahead in dealing with the powerful medical establishment and administrative bureaucracies, he warned. He told the parents, "It will be a long tunnel for us."

Okuyama did not pretend to have the answers. He himself was fearful and frustrated. He readily acknowledged that they all needed to learn much more about *hikikomori*, what caused it and how it might be treated. To help spark conversation, Okuyama introduced a panel of experts to discuss their assessment of the malady.

Kazuki Ueyama, who had been a *hikikomori* for most of the past two decades, stepped first to the microphone. Kaz, as he liked to be called, wore a blue blazer over a plaid shirt and khakis and was smiling tensely, though even sitting near the back of the room, I could see he was trembling. Squinting a bit through narrow, rimless glasses, he traced the spiral of emotional difficulties that had kept him locked up, out of sight, for so long. His seclusion had begun at age fourteen, when he was a junior high school student in Kobe, the large port city in western Japan that was devastated by the 1995 earthquake. Like many other *hikikomori*, his troubles started after he'd been subjected to the sort of fierce and cruel bullying that occurs every day in most Japanese schools. Over the past four years Kaz had not left his room in his parents' house. He had emerged from seclusion only three months earlier.

Quietly, hesitantly at first, he recounted his retreat. "Other people who are making money, going to bed, going to work each day, they are on the opposite side of the wall from me. How can I explain this to you? *Hikikomori* kids don't have a way out. We just can't get on the other side. I felt like an angry criminal, a victim. I would accuse my mother, shout at her, and say, 'Why did you give birth to me?' In the middle of my problems, all I could do was kick that wall."

The mothers and fathers in the audience nodded their heads slowly, sympathetically, telling me that their children acted in similar ways.

*　*　*

In a nation where children are raised from an early age to fit in, to readily meld themselves into harmonious, purposeful groups, bullying remains a distinctive and brutally effective means of "behavior modification." In the first years of grade school, teachers and parents often deliberately get out of children's way to let natural social dynamics take control of the classroom. Educators believe that young children left to themselves eventually master the skills they need to form cohesive social units and hierarchical relationships. These skills, in turn, are considered essential to navigating a successful adulthood, where one can adapt to and get on well with others.

Rarely, therefore, does a teacher mediate within this organic, group-forming process or intervene to prevent a nonconforming student from being ostracized or bullied. Such intervention might disrupt the whole process. More rarely still does a Japanese mother insinuate herself or get involved: she usually does not alert a teacher or call a principal on the carpet to ensure her child is not mistreated by bigger or more popular classmates. While a European or an American mother might insist that a schoolteacher or principal take care that her child is not beaten up at school, a Japanese parent tends to accept the supremacy the more powerful group imposes on her child. Instead of confronting the school, she would more likely ask her son or daughter, "What have you done in school to get yourself bullied?" The working assumption is that the group discerns in the child's character some inner truth that the parent cannot see.

Some clinical therapists collect enormous files of data recording Japan's most notorious bullying incidents, which go by the term *ijime*. These counselors are certain that schoolroom bullying is all too often a traumatic trigger for withdrawal by teenagers. One fifteen-year-old victim in Nagoya, repeatedly tortured with lit cigarettes and beaten so badly by his classmates that he was twice hospitalized, ended up forking over more than a half million dollars to his tormentors. In another case, six teenagers in Tokyo were arrested for blackmailing some 500,000 yen, or nearly $5,000, out of a fourteen-year-old boy, knowing that the victim's father had recently received a hefty retirement payment. These victims would either cajole their parents into giving them money by concocting a plausible story or just steal it from them—a reflection of how gullible parents could be, and how easy money was to come by in the aftermath of the "bubble economy." Some victims of *ijime* commit suicide by hanging themselves or swallowing weed-killer. Although newspapers regularly report on some of the most egregious *ijime* cases, the vast majority are so common they don't warrant public attention.

Bullying exists among children in many societies, but in Japan it is surprisingly intense and widespread, in part because there seems to be no moral imperative against it. One 1994 survey by the Ministry of Education reported that 58.4 percent of all junior high schools reported serious bullying incidents. A follow-up study released in 2003 reported that students who refuse to go to school after being bullied miss an average of eighteen months to two years of class time.

The psychiatrist Kosuke Yamazaki of Tokai University is one of many clinicians convinced of the connection between *hikikomori* and Japanese-style bullying. "Kids can use *ijime* as a method to get rid of someone who is different," Yamazaki told me when I visited him at a large hospital in Kanagawa prefecture, outside Yokohama. "And once a child gets bullied, he can no longer go to school. This often becomes the start of *hikikomori*." A syndrome known as *futoko*, or school refusal, is often the first stage of withdrawal. A student who chooses to stay away from school for a year or more can easily take the next step and refuse to leave his room at all.

Combating the bullying problem among students is so difficult, Dr. Yamazaki said, because young children are only copying the tactics they see their parents and other adults employ in factories, white-collar offices, and local PTA meetings. "Bullying has become increasingly universal, organized, persistent, vile, and disguised, structured upon complex three- or four-party interactions between the children who bully, those who are bullied, those controlling the children who perform the actual acts of bullying . . . and the children who choose to watch the acts of bullying as bystanders without becoming involved," Yamazaki concluded in a study of children who refuse to attend class.[8]

Though bullying certainly occurs in classrooms and schoolyards in the United States and other societies, its character and frequency are more ruthless and lethal in Japan, he told me. As the Japanese people share racial, clan, and cultural ties, their national dogma suggests that everyone is the same and shares identical thoughts and values. This ideology makes it easier to rationalize punishing the deviant.

Not only is bullying commonplace on the playground, but fear of being bullied is everywhere visible in the adult world. Bureaucrats in government ministries, elected politicians serving in the Diet, and managers in major corporations often report being harassed or bullied. A former member of the Diet, Koh Tanaka, once described to me in painful detail how he was hounded out of the opposition Democratic Party of Japan when he refused to back a specific policy endorsed by the DPJ's leaders. Stripped of his seniority and threatened by colleagues, he left elected office shortly afterward. "How can we claim to have a democracy here in Japan?" he asked me, after describing his harassment. "Even though I was elected as an individual candidate to the parliament, I was not allowed to hold my own opinions. I have been a victim of *ijime*, too."

Any disagreement with the ideas and beliefs of the larger group threatens its *wa*, or harmony. In his book *Straightjacket Society*, the psychiatrist Masao Miyamoto describes the various methods his colleagues used to hound and punish him for refusing to toe the group's line when he worked in the Health Ministry. Bullying, he concludes, is actively condoned even in *adult* Japanese society as a means to modify behavior, "a tool for forcing the individual to accept the logic of the group." This represents a "major difference from the situation in Western countries," where bullying tends to be associated with young children, and where adults who bully others are considered abnormal, or even sadistic.[9]

Clearly, problems in Japan's classrooms are growing worse. Despite Japan's recent prosperity, the number of students refusing to attend school has exploded. Although over the past two decades a steep decline in the nation's birthrate has caused the total school-age population to shrink, the number of junior high school students absent for more than thirty days rose to nearly 75,000 in 1996, or 1.65 percent of all junior high school students. By 1999, the official number exceeded 130,000, and this figure is certainly conservative since schools often list "medical" reasons for a child's absence to protect the child—and the school—from stigma. In August 2005, the Education Ministry conceded that 2 percent of the nation's high school enrollment never shows up for class.

No wild-eyed radical, Dr. Yamazaki is a white-coated clinician steeped in the conservative establishment of the Japanese medical hierarchy. Yet he was among the very first to insist to me that *hikikomori* is a syndrome unique to Japan, that it reflects the nation's mounting uncertainties. "I have not heard of other countries where this sort of withdrawal has become such a social problem," he told me. "This is not a mental disease," like schizophrenia or paranoia; it's "a social disease."

*   *   *

As Kaz Ueyama began to spill out his painful saga, it soon became clear that a common upset stomach nearly a decade earlier had changed the course of his life.

During junior high school he was plagued by bouts of nervous indigestion and, during class, often raised his hand to be excused to go to the bathroom. "Pretty soon, when I'd come out of the bathroom there would be thirty other students lined up there, including girls, saying things like 'Let's give him a big round of applause because he took another crap.'

"Before that, I'd been an extremely good student," he went on. "But after that humiliation, things started going from bad to worse." He was picked on by classmates, and his nervous stomach grew worse. After a teacher whipped him with a belt one day for causing "trouble," he decided he was too drained and pained to go back into the classroom. "I felt isolated in school and couldn't find the motivation to attend class."

For months, Ueyama stubbornly refused to leave his house, taking meals with his mother, but otherwise abandoning society. Eventually, his parents agreed to send him out of town to a vocational high school, but there again he was subjected to abuse and, he said, once again beaten by a teacher. "By the age of sixteen I couldn't go to school and never went out. For a whole month I never saw my own father's face."

Watching the world from the refuge of the family's small apartment, burdened with so much time on his hands, Ueyama began to see modern Japan as absurd and to question it. What's the point of working so hard? he often asked himself. Why do I have to go to a school where I'm not allowed to pursue my own intellectual interests, like history and philosophy, but have to memorize dates and names for college entrance exams? Why do I have to suppress my own ideas and opinions to become part of the business world? Why do I need to go out at all? Although he began reading Kant and Heidegger to understand his existential dilemma, those two philosophers offered him no real-world strategies to solve it.

"Parents like you," he said to the anguished mothers and fathers listening to him, "know all about how to find a job, how to live your lives, but *hikikomori* always keep asking 'Why?' " Ueyama cradled a microphone as he spoke, as if to keep his feelings in check. "I was always questioning everything. I kept asking myself, what about a job? What am I going to do? But I couldn't find any answer. I kept thinking that eventually I would come out, but I couldn't take the shameful stares I would get from neighbors. I just saw myself as unable to adapt. I figured I was just a bad person who couldn't live normally. So I gave up."

Just a few months after first confining himself to his bedroom, Ueyama came out of his room one night and angrily confronted his mother. He demanded to know whether she had divorced his father.

"Why would you ask such a silly question?" his mother replied.

"Because I never hear Dad around here anymore."

"Dad comes home every night," she said. "Maybe you don't hear him because you go to sleep before Dad gets home, and don't wake up until long after he's left for work in the morning."

"Gee, when you become an adult you have to work that hard?" Ueyama remembered asking himself. "I just couldn't possibly do it."

He fled back inside his room and didn't come out again for four months.

* * *

After his twenty-minute talk, Ueyama went out onto the patio for a cigarette. I followed him, wanting to find out more about this articulate, self-possessed, and intelligent young man.

Despite abandoning junior high school, he told me that he had eventually managed to graduate from a small vocational school in Yamanashi prefecture and began to take college courses by correspondence. At one point, thinking he'd like to become a physician, he even ventured out to a cram school to prepare for the medical school entrance examination.

But he soon found he couldn't maintain his motivation, and dropped out of this course, too.

Back at home, he would pace the floors, read books, and obsess about his future. Sometimes he would spend hours fixated on a 10,000 yen banknote, staring at the bill and wondering how he would ever support himself. He went through a series of bingeing episodes, sometimes gaining forty pounds in a month, then losing weight. "For a while, I just got drunk. I told my mother, 'I'm the defective product you produced. Just give up on me.'"

Then he discovered the Internet, which turned out to be Ueyama's lifeline, leading him out of his confinement. Though Japan was very reluctant to offer easy access to the Internet, compared with the United States and Europe (in part because its telephone monopoly insisted on charging 10 yen per minute to dial up a provider), Ueyama was an early user. Surfing the Web to learn more about his own behavior, he gradually discovered listserves and sites devoted to post-traumatic stress disorder and related illnesses. As he delved deeper, he realized that the bullying he had endured resembled traumatic stress, and he began to lurk in various Internet chat rooms, reading the conversations about the disorder but never posting his own comments.

With some trepidation, he initiated an e-mail dialogue with a Japanese woman, then living in Seattle, who was a member of the PTSD chat. She had been raped, and used the Web site to vent her emotions. Together they discussed their experiences—his ostracism, her anxiety—and their fantasies of committing suicide. She encouraged him to talk about his painful past, his social isolation, his desire to express himself, and his ambition to someday leave his room and join the world.

"In a sense, I guess I fell in love with her," Ueyama told me. "She had been married to an American and then divorced. She really listened to me and helped me think about other things in life. Her encouragement triggered me to get back into the world."

As a result of this Internet intimacy, Ueyama was finally able to move out of his family's apartment and into his own small unit. He found a job as a clerk earning about $15 an hour, enough to support himself. And he started to write a memoir of being *hikikomori*. "I want to help parents understand this disease, so that is why I am speaking out," he said. "I would like to become a counselor to help *hikikomori*, but I also want to write about my own experiences. Finally I've decided what I want to do with my life."

While alone in his room, Ueyama said, he had lacked energy or enthusiasm. "My mind was always racing, always busy. I was like a revving engine, whose clutch could never engage. I could put my pedal to the floor, pump the gas, but the tires just wouldn't go because the clutch just wouldn't lock in."

For any *hikikomori*, he told me, the challenge is to preserve your inner feelings and unique identity while still finding a way to function in the larger world of the collective. "When *hikikomori* try to adapt themselves to the demands of the economic society, they have to destroy their insides," he told me months later, when he was deeply engaged in his own book. "To survive in Japan, you have to kill off your own original voice."

*   *   *

Some anthropologists attribute Japan's collective coercion to a primordial dependence on and spiritual connection to rice. In the premodern era, rice was the source of all wealth, and rice cultivation demanded both intense, orchestrated labor and the pooling of a critical resource, water, to irrigate the crops and guarantee a bountiful return. A single peasant's refusal to adopt the irrigation schedule favored by others, or a reluctance to keep his own sluices operating properly, could endanger the communal harvest and the survival of an entire village. Rice cultivation demanded centralized control and broad cooperation. Achieving consensus and ensuring that agreements were implemented had for centuries been matters of life and death.

No longer is the rice harvest the prime concern in Japan, yet still today even the kanji or ideogram for a person, *hito*, shows one figure resting on another. American and Japanese psychologists have demonstrated that when faced with a social situation they do not like, Americans readily try to *influence* others to change their behavior. Japanese, by contrast, are far more likely to *adjust* their own behavior to the demands others make upon them, to accommodate the wishes of the collective.[10] Moreover, whereas Westerners often seek out various forms of self-affirmation and the positive aspects of received criticism, Japanese commonly maintain self-critical attitudes. Since they are constantly taught *hansei*, or self-reflection, in order to focus on their faults and flaws, they always seem aware of when they have transgressed some consensual standard, often an unspoken one.[11]

Yet today the notions of individual autonomy and self-expression so commonplace in the West are inexorably seeping into Japan. There is growing evidence that young Japanese like Ueyama are less willing or able to suck in their sensibilities for greater national goals, even as they find it difficult to conceptualize their own independence. Caught in this limbo, thousands of young people are turning into the social and economic equivalent of plankton, drifting through their working lives without plan, ambition, or direction, or simply not working at all. The government estimates that, aside from the *hikikomori*, nearly 850,000 young Japanese between ages fifteen and thirty-four are not working, or seeking a job, or in education or training.

"*Hikikomori* is not a positive choice, but a negative choice," Ueyama told me later. "You don't want to become *hikikomori*, but you can't help it. When we try to protect our minds and bodies, then we cannot make a living," he said. "When we try to make a living, we cannot protect our minds and bodies. There is no gray zone for *hikikomori*. There is no middle ground."

His words hauntingly echoed what the anthropologist George DeVos had discovered about Japan in the 1970s, long before the nation had emerged as the world's second most powerful economy. "Today, as in the past," he wrote, "an individual cannot function in any Japanese society without explicit interdependency and therefore responsibility to some group in his professional and vocational life. Those who fail to meet obligations soon isolate themselves, and a person who seeks to circumvent society or who becomes too independent finds himself almost totally alienated."[12]

4.

Most modern societies resemble a patchwork of clashing cultures, ethnic subgroups, and regional dialects. The French argue whether Muslims can wear headscarves in school. Turks debate the proper role for their Kurdish minority. Northern and Southern Chinese can read the same newspapers, but can't communicate readily because they speak completely different dialects. Japanese, by contrast, are taught to believe they constitute one giant mystical family, a harmonious clan joined together by a common race, shared heritage, and the same ancestor, the glorious sun goddess Amaterasu. According to the fable of Japan's creation, Amaterasu once hid in a cave and plunged the world into darkness after her unruly brother ravaged the earth and despoiled her garden, temples, and rice fields. Only through song and merriment could she be coaxed from her deepest isolation. In modern Japan, thousands of *hikikomori* emulate her in their response to affront and indignity.

Only in the spring of 2003, years after the problem was first recognized, did Japan's Ministry of Health, Labor and Welfare for the first time publish an official "guideline" that formally defined the nature of *hikikomori*. The ministry euphemistically termed this anxiety disorder a "home-oriented" lifestyle and provided the following specific criteria for identifying the syndrome: no motivation to participate in school or work; no signs of schizophrenia or mental disorder; and persistence beyond six months.

This declaration staked out the modest boundaries of medical consensus regarding a disease only a few professionals had chosen to investigate. The ministry offered no hint, however, of what triggers this unusual behavior, how it might be treated, or why it appears distinctively Japanese. But in the course of my investigations, I found a number of individuals whose treatments of isolated *hikikomori* and whose understanding of this syndrome deserved wider consideration.

*   *   *

Tamaki Saito was probably the first clinician to write extensively about the pathology of *hikikomori*. This mop-haired psychiatrist operates a clinic in suburban Chiba prefecture where he treats hundreds of *hikikomori* patients and their families. After his guide to the disorder targeted to a nonmedical audience was published in 1998, Saito became something of a celebrity, popping up frequently on documentary segments and TV "wide shows," as talk-and-variety programs are called. Dr. Saito was also the first to estimate that more than one million Japanese adults are plagued with this social illness—a claim that, as he told me, he had based on the number of schizophrenics found in Japanese society. His own clinical work had convinced Saito that the incidence of *hikikomori* must be at least as widespread. His estimate soon became the accepted benchmark adopted by others, including the government-owned NHK television and radio network, which frequently told its listeners that between 1 million and 1.2 million young adults suffer from the syndrome. In truth, no one knows for sure how many do. I sensed that, in part, this ignorance exists because many Japanese don't really want to know how deep the problem runs.

"In Japan, when a young person drops out, his family supports him," Saito said, when I first asked him to explain what elements make this malady unlike others and uniquely Japanese. "These young adults depend on their parents after they grow up, and really live in a parasitic state. Even at thirty or forty years old, the parents still support them. This state is very specific to Japan. It doesn't exist anyplace else in the world."

Saito was referring specifically to the intense relationship said to exist between a Japanese mother and her child. Clinical research has demonstrated that mother-child interactions in Japan tend to differ from those in the West, and the most prominent distinction focuses on *amae*, or "dependency," a noun used to describe a close, cocoonlike bond.

The concept of *amae* was first proposed by the psychoanalyst Takeo Doi, whose *Anatomy of Dependence*, originally published in Japanese in 1971, was well received by Western clinicians upon its translation two years later. Doi argues that the craving between mother and son for close contact works to partially counteract individuation, and that while Western societies suppress these urges for dependency, Japanese society actively encourages them. Such dependency relations can also exist with daughters. In a Japanese household the father is often absent and chooses not to share nearly as much of the child-rearing responsibilities as in a contemporary Western home. While such close mother-son contact is by no means unknown in the West, the fact that it is encouraged, not discouraged, within Japanese culture and can be reproduced in many social relationships outside the home, as between a young employee and his boss, makes the dependency seem far more intense.

To a Westerner, independence is, like freedom, a virtue or a moral imperative, while the word "dependence" conjures up negative images of welfare or drug use. In Japanese, however, freedom, or *jiyu*, is a concept laden with ambiguity. One political party, the Liberals, calls itself the Jiyuto—literally, the Freedom Party. But *jiyu* can also denote an individual who willfully asserts the right to behave as he pleases *despite* the wishes of the group, of one who exhibits selfishness by putting his own needs ahead of others'. In a society that did not abandon feudalism until the mid-nineteenth century, where the vast majority of Japanese lacked a family name until the 1870s, and the Emperor was considered divine until 1945, the boundaries between state and divinity, state and nature, and society and self—ones that Westerners might take for granted—were never clearly differentiated.[1]

Japanese see modern America as a "hunter's" society, where man roams freely across an open frontier to stalk his prey. Theirs they view, by contrast, as a "farmer's" society, whose inhabitants remain fixed in one place year after year to cultivate a perpetual rice crop. According to Chie

Kanagawa, a cultural psychologist, the Japanese self is typically understood as flexible and determined both by situation and by setting or context. Even the expression of "I" in Japanese is context-dependent, with many different word choices available to the speaker to signal relative status. When a male talks casually to a friend, "I" is *boku*; to a superior, it is the humble *watashi*; to his wife, the crudely familiar *ore*.[2]

It is no accident that a Japanese first associates himself with his company or group affiliation before giving his family name. "I am Sony corporation's Suzuki," or "I am the Education Ministry's Ozawa," is the proper way for a Japanese to introduce himself to another person as they exchange *meishi*, or business cards. Without business cards and titles, how can strangers determine which person is senior and therefore demands greater respect and a deeper bow? Without some association to an institution— a company, a university, the family—who exactly *is* a person?

Doi writes that he was first struck by the social significance of *amae* (dependence) when he was entertained in an American home. The polite American host asks his guest to choose from among a variety of beverages—hard liquor, wine, or a soft drink, for instance—and how he wants it served. A Japanese host, in contrast, produces a beverage for the guest with a deprecatory remark—"This may not suit your taste, but . . ." A Japanese would be appalled by the mandate "Please help yourself." The Japanese sensibility demands that the host help his guest and anticipate his wishes. "To leave a guest unfamiliar with your house to 'help himself' would seem excessively lacking in consideration," Doi writes.[3] Thus—according to the prominent psychiatrist Dr. Satoru Saito—when a *hikikomori* faces conflict or tension, he expects his mother to be able to anticipate the difficulty he is facing without his even having to speak. " 'If I have to articulate my problem [the *hikikomori* says], then I have to recognize it,' which will lead to shame or frustration." As a result of this fear that the mother will fail to anticipate her son's needs—and thus demonstrate the weakening of their *amae* attachment—the *hikikomori* often stops talking altogether and withdraws from contact. His accumulating frustration can cause him to rage against his parents.

So well understood is this parent-child *amae* attachment that it becomes the yardstick for judging all other connections within Japanese society. "A relationship between two people becomes deeper the closer it approaches the warmth of the parent-child relationship, and is considered shallow unless it becomes so," Doi writes. Japanese simultaneously inhabit three worlds of dependence: the parent-child realm; the workplace, where dependence is an implicit element of the social contract; and the world of strangers in which mutual dependence does not exist. This construct helps explain why Japanese maintain a strong division between those "inside" or "outside" their specific family or group relationships. They lavish attention and deference on those inside their *uchi*, or house, and ignore those outside, or *soto*, as strangers—*tanin*, unrelated persons—and accord them no special treatment. The Western belief that all people should be treated equally whether *uchi* or *soto*—inside or outside the "network"—seems strange to most Japanese. In a deeper sense, they carry psychic double ledgers: one set for the outside world, and another held closely within. For if one is expected to hold both "inner" and "outer" feelings, then truth itself should be Janus-faced. Japanese acknowledge that there is a public face, or *tatemae*, visible when one speaks formally, officially, or to strangers. One expresses true feelings, or *honne*, only among the closest friends, late at night over a glass of saké or whiskey. "That a man's standard of behavior should differ within his own circle and outside it affords no food for inner conflict," Doi explains.[4]

This separation between public and private is a reason Westerners often feel that their Japanese contacts or business partners "don't tell the truth" during business negotiations. The Japanese are telling *a* truth, a contextual truth, but it is not universal truth as Westerners understand it. Japanese may say *hai*—or yes—during a negotiation, for instance, but the word does not signify agreement with what the other party is saying; it means only that they understand what is being said. President George W. Bush may have learned this best when, in September 2004, just weeks before the U.S. presidential election, he met with Prime Minister Junichiro Koizumi and won assurances that Japan would soon permit the resumption of U.S. beef sales to Japan, a $1.7 billion annual export market which had been cut off in December 2003 after a single American cow was discovered to have contracted mad cow disease. Six months later, however, Bush was again forced to telephone Koizumi, his single closest Asian ally, to ask again when the ban might finally be lifted. Agreeing on a "framework" for lifting the ban had not actually meant that beef import sales might resume. (U.S. beef exports to Japan only resumed in December 2005, but were suspended again four weeks later after a New York–based meatpacker violated export rules designed to prevent the spread of mad cow.)

Like one's own identity, truth in Japan can depend on the context: something is not always and universally true. Some psychiatrists believe that because the split between true feeling and public "face" is so deeply ingrained in the Japanese, they suffer far fewer cases of multiple personality disorder than do Westerners. "Because all of us Japanese grow up with multiple personalities, we almost never see this disorder in our patients," the psychologist Yuichi Hattori told me.

The yearning for *amae* serves as a powerful paradigm. It explains why, in a Japanese corporation, bosses depend on their employees and employees on their bosses in a paternal bond, and why firms tend to rely on a lifetime employment system, which permits mutual dependencies to evolve and play out over a period of many years. It explains why the most talented managers often do not become top leaders in Japan: if they are too smart, they might not depend sufficiently on their subordinates and so will disturb the group harmony embedded in organizational behavior. Dependency relations also justify hierarchies in Japan, since lines of authority are easily clarified, and identities are both formed and held together around group orientations.

Many *hikikomori* simply cannot abandon their *honne* because they find it painfully difficult to navigate this split between the social artifice the "real world" seems to demand and their genuine emotions. Others just refuse to make the shift. Some therapists categorize their unwillingness to revert to *tatemae* as a communication disorder that only exacerbates their social isolation.

*   *   *

In his clinic, where he comes in contact with hundreds of patients each week, Tamaki Saito's tangible experiences seem to bear out Doi's theoretical analysis of *amae*. In Western society, Saito told me, any "grown-up person should be independent. But in Japan, we are not ashamed not to be independent," using a classical Japanese construction, the double negative, to emphasize with indirection. "After we have grown up, we depend on our parents sometimes, and sometimes our parents depend on us. This is a natural attitude for Japanese people."

The power of *amae* can also explain why a mother often encourages and abets her son's antisocial behavior instead of helping her *hikikomori* child break free. Whether her son is needy and afraid or just willfully indulgent, many a *hikikomori*'s mother cannot simply refuse to provide care for him. Yet such codependency enables the condition to persist for months or years. "The symbiosis of mother and son is a common state of the *hikikomori* lifestyle, and the mother doesn't care about the husband or other parts of the family—only the troubled son," Saito told me. "She expects her son to be independent someday, but Independence Day never comes." Fret as she may over her isolated child, the mother also finds herself empowered by him. The child simply cannot survive without his mother, and her identity as nurturer and protector remains secure as long as he remains sequestered. If her son emancipates himself and becomes independent, what then does she become? In 95 percent of the cases he treats, Saito asserted that the mother plays an active role in supporting the isolation of this "problem child," even though her reputation will inevitably be stained and the family shamed and embarrassed if outsiders learn of the child's condition.

Having screened many of his *hikikomori* patients using the standard Western diagnostic guide to mental disorder, the DSM IV, and finding that their symptoms fell into no recognized disease category, Saito believes that the syndrome is utterly new and different. "This is not a psychotic disorder, or schizophrenia," Saito said of *hikikomori*. "Westerners have trouble understanding the distinction.

"If you meet a schizophrenic patient, there is real miscommunication. Maybe you can't understand his speech or his words. Maybe he hears voices or has hallucinations. His cognitive processes are out of whack.

"But if you meet *hikikomori*, they never display these symptoms. They are very intelligent, and when they relax, they are very communicative and very coherent. That is the biggest difference."

Nor is the *hikikomori*'s condition similar to agoraphobia, the fear of being in an unsettled, unpredictable public setting. While an agoraphobic may not willingly venture out into an environment he cannot control, he readily welcomes an old friend to visit him at home. A *hikikomori* resolutely cuts his connections with everyone; he cannot bear coming into contact with old acquaintants and often refuses to establish eye contact with his parents or siblings. Though he continues to rely on his dependency relationship with his mother to survive—someone has to place food outside his bedroom door, after all—he may refuse to speak to her.

Despite repeated investigations by Japanese and other Asian psychiatrists, this withdrawal syndrome has been found in no other culture, not even in neighboring South Korea, which shares so much of Japan's Buddhist and Confucian past, as well as its state-guided model of economic development. (At least one South Korean psychiatrist has reported finding what he terms a "lonely person" syndrome among teenagers in Seoul, but the symptoms he describes are far less severe than those plaguing *hikikomori*. Many Korean "loners" surf the Internet and chat online with friends; and by age eighteen the syndrome passes because, unlike Japanese, all South Korean males face compulsory military duty.) A few Japanese living in Hawaii or Europe have also been reported to suffer a similar disorder.

*   *   *

If the nature of dependence within Japan is an important element enabling *hikikomori* to take hold, the changing nature of Japanese family life also contributes. Japanese households were once busy and crowded settings, gathering together uncles, cousins, and grandparents to form broad extended families. Modern Japanese homes, however, tend to be nuclear families populated by far fewer children than in the past, and as the size of the household has continued to shrink, an intense dependency between a mother and her only son can become magnified.

For centuries, the traditional kinship household, or *ie* system, upheld continuity within Japan. Ensuring the survival of one's *ie*, or stem family, customarily superseded any individual's autonomy. Yet in just two generations, the *ie* began to come apart as a result of the nation's rapid industrialization.

In traditional Japan, the *ie* or lineal family was far more than a simple household; it tended to resemble a vast tribal corporation with multiple subsidiaries. The *ie* arranged marriages for children of the household; if there were no male child, the clan "adopted" a male to marry into the family and carry forward the family name. The *ie* system dictated that the oldest male would inherit a family's assets, while the younger sons would move out of the main house to form branch homes that remained subordinate to the male authority residing within the main house. To help reinforce the unbroken line of inheritance, the wife of the eldest son moved into the main house to apprentice with, and eventually nurse, the mother-in-law until the latter's death; likewise, the wives of the younger sons maintained subordinate relations to their mother-in-law and the wife of the eldest son.

The *ie* also controlled occupations. In prewar Japan, the *ie* supervised small farms and manufacturing enterprises, which were the foundations of society. (It is no coincidence that the characters that comprise the word "corporation," or *kaisha*, become, when reversed, the word for society, *shakai*.) Family clans who weren't engaged in farming tended to specialize in a single occupation, like weaving, sword making, or trading, and sometimes brought in nonfamily workers to assist. Naturally, the *ie* was a bustling, multigenerational enterprise, where uncles, grandparents, servants, and cousins frequently interacted. In the rural poverty of traditional Japan, men produced large families to help with the backbreaking demands peasant life presented, and women actively participated in rice planting and other labors. The configuration of the traditional home with its series of sliding doors and common areas for eating and sleeping also allowed many generations to interact easily. Whenever I asked older Japanese to reminisce about their prewar youth, they readily recalled playing with cousins, listening to stories from their uncles, or battling it out with older siblings. Not unlike American family life until early in the twentieth century, several generations regularly came and went through the broad doorway of the wide-open family home.

The *ie* may seem old-fashioned, yet it still informs many social customs. Even today, the wife of a first-born son is expected to nurse her ailing mother-in-law, and a man and woman who wed must, by law, share a single family name. (Contemporary women find both these strictures a considerable disadvantage. Young women often say they will never marry a first-born son unless his mother is dead, because they don't want to become her nursemaid. Career women are equally reluctant to ditch their professional names for the sake of matrimony.)

Hayao Kawai, perhaps Japan's most eminent clinical psychologist, believes that maintaining clan existence has always superseded the quest for individual identity in Japanese society.

"*Ie* is different from family," said Kawai, president of the Association of Japanese Clinical Psychology and an advisor to Prime Minister Junichiro Koizumi. "The Kawai *ie* is important, not my family. It's about clan. If my son proves himself incapable, I simply abolish him and adopt another son. It's about ensuring continuation of the name Kawai, not necessarily a blood tie. This was the Japanese system before the war. I would easily sacrifice myself because I'm not important. Maintaining the *ie* is important."

As a result of rapid industrialization and a large migration to the big cities from the countryside, the smaller, Western-style nuclear family began to replace the larger *ie* even before the outbreak of World War Two. This trend accelerated after the war, in which massive U.S. fire bombings devastated major cities. The subsequent construction in the 1950s and 1960s of dormitory-style apartment complexes and tiny houses, which were too cramped to hold several generations of a Japanese family, further fragmented domestic life. As the postwar baby boom generation moved to the new suburbs during a period known in Japan as *mai homu shugi*—when imported TV programs like *Father Knows Best* began to re-shape culture and values—the roots of *ie* shrank further.

The U.S. occupation did not just abolish the Imperial system and in-troduce a new constitution after the war; it also revamped the formal, le-gal status of the *ie* household. "The Americans thought the *ie* too feudal, so they tried to destroy the system," Kawai said. Rather than abandon the concept of *ie*, however, the Japanese displaced these sentiments, project-ing them instead onto corporate life. "We began to believe, 'I am part of the Matsushita *ie* or the Sanyo *ie*,'" Kawai said. This deep psychological transference helps explains the slavish devotion of many Japanese to their companies ahead of their own families. "Everyone is eager to spend so much time and energy for the company, because if the company con-tinues, their identity remains the same," Kawai explained.

The collapse of the traditional *ie*, combined with the persistent eco-nomic downturn of the past decade, has left today's young adults increas-ingly alienated and rootless, Kawai told me. They no longer yearn to wear dark blue suits and live out their lives as a stable *sarariman*, and seem in-creasingly alienated from the rigid composition of Japan Inc., the highly organized system that distributes power among corporations, the power-ful bureaucracy, and the politicians. But they remain unable to envision new alternatives even as they seek to assert more individual autonomy. "These days, young people say 'Matsushita [the owner of the Panasonic brand] is not so important. What's most important is myself. So then I would like to do whatever I want to do.' It's completely contrary to the traditional Japanese thinking, so it seems quite selfish," Kawai said. "They forget about relations with others and think only about them-selves."

While young Japanese glean superficial images of what they believe to be "individualism" from the Western movies and TV shows they watch, they don't grasp the deeper Western sense of individual responsibility that accompanies such freedom, Kawai told me. "Their appreciation of individualism remains quite shallow," he said. "In your country, individu-alism is at first really based on Christianity. Even though you do what you like, you never forget about your God. God is looking down, like an ego, judging you. But in Japan, there is no God but the *ie*," and no one to judge but the group. "Westerners have a long history of becoming individuals, and you have established how to create relations with others. But we don't share that experience in Japan . . . I often think that our challenge now as Japanese is to come up with a new way to become individuals without relying on Christianity."

The collapse of the *ie* and the transformation of Japan's residential and occupational patterns also radically changed the environment for child-rearing families. The typical modern child today grows up alone, with one or no siblings, in a rootless new suburb without close connections to other children, other families, or other people in the neighborhood. According to government census data, as late as 1955, 36.5 percent of all Japanese households lived in extended families; by 1995, the proportion had fallen to just 15 percent. Japan's plummeting birthrate also shrinks family size. Even as late as 1960, the census shows, 42 percent of Japanese households contained five or more members; in 1995, only 14 percent did, and the average household contained only 2.82 members.[5]

Without cousins or aunts or grandparents streaming through the family home each day, the modern Japanese male teenager essentially grows up alone with his mother, who, if she works, may only do so part time. The Japanese father—the "absentee father," as psychiatrists commonly refer to him—is seldom home. Dad typically commutes an hour or more to his job, works late into the evening, and is expected to stay out even later, drinking and bonding with clients and colleagues from work. As Kawai said, the corporation has become the *ie*. Japanese dads do not leave work early to go to their son's Little League baseball games. No more do Japanese live in the mythical *furusato*, or hometown, of Japanese song, where many neighbors and acquaintances actually were blood relations.

*   *   *

What happens when the narrow nuclear family fails? Who teaches a child how to socialize and function in the world outside?

Dr. Satoru Saito suggests that Japan has entered a period of profound "discommunication," of which *hikikomori* is a natural consequence. The *hikikomori* children are protesting—silently but powerfully—the life-styles of their parents. "In this country, we haven't cherished relationships with people; we've only chased economic efficiency," this psychiatrist told me. "So children today are fragile and have to survive in a place where they no longer have sufficient support structures."

Saito agrees that modern nuclear families rarely share blood ties with others in the community. As atomized communities of strangers file into suburbs, newcomers tend not to get involved in local politics or in school activities; nor do they attend the local *matsuri*, or community festival. These new residents usually find it difficult to connect with neighbors because the social networks that connect strangers are fragmentary and distorted by the old rigidities of *uchi* and *soto*, or inside and outside.

"Because the parents don't participate in the community, the children have no exposure to outside forces," Saito explained. Ultimately, "the community's values cannot become integrated with the family's values," as no outside forces are powerful enough to invade the insular space of the nuclear household. Fathers become workaholics. Mothers pressure their children toward academic achievement and admission to a presti-gious college. "The mother's expectation for the child is very high, and if the child violates that expectation, he feels guilt and shame."

The close knit *amae* relationship between mother and child exacer-bates the anxieties of the socially withdrawn, Satoru Saito believes, and places them in a perverse sort of double-bind. "Of course the father's role should be to loosen that tension" between mother and child, "but the fa-ther usually isn't there."

*   *   *

Since 1999, Yuichi Hattori, a baby-cheeked counselor who studied at California State University, Northridge, has treated more than thirty *hikikomori* patients in the modest office attached to his house in the Tokyo suburb of Sayama, just a few minutes' walk from a sprawling Honda auto factory. While Satoru Saito believes that involving the whole family in therapy is critical in treating *hikikomori*, and while Tamaki Saito often relies on drugs, Hattori believes his patients need to burst through the internal barriers that suppress their *honne*, or true feelings. Usually that means separating the patient completely from the family.

"The main cause of this problem comes from the suppression of individuality," Hattori told me the first time we met at his clinic. "This culture does not permit you to express your individual feelings or thoughts, so you must hide them."

All of Hattori's patients come from middle- and upper-class households, and more than two-thirds are men. He describes his patients as emotionally starved. "They often don't understand their own situation. *Hikikomori* are often like three-year-olds who wander lost in the woods," he said. By his estimate, 60 percent of his clients have attacked one or both of their parents.

Hattori's patients have all struggled to become model "good boys and girls" in hopes of gaining the affection of parents who not only have difficulty communicating or expressing love to each other, but who live in a society where open expressions of affection are almost never encouraged. (The psychiatrist Kawai once confided that if he ever told his wife he loved her, she would look at him as if he was crazy.)

Hattori believes *hikikomori* are at war with their insides, their authentic personality constantly struggling against the personality they think they must create in order to gain love. Having abandoned their own will and innate emotions, his patients suppress their natural identities. Hattori calls this adopted persona the "front personality," and said young Japanese create this "false front" at an early age out of fear of abandonment should their true selves become visible. "The front personality can't have intimate relations with others," he explained. This front personality avoids confrontation and suppresses the patient's authentic, individual personality, hindering a patient's healthy emotional development. Because these children fear rejection if they let their real or "back" personalities emerge, they create false personalities in an attempt to capture the parent's attention.

Yet the patient's core, or original, personality doesn't completely disappear. It is actively suppressed by the front personality, which denies the conscience, critical judgment, and decision-making skills of the core self. With one personality suspended but not eliminated, these two personalities continue in constant struggle. Eventually, Hattori says, most of his patients "burn out," emotionally exhausted from the struggle taking place within them. Ultimately, they become defeated, emotionless zombies.

In Hattori's analysis, I recognized Kenji, the wispy thirty-four-year-old baseball fan whose inability to master the skill of *tatemae* had, as he told me, kept him from engaging with others. As a teenager he remembered attending parties and laughing at jokes he didn't think were funny, just to become an accepted part of the group. "It was another kind of bullying," he said, "being forced to fit in . . . It was so tiring to keep up the pretense and to pretend to be like the others that eventually . . . I just burned out."

Hattori argues that it is natural for the conflict between "front" and "back" personalities to emerge among adolescents—especially in the stressful social environment of the school setting. Successfully developing a "false front," or front personality, is essential for young children if they hope to survive within the rigid Japanese education system. After all, he says, look at Japanese schools where children each day study from the same page of the same book as their peers in other, nearly identical classrooms; where children are usually required to wear identical, military-style uniforms; and where teachers follow a detailed set of exacting, intrusive regulations prepared by the Education Ministry and are asked to emphasize rote learning over the development of critical thinking skills. In such a system, there is little room for the deviant, someone who might "cause trouble" by expressing his own creative flair. (This thought often came to me in the grocery store, where the only cucumbers for sale in the vegetable bin were stick-straight. Where did they ship the curvy ones?) Those who can't navigate the contradictions, who can't develop the proper "good boy" front personality in order to fit in, who can't keep their *honne* under wraps, often find themselves bullied.

Hattori uses a curious procedure to draw out the "inner" self, or *honne*. Often, he takes off his oversized, rectangular glasses and rolls his office chair to within inches of the young man, staring directly into his eyes, talking to him softly, calmly, as if cooing to a pet bird. It's Hattori's belief that this direct gaze—a look Japanese seldom experience in daily life—can so unsettle his patient as to eventually force his hidden personality to emerge. Invariably, on the half-dozen occasions when I watched Hattori use this technique—sometimes in person, sometimes on a videotape—a dramatic change in the patient's bearing was clearly visible.

Hattori believes few Japanese therapists understand the sort of therapy he uses, or even the nature of the syndrome, because they do not appreciate how deeply *hikikomori* is associated with post-traumatic stress. Hattori also believes that his patients are likely to open up and become more communicative with a Westerner than with a fellow Japanese, so he invited me to attend some of his counseling sessions, after securing the patient's approval.

During one three-hour visit to his clinic, I watched quietly from the side while Hattori worked with Mariko, a twenty-two-year-old woman who suffered from a mild form of *hikikomori*. A graduate of a junior college, she could hold down the occasional odd job and had attended about one-third of her university classes. Nonetheless, she was frequently immobilized, could not form normal emotional relationships, and said any form of social conversation made her utterly exhausted. She usually stayed closeted in her bedroom.

Now, sprawled on the red cloth couch in Hattori's office, this intelligent adult transformed herself into what seemed to me to be a whimpering five-year-old, peevishly kicking her legs out in an obvious bid for attention. Sometimes, she seemed torpid and tranquil, a needy child in search of love. At other moments, she lashed out, saying she wanted to kill her father.

"He's a coward, he's not respectable," Mariko said, spitting out her anger. "I can never understand what he's thinking." Later, in a distant, trancelike state, she described his emotional absence. "He never played with me. I don't want to become like him." Prompted by Hattori, she vividly recalled the time when she was a small child, and her father put ugly cicada bugs on her arm, frightening her as she watched television.

During those three hours, Mariko often wriggled her shoulders, hunched up her back, narrowed her gaze, and turned into a grade-school student, her face flushed, describing how she tried to fit into a group without being bullied. "I wasn't allowed to make mistakes," she whined. "I wanted to express myself, but I couldn't. I played a role so I wouldn't be bullied by others, but I got very tired trying to keep up appearances.

"When kids get bullied the parents should understand, but they don't," she whimpered. "They yell at their kids and tell them to fit in. I only wanted to be regarded as a normal person."

During this therapy session, Mariko told Hattori that she worried about what others thought of her. "I don't want to be an adult, I want to be a spoiled child, I want to be indulged," she said to the therapist dreamily, as if under hypnosis. "I wanted to commit suicide, but couldn't go through with it."

Just a few weeks before this counseling session, a man in Osaka invaded an elementary school with a kitchen knife, running wildly through the classrooms and killing eight students. It was the sort of shocking, violent crime seldom associated with life in Japan. Immediately after the crime, Hattori speculated that the assailant was probably fixated on the times when, as a child, he himself had been bullied. (Later, in fact, the man's fragile psychological state would be used by the defense attorneys at trial in a failed effort to spare his life.) Like many of Hattori's other clients, Mariko said she completely understood the attacker's state of mind. Her personality sometimes raged out of control, she said, and she was also capable of committing violent attacks. "I get angry just like that."

Hattori wondered if I had a question to pose. I gently asked Mariko whether she might feel better by being openly defiant. Might she one day impulsively just open a window, stick her head out, and scream, "I am my own person!"

"I couldn't ever do that," she responded, shaking her head, downcast. "It's impossible. This is Japan."

5.

As the plague of *hikikomori* spreads among the nation's young, someone needs to develop effective countermeasures. Yet Japan's central government, which should be taking the lead, seems paralyzed or uninterested. Such official indifference hasn't prevented a wide variety of self-appointed experts from prescribing everything from drug therapy and couch counseling to manual labor in the fields as "cures" powerful enough to overcome such deep disillusion. Dozens of centers have sprung up across the nation, many run by those without clinical training, counseling experience, or medical supervision. And while some of these represent well-meaning efforts, others are run by charlatans. In an environment suffused with shame and secrecy, there is no way of knowing whether any of these approaches really works. By early 2004, no peer-reviewed journal had published any research on the nature of this malady, nor had any rigorous field studies into its causes been disseminated. My conversations with both the Health and the Education Ministries suggested that despite my sense that a national mobilization might be needed to address this behavior head-on, neither agency was eager to probe deeply. Yet parents who are desperate, demoralized, and shame-filled flock to any treatment that offers even a glimmer of hope.

A few psychiatrists, counselors, and low-paid teachers work at the periphery of the official radar and wrestle each day with the lost and disaffected tribe of *hikikomori* and their volatile emotions. Of this small cadre of activists, three stand out for their imaginative and determined approaches to the problem: Nobuyuki Minami, a layman; Dr. Hisako Watanabe, a child psychiatrist with extensive European training; and Sadatsugu Kudo, a counselor. Each believes that a *hikikomori*'s condition cannot improve unless his environment is changed—an insight borne out by one *hikikomori*, Shigei, who said, "When doctors look only at biological symptoms and give me drugs, they don't solve the problem . . . The environment is the underlying cause."

*   *   *

Nobuyuki Minami gave up his career as an advertising copywriter and designer in order to offer troubled youth a lifeline. Since 2000, he has operated his unlikely refuge, called a "free space," in the one-time farming village of Shiki, Saitama prefecture, now swallowed up into the vast Tokyo suburbs. His center is a broad, ramshackle building constructed of flimsy wood panels and metal siding, with a gently sloping roof. This spacious old farmhouse accommodates a communal kitchen, an indoor playroom, and a large dining area, while vegetable gardens, rope swings, and a recreation area are set out back. To the right of the farmhouse sits an asphalt parking lot and a ferroconcrete apartment block yellowed by age. To the left, green onions still poke up audaciously from the damp black soil—testifying to the area's past as a farming community. Sometimes, during a game of catch, Minami's kids tramp through the field to fetch a stray tennis ball.

"We try to create another home, like a family relationship, for the kids," Minami explained as they played.

Minami has no academic credentials or training to justify his work with *hikikomori*, only his sense of urgency. "We just can't treat kids as kids anymore," he told me, as if speaking for his young clients. "We have to treat them as humans. You can't cheat kids and just order them to do things. You also have to explain to them why they have to do them.

"These kids have been rejected by the school culture which forces everyone to be the same," Minami continued, after he'd led me into the living room to talk. "But each kid is so unique; each one of them is different. I don't want to do anything to damage that. I don't want to suppress them at all, so that puts me at odds with traditional Japanese culture."

For six years Minami has worked primarily with adolescent dropouts, known as *futoko*, as well as with the *hikikomori* who isolate themselves at home. He distills his school's lessons into two basic principles. "Choice and responsibility," he told me. "Choice and responsibility is what I want these kids to take away from here. If they can learn to make choices for themselves and take responsibility for those choices, then really, what else can I teach them?"

I was struck by the simplicity of this credo. Give a Japanese teenager genuine choice? Demand that he take real responsibility for his own decisions? In Japan's collectivist culture, even parents and corporations usually eschew such accountability. But Minami nudges his students to accept autonomy and thereby slowly gain self-confidence. Most days, students choose which subjects they study, and are allowed to focus on areas they like, rather than shift, hour to hour, from math to science to history. They also take responsibility within the school for cooking and cleaning and do some of the gardening chores. From Minami's perspective, these "troubled" kids are actually less troubled than many of their parents and teachers. Like barometric gauges, they sense atmospheric changes most adults can't discern.

Just as with a discreet hostess club in the Ginza, there is no way to learn of Minami's unassuming "free space" unless someone in the know leads you there. I had been brought that day by Hiro, the gangly nineteen-year-old *hikikomori* who loves to draw spacecraft and build models and who is gradually cracking out of his shell. His willingness to bring me along and introduce me to Minami was the climax of my year of conversations with him and his mother.

I felt great sympathy for Hiro, who seemed genuinely intelligent, gentle, and lost. There are many detached young men in Japan today and I wanted to see whether there was even a chance Hiro might find his way back into the mainstream, or have the courage to eventually discern his own path. Talking to a caregiver like Minami might provide some answers—both for Hiro's life and for others who suffer from *hikikomori*.

Most of Minami's students are significantly younger than Hiro and attend this free space three times a week. Hiro comes about once a month, taking a twenty-minute train ride to the school to play on the group computer, hang out with some of the other students, whittle some wood with a knife, help with the cooking chores, and work on the designs for some of the techno-warriors and space rockets he plasters all over his bedroom. More of a floating than a "regular" participant, Hiro told me he felt comfortable and relaxed around Minami, and seemed proud that he had made a place for himself within the protected community. To him, these loose and casual connections prove he is no misfit. He did not seem to notice that he was two heads taller than his thirteen- and fourteen-year-old schoolmates; or that, with his shoulder-length hair and sprouting mustache, he stood out among them as a physically mature man. He came here simply because he could have fun, he told me. "This place has lots of good information and materials, so in addition to meeting other kids, I can do many things here I can't do by myself at home."

That day of my visit, as Hiro worked at the school's personal computer, Minami gave me a tour of the living and dining area of the rambling house, where a dartboard hung on one wall and a guitar lay against the wall adjacent to a TV set. "We really don't have a schedule, but every day I ask the kids to cook," Minami explained. In the kitchen, six teenagers, girls and boys together, were preparing lunch after a morning of math practice. "Today they decided to prepare *chahan* rice and wonton soup. It's important they decide for themselves what they are going to eat."

As Minami offered me coffee, he explained how child-rearing in Japan has been warped by the pressure to create harmony. "In Japan, as you know, everybody has to be good friends. When it works, that's okay. But when it doesn't, you face pressure to push everyone together or exclude a person who somehow is different.

"In that way, traditional school culture is typical," he said. "The kids who come here are those who have been rejected by those schools." The Internet, MTV, video games, mobile phones, and movies are rapidly exposing a once-homogeneous and nearly indistinguishable body of students to new ways of acting, dressing, thinking, and communicating. Yet Japan provides few outlets for youngsters who have absorbed and been changed by these new media.

Nearly since the beginning of public education in Japan a century ago, Japanese schools taught group solidarity and excelled at imparting basic education. Now schools lag, and student performance has tapered off. Although schools still prepare students diligently for standardized exams and drill them to memorize obscure facts and dates, teachers do not encourage pupils to acquire critical thinking skills—analysis, creativity, or independent reasoning. Teachers lecture, and students dutifully take notes but are not expected to form their own opinions or judge the relevance of the evidence presented. Give-and-take in the classroom is discouraged. Though the demands of the twenty-first century require teaching students how to pick apart problems by using complex reasoning and how to apply one's accumulated knowledge to real-world situations, Japanese schools still emphasize rote instruction. Some teachers now even carry stopwatches, to ensure pupils spit out their answers quickly enough. In a world being transformed by the diffusion of global technologies, the rise of knowledge-based industries, and an accelerated flow of vast pools of information, these students are not being prepared adequately for the world they will face, yet school curriculums have barely changed.

"During our long period of high economic growth, kids didn't stay home from school or become *hikikomori*," Minami told me. "Only after we reached the summit did people find themselves lost. They wondered, what should we value? Our strongest virtue as Japanese is that we never got fazed and never got puzzled, we just marched straight ahead. But kids sensed the moment [of change]. They looked at adults telling them 'You have to study hard or you won't be successful,' and the kids, they just didn't trust it. They didn't believe it. This was when *futoko* and *hikikomori* started—which is something most people, especially officials in the Education Ministry, simply don't understand."

The evidence suggests students know their schools are failing them, which is why they are abandoning them in record numbers. In 2002, more than 131,000 children, including nearly 3 percent of all junior high students, simply did not attend school at all, according to the official figures; and these statistics probably understate reality.[1] Yet schools seldom try to woo students back into the classroom once they leave, and parents are not prepared to drag them back.

"When you look carefully at the kids in this school, what they are seeking is community with others; they are seeking friends," Minami said. "*Futoko* are not rejecting others, it's just that they can't find a single place where people will be patient with them" and let them pursue their own interests. When so many thousands fall out of the government system, private groups or individuals like Minami have to step in.

Most efforts to rethink the nation's rigid educational doctrines have been blocked not only by Education Ministry bureaucrats and teachers' unions who detest change, but also by parents themselves. Indeed, parents were the most vehement opponents of the government's decision to abolish half-day classes on Saturday to give students more time for play and relaxation. Less classroom time, mothers feared, would make it more difficult for their sons and daughters to pass college entrance exams. Many mothers also didn't want to commit more time to watching over their children. In swift reaction, enrollment surged in *juku*, or private "cram schools," where students often study until ten or eleven every night, being drilled on the subjects likely to appear on their exams. (In Minami's own neighborhood, he told me, one *juku* sent its students home at three in the morning, and another class started at four.) Although cram schools crowd out sports or socializing, parents still fervently believe that "the number one route to power in Japan," as Minami called it, is passing a college entrance exam.

Minami found an opening to attract students, however, because his village was among the first to permit some forms of "home schooling." His program is now authorized to issue certificates that entitle students to return to a traditional classroom someday, if they choose.

As we looked out at a living room full of rambunctious teenagers, Minami said it is impossible to determine whether a child truly is condemned to a long bout of *hikikomori* or *futoko*, or whether proper intervention can fundamentally alter that course. He pointed to one thirteen-year-old girl in a pink sweater, who giggled as she soared on the swings. "She was home for more than six months and refused to go out. The first time she said she wanted to go out, she was so afraid . . . she almost couldn't speak. But now that she's here, she is laughing and interacting with the others like a normal child. She might even return to a normal school next year.

"These children are so afraid and so mistrusting. They feel that other children might betray or bully them at school." Most children instinctually want to communicate and be with their peers, he said. "That's why it is so hard for them—these children want to go out and just can't!"

*   *   *

"It's not with the children, the *hikikomori* children," that most problems lie, says Hisako Watanabe, a child psychiatrist at Keio University Medical Center in Tokyo. "It's with the unhappiness of the mothers." She believes the roots of this disorder can be traced to intergenerational tension, and to adults whose own childhoods were traumatically jarred by the national experience of Japan's finally having to embrace defeat in 1945. Soldiers returned from war and silently buried their guilt over battlefield atrocities, but their sins now visit a generation of anomic youth. This is why, in her clinical treatment, Watanabe told me, she often spends as much time working with parents as with their *hikikomori* children.

Watanabe speaks in the fluent, clipped British English she learned as a teenager in London while her father was stationed there as a foreign correspondent for a prestigious Japanese newspaper. Later, she returned to study psychotherapy at a prominent British institute. Though she graduated from Keio, "I was rebellious. I hated Japanese society," she admits. "I hated cram school," and when she returned to Japan after living in England as a child, she also endured bullying and ridicule from classmates who said her Japanese was too bookish and formal. "Yet here I am working as an advocate for children, trying to change Japan," she chuckled.

When I told her about my encounters with Hiro and other *hikikomori*, Watanabe said she well understood the syndrome. She described working with one twenty-nine-year-old patient who became "school phobic" at age eight.

"He was a very sensitive, very clever boy, yet he suffered a fear of going to school," she said. "He hated the mass, the group. His point was that the group is so crass, so insensitive. Even now it's very much like a military stereotype . . . and I want to emphasize that we in Japan have not yet overcome our stereotypical, oppressive-style behavior after the war. We could not throw it away, because it had been so successful in mobilizing our talents and energies to the utmost. After the war we used it to rebuild the country. It was good because, you know, we are living quite an affluent life, so it worked well, but at the cost of each individual's private life and family life and individual maturation.

"To use psychological terms, I'd like to say Japan has taken on a manic defense after the war, manic defense," a defense mechanism created to mitigate the narcissistic wound caused by defeat. Japanese soldiers had been well trained; its kamikaze pilots had willingly sacrificed their lives for the glory of their nation. Yet their spiritual sacrifice was bluntly deflected.

Even in defeat, she emphasizes, the Japanese remained a fiercely proud people. "We could never afford to have our country colonized like other Asian countries," she said. The nation could not willingly bear the humiliation of defeat. Japanese even ordered other Japanese to mount suicide missions against American troops during the battle for Okinawa, where peasants brandishing bamboo sticks were forced to launch hopeless missions against GIs toting machine guns and rifles. Others were ordered at gunpoint to commit suicide. "We did this so that we might survive as a nation—not to survive as individuals. So individuals became the victims." Some sixty years later, "this sort of mentality is still maintained and this mentality of 'we will not be defeated' is still ubiquitous, pervasive in every family, especially in high-status families."

This struggle for conquest was readily transferred to a new field of combat. "Today, instead of the Pacific war, it's the economic war we dare not lose." For a new generation of young Japanese who have never known war, trauma is reproduced through what Watanabe describes as "transgenerational transmission of oppression," especially among elite families. "They have totally sacrificed the happiness of their own offspring and made their children their sacrifice to the gods, for Japan, to a god named Japan," she told me. "I have worked in the clinical field for twenty-nine years, in pediatric medicine, psychiatric wards with handicapped, and it's repeatedly so."

Japan's soldiers returned home deeply traumatized, yet a rigidly disciplined society demanded utter self-denial. Men dared not express their horror and shame over the atrocities they committed, whether in the massacre of civilians in Nanjing, China, or with the forced induction of "comfort women" as sex slaves.[2] To compensate, these veterans grew determined never to be traumatized again and so created meticulous, fussy households, often neurotic environments, in which their children were expected to be scrupulous and always vigilant. "This process created very good, maybe 'perfect' children, but at the cost of their own individuality," Watanabe said. "They were not allowed to explore, to try or to fail, to have the experience of trial and error. They became good children, the sort of child of whom the traumatized parent could say, 'Oh look, I succeeded. I made a new version of success to mitigate my traumatic experience'— a Golden Egg."

During an era of stress and dramatic transition, however, such "perfect" children have proven ill-equipped to parent their own children. A new generation has been raised in material affluence, not in deprivation, and is constantly exposed to new technologies and forbidden foreign values. Their parents, who were raised in suffocating homes by strict and unhappy parents, cannot regulate their own desires, Watanabe concludes. "Outwardly, they look like they have very good control of themselves, but inside [their emotions] are actually very primitive, impulsive, and underdeveloped," a consequence of their childhood repression. Such parents often explode in rage at each other, or scream at their infant children, and create households in which nurturing expressions of love or real conversations are totally absent. And like Hiro and the other *hikiko-*

mori I've gotten to know, young Japanese of this generation often grow up alone, as a single child, without other relatives close by to mediate. Many mothers like Keiko, Hiro's mother, may turn their children into *hikiko- mori* to punish their husbands for the inequities built in to family life, be- cause most Japanese husbands believe they fulfill their parental duties simply by providing the money needed to buy groceries and pay the rent. "It's a form of retaliation. When a child becomes *hikikomori*, the mother can say to the father, 'You created this!' "

Now in her fifties, Watanabe said that she well understands the sort of life baby boomers like her endure in modern Japan. "We don't talk much about it . . . but I have seen my mother suffer, my aunt suffer, and through my clinical work I have heard lots of stories of, well, massive abuse within families. Not only is there absence of communication be- tween parents, there is hatred—hatred of the wife toward the husband." (She also believes that Japanese couples have little intimate contact, which is why men look for sex outside the home.)

This background naturally makes her extremely sympathetic to *hikiko- mori*, and she actively supports the right of young adults to seclude them- selves. "The child has been exposed to the constant denigration of the father and the resentment of the mother, so it's impossible for him to hold an image of a healthy family life . . . He becomes frightened of the outside world."

Her insight was consistent with what Yuichi Hattori, the clinical psy- chologist, had also observed: few of his *hikikomori* teenagers could recall ever being held or embraced by their own parents, and grew up emotion- ally starved. "The parents are incapable of communicating any emotion, especially love," he told me. Some of his clients were so shut down that sometimes he asked his wife to role-play as mother, caressing and hug- ging a patient to provoke an emotional response from one seemingly in- capable of expressing any feelings at all.

Watanabe's child therapy often tries to induce mutual interaction be- tween father and mother. "They are very lonely. They cling to the so-called mother and father roles, but without any mutual reciprocity or gratifica- tion. There's no real content, not even ordinary conversation, ordinary relaxed conversation. That's where I put a lot of energy. In most of the cases, the children are fine. It's the parents . . . the inner sad, deprived children who have become parents, who are the main objects of my work."

I found Watanabe's speculations about the roots of *hikikomori* powerful and persuasive, but she never permitted me to observe or evaluate her treatment regimen. She would never let me see the inside of her clinic, which operates within the pediatric wing of the Keio University Medical Center, or interview any of her patients.

She told me that she incorporates Western psychiatric principles into her practice, and brings *hikikomori* patients into the hospital ward to live. There, isolated behind the curtains of their beds, they have no choice but to hear the sounds of other patients. "The pediatric ward is an ideal place because there are babies, toddlers, preschoolers, schoolchildren, and other adolescents all around," Watanabe said. "I attempt to conduct an orchestra of human relationships within the ward . . . so young people can create a relaxed and nurturing kind of enjoyable community in which the patient feels at home, feels respected, feels love, and feels free to speak or not to speak. There's no pressure."

A common area, roped off by curtains, helps her create this artificial, familial neighborhood. "I call it a village. I tell the children, 'Let's make our ward a village' because we need a village to regrow a healthy child. Because that's what we're losing, the community life. We are losing trusting communities.

"Think about an elephant growing up in an African herd, and the elephant raised in a cage in the zoo," she continued. "That's how different it is for today's *hikikomori*. They have not learned group activities, group rules, group solidarity, group harmony. So they come here, into the hospital. We let them be *hikikomori* in their own beds, in the hospital.

"What I'm trying to do is minimize the secondary injury or disturbance" that the *hikikomori* endures, Watanabe added. "Over twenty-five years ago, when I was young, school refusal itself was considered a stigma. Yet nowadays I have lots of so-called graduates who have never gone to school yet are successful in international fields as artists or journalists. So I have no fear of children refusing, or not going to school. I tell the mother, it's like you refusing an arranged marriage." Women can choose to remain single, so children should be free to abandon school, too.

Watanabe told me that in counseling she tells her patients that they are actually more advanced than their chronological age, but that social demands suppress their innate abilities. "From an outsider's point of view, you have achieved quite a lot," she often tells them, "but your inside is timid, shrunken, and even immature. So this twelve-year-old has a twelve-year-old's *honne* or true feeling, but also has dreams and imagination which allows him to perform like a twelve-plus-twelve-year-old—or like a twenty-four-year-old. Instead he functions like a twelve-minus-twelve-year-old—like a baby.

"I tell them 'Stop this. Don't go to school. Stay in this hospital. This is a place where children fighting leukemia or congenital heart disease are enjoying life, and enjoying trustful relationships with us doctors. So learn from this. This is the life principle, not a business principle. Forget about business principles and go back to your infancy.' And lo and behold, a sixteen-year-old, after two years of intensive therapy, could last month start to cry like a baby. It's been a release. And now she says it's much easier for her to get through even one day; her day-to-day life has become much easier because she's now allowed to cry. She's a very bright girl.

"There are lots of children like her. I have treated hundreds of children in this way. I don't want palliative therapy. I want radical therapy. Yes, so I give them time and a protected setting in which there is security to confide true feelings."

She seldom prescribes antidepressant drugs, which she says are tools only "lazy doctors" rely upon. A few of the patients brought to her as *hikikomori* are actually schizophrenic, but most "are far more mature than ordinary school children. I am advocates for them. I say wait five or ten more years and your era will come, or you should escape from Japan and live in Australia or New Zealand."

Like Minami, she believes that patiently offering *hikikomori* a chance to build social attachments with others at their own pace, and slowly creating networks of trust, represents the first step in eroding self-imposed isolation. Both believe that creating an environment of confidence, instead of fear, is critical and frequently overlooked.

Watanabe believes that *hikikomori* behavior will disappear only when Japanese society finally encourages individual expression. "Why does a sensitive boy have to feel so uncomfortable in this society?" she asks. "I feel it's because people in this nation are not happy, not happy as individuals. They try to be happy as a group, at the cost of the individual, which is the contradiction. You have to be happy first as an individual. You have to be honest toward yourself. But people are not honest to themselves in order to be honest to the group and to conform to the group.

"The society's stigmata are still so very, very frightening that ordinary people cannot just speak out. One has to be a really black sheep or some sort of delinquent or some sort of lunatic in order to be the eye-opener or the whistle blower. Of course, some men call me a lunatic, which is something I celebrate," she said, chuckling. "Because being called a lunatic in Japan means you are doing really good, original work."

*   *   *

Sadatsugu Kudo offers what he calls "a much more severe approach" to dealing with *hikikomori*, compared to the indulgences permitted by others. While a psychiatrist like Watanabe relies on counseling or hospitalization to alleviate the pain felt by a social recluse, and Minami lets children play, Kudo adamantly believes that work offers the most therapeutic benefits. "In our society, people have to develop the skills to survive on their own and make a living," he said. "So I first want the young adult to feel at ease. Then I want him to acquire the skills he needs in order to make his way in the world. He has to adjust to the strains and demands the outside world imposes."

For nearly thirty years, Kudo—a squat man with a broad face, large rectangular glasses, and a fifties-style crew cut—has operated the Tamejuku support center in the gritty suburb of Fussa, a town best known as the home of a sprawling U.S. airbase. A cluster of sixty-five simple dormitory rooms, metal factory sheds, and work spaces, his barebones facility offers school dropouts and *hikikomori* a refuge and a place to learn a trade.

His is the oldest shelter in Japan, Kudo claims, though he never imagined running such a place. A friend from college started a *juku* to teach English and math; when he became ill, he asked for Kudo's temporary help. When the friend unexpectedly died, the school was left in Kudo's hands. Though prepared to give it up, he couldn't shut the doors until he finished training one particularly helpless pupil, a thirteen-year-old former thalidomide baby who wanted to become a cartoon illustrator even though her hands and arms were deformed. "That was the big mistake," Kudo said. "I never did close."

Instead, he decided to operate a different kind of *juku*, "one that would open its doors to anyone with problems"; to charge only what each family could afford; and to never become a typical cram school. Some of Kudo's first pupils were juvenile delinquents, or *boosozoku*, who wear leather jackets and ride the streets on noisy motorcycles. Pickpockets and other petty criminals also showed up. Gradually, however, Kudo began to learn of lonely, isolated teenagers who refused to communicate with the outside world or to leave their rooms. "At that point, children with *hikikomori* were considered autistic, and families were often ashamed of their children and refused to let them out of the house."

At the request of a few parents, Kudo began to visit the homes of children who chose to isolate themselves. Sometimes he showed up a half-dozen times to coax individual teens out from their hiding places. "I began to realize these were not autistic children, that they were not ill. They used very few words, they hardly spoke, but they were not incapable of communicating. They just were shy kids who didn't know how to interact with others."

Kudo insists he is the only counselor in Japan who treats what he terms "true *hikikomori*," young men who utterly refuse to step outside their rooms. "There are some people who can't communicate with society at large, but still maintain friendships, have social interactions, and can go out, especially at night. They have to break through one wall. But there are others who can't even step out from their houses, much less communicate with people. I call these 'two wall' *hikikomori*." He believes that traditional therapists like Tamaki Saito, who runs a clinic in Chiba prefecture, are incapable of treating these true *hikikomori*. "If you can show up at a day care center or a clinic, then I'm not really sure you are *hikikomori*, someone who cannot go out. I focus on the 'two wall' *hikikomori*,' and no one else really does."

Kudo uses an incremental, labor-intensive strategy to cajole teenagers from their rooms. He will traipse to a child's home two or three times and speak only to the parents, but in a voice loud enough for the isolated child in an adjacent room to hear. "You have to loosen the fears of these children, so you speak with the parents in a way that the *hikikomori* gets used to the idea that you are coming." Kudo may return three or four more times just to place a letter under the child's door. Eventually "the kid opens the door for us."

It is not always that easy. Hisatada Kouno, one of Kudo's staff counselors, described in greater detail a year-long quest to get one nineteen-year-old boy from Tochigi prefecture to open up. "This man literally did not take one step outside his room in four years," Kouno said of this *hikikomori*. "He would occasionally talk through the door to his parents, but they had not set their eyes on him in all that time."

One day, the boy's mother slipped a note under the door announcing Kudo's visit. Nine visits later, there was still no response.

"Finally, on the tenth visit, Kudo said, 'If you don't come out, we'll come in,' and gently began to push the door handle. The boy said, 'Please come back next time.'

"I said, 'It's been more than one year already that you haven't spoken with your parents. Don't you think there's a limit for your parents and other people who care about you?' I was posturing, of course, but I said, 'Let's see each other and talk.'

"The boy suggested talking through the door, but Kudo said, 'Conversation through a door isn't clear. I'm going to force open the door.'

"Finally the boy opened the door. He had long hair, and a very scraggly beard. He was very shabby-looking. Obviously, he had not bathed. He said all he could do was eat and sleep."

The three sat and talked together for nearly three hours in an adjacent room, the teenager blaming society and his parents for his unhappy state. "Let's forget the past, and start from here," Kudo told the boy. "It's not that easy to start from where you are now, but we can help."

The boy went downstairs and spoke to his mother—the first time they had laid eyes on each other in four years. Six hours after that, the teenager was resettled in a room at the Tamejuku shelter. "After four years he slipped out of his noose," Kouno said. "Now, he's cut his hair, bathes regularly, and is holding down a part-time job nearby."

His case is not so unusual, Kudo said. Because the prying eyes of neighbors can prove so fearsome, and because the isolated child usually blames himself for being different and causing family shame, Kudo's technique is to immediately spirit away those *hikikomori* he can coax from their rooms. They are taken directly to his center, where they slowly learn to socialize with others, take part in communal chores, and learn a craft or trade.

"When they first come, they can do what they want. They need to develop trust and feel comfortable and learn in this new environment," Kudo said. After about six weeks, the young adult meets with a counselor to choose a series of recreational activities to help him learn communication and socialization skills and experience the joy of play. Eventually, he may go on to work in the shelter's own recycling center, nursery, bookstore, or bakery, or learn how to use a personal computer. "We have to teach them that if you want to earn a thousand yen, then this is what you have to do," Kudo said. "They need to understand what it takes to earn a living and have the facilities where they can gain experience."

This is cold turkey. There is no talk of drugs or counseling here. Kudo studied sociology in college, not child development, and has neither clinical training nor an advanced degree in adolescent development or psychology. He receives no government support, and his facility is not subject to any government supervision. This is pragmatic, "seat of the pants" treatment—physical activity, training, and work, without too many frills. Subsequently, Kudo did receive some government funding.

Kudo's newest initiative is what he calls the "Community Uncle Program," where young residents are paired up with retired farmers, crafts-men, and technicians who can pass on their expertise to a new genera-tion. One student learns how to brew saké; another how to prepare buckwheat soba noodles, which Japanese love to slurp down at lunch-time. By connecting these adrift young people with a swelling reservoir of lonely elderly Japanese, the program creates new opportunities for so-cial interaction and gives the youngsters vocational skills. "It's like a trial apprenticeship," Kudo said. About thirty students take part.

While Kudo believes that "two wall" *hikikomori* is a uniquely Japanese phenomenon, he does not agree with those who say that it reflects a re-cent behavior pattern born of affluence. He says that it is a product of Japan's anomalous culture. "The very first *hikikomori* was Amaterasu *oomikami*," he said, referring to the sun goddess. "I believe that *hikiko-mori* has existed for a thousand years," Kudo insisted.

Kudo told me that *hikikomori* shut themselves off in much the way Catholics go inside a confession box to square their sins with God. "In our culture *hikikomori* means you make your own place to deal with your own problems, while your emotions and physical body are pulled back. Show-ing your face to others in an assertive way isn't normally done. So people withdraw, go into their rooms, to deal with their lives and their problems."

Minami, Watanabe, and Kudo are, in Watanabe's definition, lu-natics—people who are "doing really good, original work" to help some of the most vulnerable members of their society. These three have no pro-fessional contact with one another. Each pursues a different strategy in counseling *hikikomori* and cajoling them out of their isolation: one em-phasizes group play; another, counseling; the third, work. Yet each oper-ates on remarkably similar principles. They want their charges to exercise individual judgment over their lives. They insist that each be held ac-countable for his actions and be able to distinguish between fixed, not flexible, notions of right and wrong. They want to encourage individual autonomy over collective sensibilities, and recognize that these lost and sometimes troubled young adults can prosper only in an open, flexible, and trusting environment—precisely the sort of surroundings modern Japan tries to undermine.

6.

In the halcyon autumn of 1991, Tokyo seemed to me the indisputable center of the universe, a gravitational force as mighty as ancient Rome. Wandering the streets of Ginza, Tokyo's most illustrious entertainment district, I felt as if I had been sucked into a strange new vortex, a dizzying universe quite unlike any that might have preceded it. A Japan once renowned for the Zen-like restraint of its aesthetics—its material simplicity, its tranquil bamboo gardens, its glassy ponds stocked with calming carp—now bathed itself in brassy neon lights and erupted in convulsions of exuberant decadence.

Each evening, as dusk fell and the lights took hold over this fabled neighborhood, an arrogant fleet of black Rolls-Royce limousines, Mercedes-Benz sedans, and luxury Toyota Crowns paraded into the narrow back alleys, cramming the sidewalks and exacting every inch of curbside as their tribute. Chauffeurs paced, smoked cigarettes, and kept fidgety vigils long into the night after disgorging their passengers, the shadowy and powerful men who would emerge again only around midnight, their ties slightly askew, their gait a bit wobbly from rounds of smoky scotch or chilled saké.

As the sun retreated, young women who carried themselves as delicately as their dresses, in fabulous silk kimonos, heavy *obi*, and white *geta*, the traditional wooden sandals, began drifting by twos and threes into inconspicuous bars and hostess clubs, whose entranceways were signified only by tiny gold-plated Japanese nameplates. Other women, sheathed in expensive European couture and stilettos, strutted toward caverns with neon-lit names like Club Royale or The Monaco. These women would linger fastidiously over their customers, offering delicate morsels of small talk and watered-down whiskey to ease the flow of conversation among the barons of finance and industry holding court.

Once again, the city's business elite was setting off on its nightly amble, a ritual of dining, drinking, and entertaining known as *nomikai*— literally a "drinking meeting." Behind sliding *shoji* discreetly shut, the nation's deals were sealed and relationships cemented. Here in the Ginza, discerning patrons could find restaurants that inserted real gold flakes into the desserts. Or clubs that offered rare single malt scotch served on icy round globes hand-chiseled from Alaskan glaciers. Waiters instructed patrons to listen for the crackle and hiss of 10,000-year-old oxygen being set free from the primordial glacial fields as the fist-sized orbs dissolved in their glasses. Corporations, it was estimated, were spending $35 billion per year on such exercises in male bonding, six times what their European or American counterparts did.

Even though the Nikkei 225 stock average, Japan's Dow Jones, was trading at nearly 50 percent below the record established just eighteen months earlier, the nation betrayed no hint of recession. Annual growth still measured a heady 3.3 percent. Nothing could cool the nation's scorching-hot real-estate market, despite a determined campaign by the Bank of Japan to raise interest rates and slow the nation's speculative appetite.

This was the "bubble economy," and strolling through the Ginza you sensed the headiness swirling. In this last decade of the twentieth century, the Japanese had emerged triumphant. Who dared rival them? They built better cars more efficiently. They fabricated the most complex computer memory chips. These Japanese had created an advanced, prosperous, and technologically sophisticated economy without the ghettos, the criminal underclass, or the social tensions that ravaged Western societies. Everything worked so smoothly in Japan, visitors marveled. No wonder these well-tailored executives seemed so invincible, if not arrogant, as they wandered from men's club to "snack bar" to consort with their favorite hostesses for hire.

What these Japanese could not comprehend—nor could most of the rest of us, back then—was that the incredibly close-knit system they had meshed together, one which allowed the nation to accumulate so much wealth so quickly, also held the seeds of its undoing; that this same incessant unity of purpose that generated such fabulous industrial efficiency might prove weakness as well as strength. The group harmony this homogeneous people struggled so obsessively to achieve—through the pressure to conform, the resistance to criticism, the repression of dissenters, and a desperate, almost pathological need to keep "outsiders" at bay—carried a dark and destructive seed. Not only did this system seriously constrain individuality to the point of "infantilizing" many of it own people, effectively robbing them of their own identities; it also stripped the nation of its ability to adjust to the unforeseen changes in the world and in business practices that the inexorable process of globalization was now stirring up. Until this moment, Japan had been able to appropriate the trappings of the modern world without creating for itself a critical consciousness, a truly democratic sensibility, or a vision of how a "unique" people might interact easily and equally with the rest of the world. "The essence of Japan is to have no essence," one famous Japanese political scientist concluded, arguing Japanese had never learned to properly differentiate between the instrumental and the ideal. His society, he said, was like a pot crammed with octopus, unable to discern a world separate from its own outsized tentacles. By analogy, he suggested, Western societies, where Judeo-Christian values had taken hold, or the Chinese culture, where Confucianism remains central, more resembled the sort of whisk broom used in a traditional tea ceremony, in which a sturdy, unitary wooden base splays itself into a finely separated tip, with space for each long and articulated tine of bamboo fiber to stand free and apart from the others.[1]

As the elements that constituted global competitiveness radically changed in the 1990s, however, the Japanese system—already heavily insulated from the outside world—ultimately proved itself far too inflexible. For just as a *hikikomori* shuts himself off in his room rather than mediate a society he finds intolerable, or "too severe," as one such recluse put it, Japan chose to ignore the obvious signs that its corporations invested and exported too much, that its webs of closed, protective relationships would never be as dynamic as open ones, and that national investment schemes that relied on government experts to envision the future could never consistently outperform those who summoned the wisdom of independent innovators, diverse risk-takers, and the signals unrestricted markets provide to guide their evolution.

* * *

To me it seems no accident that mighty Japan careened off course precisely when the age of information, intelligence, and flexible global production utterly disrupted a more rigid industrial order.

Since the dawn of the modern era, Japan's goals had been unquestioned and its society precision-engineered to conquer the industrial age. Nationalism and colonial expansion had first fueled feverish investment and rapid industrialization, as the nation appropriated and perfected the technological advances the Western world pioneered. Government-guided capital and then rising militarism dictated consumer behavior, organized family relations, and regulated life from kindergarten through retirement.

After World War Two, these same unyielding arrangements were refocused toward attaining superiority in global markets. Japan Inc. worked single-mindedly to avenge the nation's military failings and export its way to prosperity by targeting priority industries, promoting cartels to retain corporate profits and restrain competition, protecting the home market, and allocating scarce capital. It grew wealthy by mastering the mysteries of the shop floor. It pioneered lean production systems and just-in-time manufacturing, and appropriated the methods of total quality control (a system pioneered by an American, W. Edwards Deming, but mostly ignored by his countrymen). It knew how to export uniform, high-quality goods at low prices to mass markets. To focus on this single goal, seldom had a society so evenly meshed the disparate interests of business, government, and political elites. Its people accepted limits on their personal liberty in the service of this higher calling, as if newly conscripted soldiers.[2] Time after time, the nation responded adroitly to gradual, foreseeable change. Indeed, by 1990, this small island nation had vanquished its former conquerors, producing more economic output per person than the United States, and paying higher wages.

That was the war Japan knew how to win.

But when the rules radically changed in the 1990s, and change became far less predictable and far more turbulent, what once had been seen as core strengths were exposed as much deeper vulnerabilities. So obsessively had Japan focused on one single dimension of success that it lost sight of other important elements societies need in order to adapt and prosper. The nation's emphasis on industrial production, for instance, made it overlook strategic niches where specialization could boost profits. Its skill at making manufacturing more efficient made Japanese less concerned with the ways computers and software could increase productivity, and caused it to overlook the growing importance of the service economy. Its reliance on closed, proprietary systems and a bias toward vertical integration within large firms—a natural extension of the structure of hierarchies so deeply embedded within the society itself—fell out of step in an era of open systems, common standards, and horizontal alliances that cross borders. (Being confined to a narrow universe of Fujitsu-engineered products and software made little sense when everyone else in the world was using UNIX, not to mention "open source" software.)

By constantly machining its society to exacting tolerances—dressing its young boys in identical military-style uniforms and dispatching them to identical schools to study from the same books on the same day—it effectively marginalized those "deviants" whose creativity and singular insights might have set the stage for change and made adaptation less traumatic. It had no place for the sparklingly creative autodidact. Much as *hikikomori* sought the refuge of their own bedrooms for safety because they were far more sensitive and intelligent than their average classmates, many of Japan's most creative talents, whether orchestra conductor Seiji Ozawa or fashion designer Issey Miyake, eventually found they needed to abandon Japan to discover a nurturing, creative environment, free of *ijime*. How might you change a world in which it was so dangerous to be different?

As I got to understand it better, I saw that, rather than a vibrant free market, Japan actually functions more like a highly controlled, quasi-socialist system where bureaucrats feel they know best how to organize the system of production, and have the power to make life unpleasant for those who don't agree. Companies are essentially protected from failure, as long as they follow the dictates of regulators and their main bankers. Rather than consider a strategic course that might emphasize differentiation, corporations tend to converge and look the same, like bonsai shrubs artificially manipulated in a Japanese garden. Their lockstep behavior offers little incentive to one who might want to buck a trend or rely on his own ingenuity, so the individual finds himself robbed of true initiative. In the providence of an ideal Marxist state, everything would be the same and affordable for all, so that each man could contribute according to his means. In Japan, however, everything seems the same and is made exorbitantly expensive so that only a very few could have the ability to pursue their own passions.

No wonder those few entrepreneurs who defy such a lumbering and methodical system and resist the interference of bureaucrats on their path to success find the customary Japanese methods utterly contemptible. Typical is Masao Horiba, a ponytailed entrepreneur who founded his own firm in Kyoto just after World War Two to develop high-tech measurement instruments. He told me he classified Japan a "deduction universe" where as long as you don't make a mistake, there are no points taken off. "As long as you never do anything wrong, you never lose points, and if you never lose points you are guaranteed a promotion every year as well as a pay raise," he said. "So no one takes a risk for fear of making that mistake." His company, by contrast, embodied his philosophy of "Joy and Fun." Among its innovative aspects, company employees were not permitted to work late at night or on weekends.

The rare Japanese who does stand out, who does, for instance, garner a Nobel Prize in science, invariably recounts how he had been a poor student, considered "odd" or "weird" within his university or corporation, and had soldiered in relative obscurity for most of his professional life.[3] Luckily enough, such "weirdos" never felt so discouraged that they became *hikikomori*. Yet many others felt compelled to abandon Japan in order to pursue their research: thus, the bacteriologist Hideyo Noguchi (1876–1928), whose left arm was deformed by a childhood cooking accident, and who was told he was therefore too repulsive to consider becoming a practicing physician, moved to the Rockefeller Institute where he discovered the syphilis spore. More recently, Shuji Nakamura, who invented the Blu-ray technology for DVD players in 1996, transferred to the University of California, Santa Barbara, after his employer lost interest in his research and offered him only a token payment for his breakthrough.

A prominent economics professor, Iwao Nakatani, provided me with an anecdote to vividly describe how little the question of merit influences annual promotions in most firms, and how this, in turn, affects the working standards expected in the typical Japanese workplace. One day he attended a reunion dinner with a class of former students, and when he entered the restaurant his students followed Japanese custom and lined up to bow and offer their new business cards to their former sensei. These classmates were all the same age; as Nakatani inspected their cards, he realized they had all achieved precisely the same rank within their respective corporations. "Funny thing was," he recounted to me, "I did not recall that they had all been equally talented when they sat in my classroom." Nakatani later joined the board of Sony.

The traditional "jewels" of the Japanese workplace—lifetime employment, company unions, and seniority-based wages—help reinforce such conformity. More broadly, the economic turbulence sometimes needed to coerce change is usually precluded through the complex design of the so-called Iron Triangle, the arrangement of Japan's corporations, politicians, and government bureaucrats—often orchestrated by the nation's main banks—which dispenses the funds essential to keep the system running.

In most market economies, major banks aren't the only ones to decide whether a corporation obtains the money it needs to do business. A company can raise funds directly through a relatively transparent capital market, selling bonds or issuing stock to a diverse set of clients, in addition to taking loans. An individual's brainstorm can win backing from venture capitalists and a successful start-up can take itself public. In these companies, decisions tend to be quick and opportunistic, profits crucial, and efficiency prized. In nations where this system works properly, enlightened self-interest drives markets, lonely entrepreneurs take risks to start new companies, and a Darwinian style of capitalism allows the strong to survive and forces the weak to perish. Consumers express their choices in such a free and dynamic marketplace, and a company needs to respond or face extinction. Yet the Western businessman who comes to Japan in search of profits often finds himself trapped in a strange mirror world where left is right and up is down.

In the years leading up to its unrivaled prosperity in the 1980s, Japan's giant banks orchestrated most corporate decisions—from behind the scenes, not from center stage. Acting as syndicates, city banks, trust banks, and insurance companies offered loans to favored industries while at the same time purchasing stock in the companies with whom they dealt. Corporate borrowers also used some of their profits to buy shares in the banks that were, in turn, their main lenders. It was as if Citibank made loans to General Motors while General Motors used some of its automotive profits to buy large chunks of Citi stock rather than pay cash dividends to its shareholders. Imagine further that all Citibank employees drove GM cars, and that all GM paychecks were deposited in Citibank branches.

In this bank-centric system, the central government held powerful leverage to determine investment decisions and to stimulate industries it considered strategic.[4] The government, as one economist noted, "deliberately chose to emasculate the stock and bond markets," to ensure that these banks and insurers—firms over which the bureaucrats could maintain complete control—were kept firmly in the driver's seat.[5]

Independent outside influences had little opportunity to shoulder their way onto the trading floor. Domestic competitors were restricted. Foreign investors were kept away. Small shareholders had no right to demand that independent boards protect their interests or ensure efficient management of the firm. Instead, Japanese companies protected their "stakeholders"—incumbent managers and employees—by creating weak boards populated by insiders selected to rubber-stamp decisions. The notion that dissidents might try to oust incompetent managers, or force a merger to boost a corporation's performance, was unthinkable. Informing shareholders was a burdensome chore, not an obligation, and was arranged so as to thwart any protesting activists.[6]

There was no suing in court to force boardroom change. Because Japan views itself as a society that disdains litigiousness, the process of going public with criticism would be certain to damage "group harmony." Besides, Japanese courts were so understaffed that it could take years for an important corporate matter to be adjudicated. Instigating a leveraged buyout or hostile takeover was insanely difficult in courts that were loath to enforce rules of fair play—as would-be "raiders" like T. Boone Pickens learned through painful, firsthand experience. The accounting industry was hardly more open, with auditors often being held captive by the firms that employed them. Multiply the Enron scandal a thousandfold, and assume that—unlike Enron's Jeffrey Fastow, who was forced behind bars after a guilty plea—almost no one in Japan went to jail.

In the mid-1980s, there were scattered voices of prudence within Japan who counseled a change in policy lest the gathering bubble burst. Adopting such a series of reform measures might have forced Japan Inc. to loosen its obsessive grip on its people. Indeed, in 1986, the famous Maekawa Report, promoted by the government itself, advocated a series of useful changes to open up the system.[7] It called for dismantling some of the strong state-centered models of development that single-mindedly emphasized exports and advocated incentives to stimulate higher consumption at home within a less-regulated domestic marketplace. It said Japan should open up its financial markets and permit its people more leisure time by restricting work hours and enforcing those limits; it even encouraged the educational system to inculcate self-expression and critical thinking in order to create a "new age" knowledge-based economy that relied more on services than on traditional manufacturing.[8]

But like most such well-intentioned studies, the Maekawa study simply gathered dust. Japan's system proved too rigid to adapt and retool. Rather than behave like the leaders of a prosperous high-tech nation whose automobile and semiconductor industries now showed the way, Japan's powerful continued to govern as if theirs was still a poor agricultural nation, bereft of resources, where everyone needed to pitch in and sacrifice to harvest the rice fields. The Japanese people remained unusually frugal long after the nation had matured economically, because the system systematically repressed consumption in order to recycle the funds back to government and to businesses who were encouraged to indulge. With prices kept stubbornly high through regulations, the nation's household savings still measured 13 percent of disposable income in 1990, some 50 percent higher than in European nations, while the share of government spending on fixed investment like bridges and buildings, at 8 percent of economic output, was more than double the ratio of comparable U.S. spending. Even today, after more than a decade of recession in which many Japanese have been forced to draw down their "rainy day" funds, Japanese, on average, save twice as much as Americans and nearly a third more than Europeans, while the nation's consumption as a percentage of economic output lags significantly behind major industrial nations.[9]

Yet to keep the system from choking on these excess savings, the funds had to be redeployed, somehow. Japanese corporations used the surplus capital to load up on commercial assets like new factories, construction equipment, and high-tech robots as ever-decreasing returns indicated the slowing of productivity growth. Throughout the 1990s, the nation's corporations consistently invested more than 15 percent of the nation's annual output to generate barely 1 percent of growth.

The inefficiencies seemed obvious to outsiders, but the Iron Triangle feared that giving its citizens the liberty to indulge might jeopardize the bedrock values of the collective, the resolute self-sacrifice that had propelled the nation's renaissance. Besides, why give up power or tinker with success? Instead, Japan maintained its stubborn focus on boosting industrial exports while ensuring that domestic consumer spending languished. Selling yet more cars and stereo sets to foreign buyers didn't solve the problem of the nation's woeful economic imbalance, however. Japan exported far too much and at home consumed far too little in part because the government kept prices so high. As the proceeds from those exports kept coming back to Japan as growing stacks of yen, and the nation's big industries, banks, and insurance companies indulged in high-octane investment, which only expanded the bubble—ultimately, disastrously.

The nation's banks were the first to career off course since they could not possibly reinvest all this cash productively. Their very best customers, Japan's highly competitive global exporters, no longer needed to borrow from banks to fund their expansion, since they were now able to easily reinvest their own rising profits. Thus local bankers were now forced to chase after second- and third-tier clients whose business operations and projects were not nearly as sound. To recycle mountains of excess cash, they loaned for construction of superfluous factories, office buildings, golf courses, water parks, and resorts. While loans to this new class of borrowers might have seemed more risky, banks could assume that perpetually rising land prices, the collateral used for all loans, would guarantee these debts.

This logic was based on the fact that in Japan, real estate prices were engineered not to fall. Land was the bedrock on which the whole financial system was contrived. Thus, a land parcel or decrepit building was not considered a liquid asset easily bought or sold as part of a normal commercial transaction, the way you might sell rolled steel, gold coins, or pallets of detergent. Homeowners didn't constantly refinance mortgages, or move from one neighborhood to another. A house or tract of land usually changed hands only when a son was forced to pay confiscatory inheritance taxes on his father's holdings. Laws protected landholders, and the Japanese tax system discouraged mobility, and these factors helped keep the price of land stubbornly high.

Since the price of land seemed guaranteed never to stop climbing, banks felt no qualms about diversifying into new and riskier projects. Bankers rarely examined the underlying logic of a proposed loan before making a commitment. Most had never been trained to pencil out the numbers, determine risk, or assess whether a golf club or hotel, when built, might actually earn back profits sufficient to repay the loan. Actually, the bankers didn't really care. As long as a borrower owned sufficient land to serve as collateral, the loan would be approved.[10]

With so much money chasing after land, real estate prices naturally skyrocketed. The grounds of the Imperial Palace in central Tokyo were said to be more valuable than all the real estate in the entire state of California. The distortions grew so large that eventually the Bank of Japan had no choice but to step in and douse the speculative fire. On the last day of 1989, it began to jolt interest rates higher, and eventually land prices began to heed the laws of gravity. As prices began to tumble, the entire financial system sputtered and soon came undone, since the land pledged to secure speculative loans was no longer sufficient. Within months, the nation's growth rate would plummet to a mere 1 percent, not to rebound for more than a dozen years; commercial land prices in the nation's six largest cities would plummet by an average of 84 percent within the decade; millions would own homes that in 2005 were worth far less than they had paid for them in 1987.[11]

* * *

Japan Inc.'s initial response after crisis hit in the early 1990s was to deny that anything had gone awry. Its political and economic leaders acted as if the nation's mounting blizzard of debts would gently melt away on their own, if only the government would spend more taxpayer money to crank up the economic engine.

To some extent, this blithe confidence reflected the fact that not all segments of Japanese corporate life were suffering. The nation's ultra-competitive exporters like Sony, Toyota, and Canon continued to prosper because they had learned how to successfully compete in a growing global market. But the nation's inefficient domestic industries—food processors, construction companies, distributors, and textile manufacturers—remained coddled by government regulations that systematically kept foreign rivals away. Rather than force "old Japan" to streamline and adapt to an advancing era of relentless global competition, a dual economy emerged, one in which winners subsidized losers, even as the interests of both grew increasingly antagonistic.

The unfortunate reality for today's Japan is that the corporate brands Americans know well, the efficient exporters such as Canon and Honda who lay out innovative and distinctive strategies to compete against European and American rivals, contribute only 10 percent of the nation's gross domestic product. The other 90 percent is produced by obscure "me too" firms which sell only within a highly regulated domestic market. The arcane rules that once helped Japan create new industries from scratch now block potential upstarts from offering better services at lower prices or challenging the entrenched. When a Japanese entrepreneur founded a Jet Blue–like airline to provide low-cost service to the northern island of Hokkaido, government policy helped ensure its swift demise. When Toys "R" Us decided to invest in Japan and open giant new stores, it discovered arcane rules severely limiting how big its outlets could be. "If industrial policy is a matter of 'picking winners and losers,' " the economist Richard Katz concluded, "then the essence of Japan's malaise is that it gradually shifted from promoting winners to protecting losers."[12]

By protecting small and beaten-down domestic firms, the government helped guarantee that workers still were paid. But the support artificially boosted prices for land, labor, and materials so high that, to compete effectively around the world, the best firms, like Honda and Panasonic, had to send more and more of their factories to Malaysia, China, and Mexico. As this "hollowing out" accelerated, fewer efficient firms were left to subsidize the growing army of the feeble. A market more open to foreign competitors and foreign investment would have imposed more discipline and forced unprofitable firms to sink if they couldn't refloat themselves.

Japan's banks could also flout market discipline thanks to their incestuous ties to their corporate borrowers. Banks and insurance companies kept rolling over unpaid loans rather than acknowledge that traditional clients had now become insolvent, and kept paying dividends long after they began hemorrhaging red ink. Shutting down scores of bad borrowers and throwing millions of people out of work would violate the nation's sacred social contract, and cause bankers to lose credibility. Calling deadbeat borrowers on the carpet, or reducing the dividends they paid to shareholders might call attention to management's own decision-making and raise the issue of its accountability. This leniency, however, only dragged the banks—already hobbled by the collapse of land prices—down farther.

Since so many corporations and banks owned a stake in one another, no one pushed for a day of reckoning. Instead, Japan Inc. preferred to keep its dying companies on life support, hoping that if they just held on a bit longer, the economy might somehow return to growth on its own, or that a miraculous rise in land prices might someday restore balance sheets. The Ministry of Finance was also reluctant to pull the trigger as bad debts continued to swell. But such mercy exacted its own costs, too. As all-but-defunct corporations kept producing, their existence continued to distort the market by keeping wages higher and prices lower than they might otherwise become.

By 1998—after two securities firms and the largest bank on the northern island of Hokkaido ignobly collapsed—the government was forced to dip into the national treasury and put $18 billion of taxpayer funds into the nation's largest banks to prevent them from failing, too. It also created a new Financial Supervisory Agency to oversee a gentle, Japanese-style cleanup. In a culture where corporate responsibility remained diffuse, the government did not force top bank managers to quit, and quietly indicated that it would pursue a policy of forbearance rather than inject the upward of $700 billion it would take to make sick banks healthy again.

The decision to delay and defer reflected the equally unappealing alternatives the politicians faced. Voters would be outraged if even more of their taxes were set aside to resuscitate troubled lenders. Yet forcing tattered banks to seize the assets of their deadbeat borrowers would put many more mom-and-pop factories out of business forever and trigger a startling jump in unemployment. Unwilling to endure the political fallout from either course, the government authorized loan guarantees to keep banks in business, maintained deposit insurance on individual savings accounts to mollify taxpayers, and drastically sliced interest rates, pumping massive quantities of money into the system to keep dodgy borrowers afloat.

As companies tried to sell off excess assets and gradually pay back their groaning debts, prices and then wages started to sink. Banks stopped authorizing loans to new borrowers as they tried to recoup old losses. Japan soon entered a nuclear winter of deflation, with too many goods for sale and not enough buyers. In such a desolate, upside-down economy, consumer prices began to *fall* by 1 percent each year, which, perversely, made the savings left in bank accounts ever more valuable even though they earned only the minutest rates of interest. Like an acid eating away at self-confidence, deflation also worked to discourage consumption: Why buy a refrigerator this month if it will likely be $30 cheaper next month?

As spending plunged, corporate profits sank further, and there were ever fewer jobs. This downward spiral—not seen since the Great Depression of the 1930s—proved very hard to reverse. How could you jump-start an economy if real interest rates were already zero?

In this unsavory stew of sinking land prices, rising unemployment, shrinking profits, and looming bank failures, citizens lost confidence in their government and in their own future, and the nation's prodigious savings rate began to erode. As society grew anxious over bank failures and unemployment, many took their money out of the banks altogether, installing heavy metal safes in their homes to safeguard their cash. Others bought gold bars as a hedge against the anticipated collapse of the yen. Both measures reduced the amount of capital banks had to work with. Savings also fell because the nation was getting older and because those without jobs had to fall back on their "rainy day" funds. From 13 percent in 1991, the household savings rate plummeted to 6 percent a decade later, a sign of how much stagnation had eaten into the nation's marrow. By this measure, at least, Japanese behavior was beginning to resemble that of Westerners.

But not always. After a 1998 deregulatory change made it possible for Japanese to invest their savings abroad without fear of audit or need for government permission, American brokers Merrill Lynch and Charles Schwab opened large Tokyo offices and a slew of retail branches in a bold effort to attract new customers. Yet most Japanese believed that investing in equities was like betting on horses at the track, and that sending investment money offshore was downright unpatriotic, if not excessively risky. While Americans on average invest more than 40 percent of their savings in equities or mutual funds, Japanese "gamble" only 11 percent in equities, stashing the rest in low-yielding time deposits or insurance policies.[13] I once watched a prim, silver-haired Japanese widow dump ten thousand dollars worth of yen into a postal savings account that would yield her only $12 a year—or 0.012 in interest for a ten-year bond—instead of entrusting the funds to a foreign manager like Merrill or Schwab, who offered a higher reward overseas.

"I'll be able to buy a bowl of soba noodles next year on what I'll earn," she told me, shrugging her shoulders.

She confided also that she liked it that her post office branch manager came by car to pick her up whenever she needed to make a deposit, and the unswerving loyalty of thousands of customers like her made Japan's postal savings system, which sold life insurance policies and certificates of deposit along with stamps, the largest single financial institution on the planet.[14] Just a few years after launching their retail operations with much fanfare, Schwab and Merrill quietly retreated from Japan's inhospitable shores, having failed to attract sufficient funds for their pension management businesses.

Thus, Japan Inc. transformed a potentially short and brutal readjustment into one that still remains unresolved. A dozen years after the bubble economy deflated, in March 2002, the official figure for nonperforming commercial loans still totaled more than 10 percent of the nation's output, or some $422 billion. But many experts estimated the real amount of distressed debt—including loans being paid on time by corporate customers who still remained wobbly—totaled more than twice that, perhaps as much as one trillion dollars, or some 30 percent of GDP. This overhang of debt was at least twice as severe as the savings and loan crisis that crippled the U.S. banking system in the early 1980s. Never in world history had so many owed so much for so long. And the costs of digging out of this hole only increased the more Japan delayed and deferred.

As of September 2004, some progress had been recorded, but more than $250 billion of nonperforming loans remained unresolved according to official estimates of the FSA. The public saw the glimpses of the contraction during the downturn, as a series of "zombie" companies were finally forced out of business; struggling firms like Nissan Motors and the failed Long-Term Credit Bank were placed in the hands of foreign owners; and banks radically reduced their loan portfolios to boost earnings and reduce their bad debts, triggering a "credit crunch" among small firms. Big companies stopped hiring new recruits for life, preferring to take on part-time workers. But much of the inner turmoil that surrounded such dealings was never fully disclosed to the Japanese public at large. And Japan was still not healthy enough for its mid-sized firms to reemerge as aggressive players in foreign markets.

*   *   *

During the entire decade of the 1990s, and as a direct consequence of this denial and delay, government deficits soared as politicians injected massive amounts of government money into the construction industry to boost the macroeconomic blood flow and maintain a stranglehold on power. They spent billions of the nation's accumulated postal savings to build four-lane expressways that led into deserted forests, parking garages submerged below riverbanks, and lavish resort hotels erected in remote hamlets. In the southernmost island of Okinawa, the government proudly inaugurated the nation's longest, toll-free bridge in 2005. The 1.2 mile link to Kourijima Island cost $250 million to build, and services a population numbering 361. In northernmost Hokkaido, the government will spend $46 million per mile over ten years—a total of $4.3 billion—to extend bullet train service to the town of Hakodate, whose population totals 280,000. While the U.S. government only spends about 3 percent of GDP on fixed investment, Japan's government consistently allocated 8 percent to public works.[15]

In the good times, soaring tax revenues had funded these government boondoggles. Historically, these expenditures had been justified as reconstruction projects for a war-ravaged nation. Later, during the 1970s, infrastructure projects brought first-class roads and bullet trains to neglected areas of the countryside and generated ample opportunities to reward friends and earn chits. But even after the bubble burst, and tax revenues buckled from recession, the government remained addicted to public works spending. Japan's "construction state" cruised like a bicycle: if the wheels stopped turning, if the pipeline of new projects emptied, the whole contraption would keel over and toss millions of blue-collar workers out in the streets, since one in every six Japanese jobholders worked in construction. New projects, like an international airport constructed on landfill in Osaka Bay, were now passed off as measures to overcome the ill effects of recession. When the runway and terminals literally started to sink, more money was allocated to shore them up.

Promoting massive building projects in the teeth of recession also helped ensure that the ruling Liberal Democratic Party would continue to replenish its giant campaign coffers from the contractors whose crews paved riverbanks, dammed tiny streams, and liberally smeared concrete over rural hillsides, ostensibly to prevent rockslides. Environmental destruction became an inevitable by-product. Fixated on public works spending to create jobs and garner votes, the LDP government raised the nation's consumption tax from 3 percent to 5 percent in 1998, even though the nation was just beginning to emerge from four years of recession. This 67 percent tax hike cost the prime minister Ryutaro Hashimoto his job and triggered another recession after consumers closed their wallets in panic. Yet government spending still continued to outstrip tax revenues.

Four years later, by 2002, even the government had finally over-reached. As the national debt neared 150 percent of annual economic output, soon to top 160 percent, economists began comparing Japan's plight to that of debt-plagued Argentina. ("What's the difference between Japan and Argentina?" the joke went. "Five years.") While individuals might still hold passbooks containing staggeringly large sums of yen deposited in the postal savings bank, still the world's largest financial institution, the national coffers were bare; Japan was now more insolvent than any other major industrial power. And as the nation aged, fewer of working age would be left to support the pensioners.

Between 2002 and 2005, Japan enjoyed periods of momentary updraft as well as recessionary reversals. A surge of business with a fast-growing China, as well as a rising yen, gave many large firms a brief window to restore profitability, even if they sharply cut back on hiring new workers or on taking out new loans to invest in new business lines. The rate of household savings fell further, as workers found it increasingly difficult to secure full-time jobs. But thousands of small and medium-sized companies still lurched in a profitless twilight zone while regional banks scraped to stay alive. Land prices still fell. Unemployment among recent graduates climbed above 10 percent while nearly half of young workers quit their first jobs. And Japanese productivity remained 30 percent below the United States—the lowest in the OECD. Finally in the second half of 2005 foreign investors clamored for Japanese equities, driving the market 40 percent higher. Yet Japan continued to resist deeper "structural reform," and it was not clear how a once-vibrant economic superpower, now also confronting the prospects of a rapidly aging population, would ever regain its world-beating dynamism. For nearly half of the fourteen years since its stock and real estate bubble burst in 1991, Japan had been mired in recession.

*　　*　　*

When Japan had last been forced to retool and rebuild, after World War Two, the route ahead was obvious. Japan simply followed the leaders on a path of industrial catch-up, while America acted as the protective parent, guarding its island shores and buying up the goods its factories produced. Then, as in its reemergence from seclusion in the late nineteenth century, the Japanese appropriated from abroad and adapted the best technologies to suit local needs. Mandarins told workers what to do, and an obedient, hard-working society complied. Besides, a nation still licking its wounds from horrific defeat was eager to overcome its many hardships.

But in that era, the Japanese had little competition. Now, in the shrinking globe of the twenty-first century, they do. When they first built state-of-the-art factories in the 1950s and '60s, the Japanese were able to steal a march on any other potential rival in Asia. Now, Taiwanese bake semiconductor chips, Koreans build flat-screen TVs, and Chinese are the lowest-cost producers of industrial goods, often using Japan's excess capital equipment, purchased on the cheap. Moreover, the powerful and chaotic currents churned up by globalization have helped erode the very core of Japan's manufacturing competence and social cohesion. In a new world of flexible adaptation to discontinuous and unpredictable change, software—not just hardware—creates wealth; services and marketing, not just manufacturing, add value. By harnessing information technology, foreign companies learned to leapfrog Japanese rivals. Japanese might endlessly refine the tiny motors that power disk drives and hone the process technology needed to build ever-cheaper semiconductor memory chips, but they could never master the revolutionary architecture of the Pentium microprocessor or the software to run it. Nor could they emulate the supply chain management, customer relations software, Internet commerce, or outsourcing processes their American competitors pioneered to make their firms more productive and their marketing and design more specialized and strategic.

Now, too, Thais or Chinese can do many of the things Japanese did, and often they can do them cheaper. Even more troubling, those very innovations in information technology that were transforming Western societies, accelerating upheaval, and ultimately making them more productive, threaten the very architecture of control intrinsic to Japanese-style management. Now it is possible for corporations to outsource many of their services, level their corporate structures, and let customers interact more closely with producers and with one another. Instant messaging and data-sharing now eliminate vast numbers of corporate meetings. In this new world, Americans and Europeans, as well as Japan's South Korean and Chinese neighbors, eagerly employ computers and the Internet in daily life; and, as they do so, their productivity increases.

But the Japanese proved not nearly as avid in moving in this direction, toward open collaboration. Those same Japanese who built computers didn't like to use them, and the Japanese office long resisted the invasion of PCs and the Internet because by empowering the individual, these devices undermined traditional levers of centralized control. Long after e-mail became ubiquitous in U.S. corporations, documents in Japan are still routinely hand-routed from branch to branch and from department to department. In a typical medium-sized firm, each department manager fixes his red *hanko*, or personal seal, on a document before it can be passed on, and there's no way to stamp an e-mail. Information is not broadly shared among divisions of a corporation, but parsed out and brokered among divisions, so that some factions can gain advantage on rivals. In government, appropriations for even the smallest items in a municipal budget still have to be checked, stamped, and approved by bureaucrats in Tokyo.

When I first moved to Japan in 1996, most government agencies and businesses still didn't use desktop computers. Statistics showed that even though Japanese firms like Toshiba and NEC were major computer manufacturers, Japanese didn't rely on computers and didn't trust e-mail. One business executive, a retailer who rented office furniture, described how she had begun using e-mail to do business, quoting prices and confirming transactions through her own desktop PC. One day, her boss furiously confronted her. "He told me it was completely improper to do business through e-mail," she said. "He suggested that somehow my use of the Internet might be costing the company some money, but in fact he was upset that I was leasing furniture and equipment directly, without his putting his own *hanko* on the agreement."

The sales agent was instructed that, from then on, she could do business only with customers who completed transactions the old-fashioned way, by fax. "It doesn't matter that it's more expensive," since she was now faxing back and forth on paper instead of using e-mail. "But the boss doesn't want to lose control by letting me use the computer."

Other factors also slowed Japan's acceptance of the Internet. It was relatively expensive to "dial up" an Internet service because the monopoly phone company, Nippon Telephone and Telegraph, kept rates high. Typing a Japanese kanji character into a computer is hard, one character sometimes requiring two or three steps. Since acquiring computer skills wouldn't help students pass entrance examinations for high school or college, Japanese schools hesitated to open computer training labs. Even after broadband Internet began to spread, the result of a vicious price war instigated by a Berkeley-trained entrepreneur in 2002, Japanese were still more likely to exchange short text messages on their mobile phones than use the keyboard of a laptop computer and the Internet to conduct research or transact business.

*   *   *

In Japan, many of the mechanisms that in other countries may force political or social adaptation—talk radio, class-action lawsuits, direct-mail and petition campaigns, protests in the streets—do not really function. Price signals are often short-circuited by regulations. Obedience and group harmony stifle independent action. With authority distributed from above, there are no checks and balances, no way to say for certain who really controls the system. If no one person is truly accountable, whom exactly do you blame?

Since 1955, a single political party has ruled the nation and has become expert at deflecting change through ignoring demographic changes, co-opting the press and other mass media, and wielding the formidable patronage of incumbency to keep opposition at bay. The Liberal Democratic Party relies on the expertise of the nation's powerful bureaucrats to buy off or suppress opponents. Until 2005 an LDP policy board had to approve a prime minister's legislative proposals before they were even presented to the Diet for consideration. This panel was made up not of policy experts, but of elderly party hacks far more concerned with their ability to raise cash from vested interests like dentists and construction companies than with the subtleties of regulatory reform. One young LDP legislator, Taro Kono, the son of a former foreign minister, told me how shocked he was to attend his first session of the Foreign Affairs committee and discover there was no opportunity for debate. "Everyone reads from a prepared script," said Kono, who had studied international affairs with Madeleine Albright at Georgetown University. "I don't even have to show up." Party dissidents, the few that speak out, inevitably find themselves expelled from power and kept out of policy-making circles. Disloyalty means political exile.

Change is also obstructed through Japan's lack of a policy of "one man, one vote." Although the Japanese people have largely abandoned the countryside for the cities and suburbs, the courts have upheld the electoral inequality that allows rural voters to hold three times the influence as urbanites casting ballots in metropolitan Tokyo or Osaka. Thus, politicians representing declining rural districts vociferously protect the agricultural subsidies, construction projects, and high-tariff barriers that keep their local constituents prosperous and protected. Its rural bias also allows the ruling party to continue to favor older, rural residents over younger city dwellers: for example, in 2002, over 400,000 urban dwellers in Yokohama elected a single representative to the Diet—as did fewer than 150,000 voters living in the third district of the rural Nagano prefecture. Japan did change its voting methods, eliminating a system where multiple candidates were elected from a single district to create single-member districts, ostensibly to foster the development of a "two party" political system. But the effects so far have proven negligible—the ruling party is now stronger than ever.

As for Japan's mass media, infamous *kissha curabu*, or "press clubs," regulate the flow of information between important government ministries and the general public. These powerful "clubs," comprised of the biggest newspaper and television groups, hold the power to bar nonmember journalists from attending regular press conferences and briefings. Information is not freely disseminated. In my first year in Tokyo, at a press briefing held by the health minister, Naoto Kan, I was forcibly pulled by my lapels and shoved out because a member of the Ministry's "press club" believed I had not requested proper permission from its "captain" before entering the room. Freelance journalists and foreign correspondents like me have to request special permission to attend briefings and press conferences, and frequently are barred.

Members of these press clubs often sit together to jointly determine how news events should be portrayed to the public. After a press briefing, club members routinely compile a memo framing the "news" disclosed during the briefing, and determine how it should be dispatched to their editors. Thus, Japanese newspapers carry virtually identical stories each day. One Japanese journalist confided his frustrations. "We run around all day making sure that when each newspaper appears the next day we are all exactly the same."

After more than two decades in journalism, I was shocked the first time I attended a prime minister's televised "press conference" to discover that it was as spontaneous as an intensely scripted Kabuki play. Not only did the prime minister mouth answers written for him in advance, but the questions the reporters posed had also been dictated, word for word, by government bureaucrats. A reporter who dares improvise and asks his own question will soon find himself stripped of his privileges and barred from the press room.

Japanese journalists also forge surprisingly intimate relationships with the politicians and bureaucrats they cover. Whether assigned to a cabinet member or a prominent policy commander, a reporter is expected to greet the official in the morning at his home as he leaves for work, and to go back late in the evening to await the politician's return from dinner and drinks with his benefactors and colleagues. In the ritual of the "night attacks," as they are called, the newsmaker invites reporters into his personal quarters for late-night beers and "off the record" conversation. One night I counted more than twenty pairs of shoes lying outside the dormitory apartment of Hiromu Nonaka, then Japan's powerful chief cabinet secretary, as reporters crowded into his living room or made their way to his refrigerator to get a cold beer. Little, if any, of such an evening's conversation usually finds its way into the next day's newspaper. Yet inevitably journalists grow so close to their subjects that they become secret advisers and confidants rather than independent analysts. Few independent watchdogs crusade to protect the public interest.

Even the language Japanese newspapers use serves as a soporific: rather than illuminating its readers, it seeks to calm them, to deflect responsibility, and to obfuscate. Newspapers seldom identify their sources directly or clarify who is responsible for brokering or implementing a policy, but rely on constructions like "it was learned" or "it was said." Ambiguity is considered a virtue. One editor at NHK, the government-owned broadcast network often described as the "BBC of Japan," recounted how a superior chastised her: he handed back a script and instructed her, "Could you make this story *less* clear?"

Real "scoops" are most often published by the weekly magazines, which are barred from membership in the influential "press clubs." Often these stories come from mainstream reporters themselves, journalists who, knowing their enterprise pieces or "scoops" cannot be published by their own newspapers, give them to a competitive "scandal sheet."

Despite the collusion, Japan's media is both powerful and exceedingly widely read. The circulation of Japan's mass-market dailies, like the conservative *Yomiuri Shimbun* or the more liberal *Asahi Shimbun*, is eight to ten times greater than the largest U.S. papers—in a nation with less than half the population of the United States. The papers enjoy exalted status, including rules that prohibit discounting and declare "press holidays"— twenty-four-hour periods when no papers are printed, to give printers and deliverymen a day off. Thus, Japanese newspapers seem to have no idea of the crusading tradition of investigative journalism, of supporting the underdog, of afflicting the comfortable, and of battling for the public's interest that is familiar to Western societies.[16]

*   *   *

Civil society is equally enfeebled, from the top down. An "us" and "them" mentality characterizes corporate *keiretsu*—Japan's giant, interconnected conglomerates—as well as government ministries. In the world of the "octopus pot," subordinates are responsible to their superiors, not to the wider society. Superiors shrug off individual responsibility, suggesting that a larger group of senior managers is ultimately responsible for resolving any difficulties. There is little institutional memory in a system where managers are routinely transferred from department to department or from branch office to headquarters and then back every two or three years. In Japanese firms or government agencies, employees don't really learn from mistakes or take responsibility for past errors, just as Japanese still find themselves unable to plainly dissect their nation's conduct during World War Two regarding atrocities committed against civilians or the role of "comfort women" forced to give sexual services to soldiers of the Imperial Army. Japan's most famous movie director, Akira Kurosawa, powerfully exposed this mind-set in his 1952 cinema classic *Ikiru*, or "To Live," the story of a bureaucrat who works for thirty years at City Hall and never accomplishes anything. More recently, even after massive government public works spending failed to lift the domestic economy out of its long stagnation in the mid-1990s, Japan's leading politicians insisted on digging even deeper and spending more. Their strategy wasn't flawed, they insisted; it was that the amount appropriated had been far too modest!

In Japan, no vigorous, independent think tanks monitor how government spends taxpayer funds or how bureaucrats behave. Mavericks don't win followings by attacking the status quo. On the contrary, social activists are often forced to endure extreme social ostracism; the few "whistle-blowers" who try to document wrongdoing or injustice in Japanese society invariably find themselves bullied or punished. In a memoir describing his difficult years working as a Health Ministry bureaucrat, the psychiatrist Masao Miyamoto described in agonizing detail the hazing rituals and harassment he was forced to endure because he would not adapt to the "party line."[17]

People who try to blow the whistle on corporate malfeasance or government scandal are often punished, without recourse to the courts. Kei Sugaoka, an American of Japanese descent, was quickly dismissed from his job as a safety inspector for General Electric after he disclosed a cover-up of safety violations at a nuclear reactor in Fukushima. Sugaoka said he watched his supervisors carefully erase videotapes showing cracks in a critical component of the reactor, yet when he "blew the whistle" and told regulators, his name was improperly disclosed to the utility and his employer.

"The Japanese say they will protect whistle-blowers," Sugaoka told me, "but that just isn't true." Japan nearly endured a national energy shortage in the summer of 2003 when the utility was forced to shut down all its nuclear-fired power plants temporarily to repair the damage Sugaoka had uncovered, and check whether other reactors were similarly vulnerable.

The whole purpose of this system of coordination and control has been to keep the economy humming, but now that goal no longer seems possible. In a world being leveled by global competition, a Japan marked by high wages and low productivity faces a difficult future. The "crown jewels" of lifetime employment and a seniority raise every year can no longer be guaranteed for the vast majority of Japanese workers, yet labor markets remain so inflexible that a mid-career employee can find it very difficult to land a new job, no matter how sterling his résumé. Corporations who need to pay back long-overdue debts have started to trim their labor costs by refusing to hire new employees and by limiting the raises they give older ones. Men who had been promised a job for life are suddenly losing their places. Their neighbors struggle to pay off mortgages on tiny homes that have lost two-thirds of their value in a decade. By 2004, youth unemployment stood at record levels, above 9 percent, and an estimated 630,000 young adults were said by the Labor Ministry to be neither in school or training, nor in a part-time job. To a new generation raised in a world of unfathomable affluence, the authoritarian mind-set that still drives Japanese life seems increasingly pointless.

*   *   *

The networked relations circumscribed within the Iron Triangle breed collusion, undermine transparency, and effectively interpose themselves into all matters of personal space and private relationships, thus insulating individuals from the need or will to assert responsibility. One trenchant observer, the Dutch journalist Karel van Wolferen, suggested that so expertly engineered was this Iron Triangle it needed no one at the top to run it; it was, in effect a power structure that was hollow in the center.[18]

"We lost our own narrative," Haruki Murakami, one of Japan's most prominent contemporary novelists told me one day, when I asked him to explain the meaning he drew from his nation's lost decade. When the bubble collapsed, "what we lost was confidence. Confidence in ourselves—socially and economically."

Japan's postwar story had been constructed around feverish economic conquest, and relentless growth had served as a sort of national religion binding citizens together, Murakami said. "We believed in the strength of the society and the power of our economy. And we believed that things were getting better and better, year by year and day by day . . . That's a kind of confidence, but that was lost . . . Once the Cold War ended, everything changed. We couldn't adjust to the new situation. It was a kind of chaos and we lost [our] sense of direction."

7.

THE IRON TRIANGLE OF THE PSYCHE

*To . . . understand the Japanese, to anticipate their behavior, we must
know the why's behind the what's; we must know the values driving the
culture.* —THOMAS KASULIS, *"Intimacy: A General Orientation in Japanese
Religious Values"*

The more I entered into the concealed realm of the *hikikomori*, the world
in which they shut out the sun, the more I understood that these men
were renouncing a complex web of values that made them feel impotent
and without worth, one that curbed their innate individuality and suppressed the very qualities their nation needed to shake off its own
inwardness. In Japan's extraordinary transition from feudalism to modernity, I came to see, the adjustment has proven incomplete: nothing in this
system, forged through stress, obligation, and mutual sacrifice, seems to
inculcate fundamental tolerance and compassion.

This can be hard for a casual visitor to Tokyo to sense. A tourist sees
the gleaming high-rise buildings decked out with video walls five stories
tall, the bullet trains and conveyor-belt sushi restaurants, the rave clubs
and whiskey bars and high-tech robots, and assumes that Japan sailed
smoothly into modern prosperity, easily adopting the mores, business
practices, and social organizations of the Western world. After all, if the
Japanese play golf, design semiconductor chips, and wear suits and ties
to work, it is natural to suppose that they have also adopted our own social values along with our technology. Besides, Japanese are among the
world's most gracious hosts, and always treat temporary foreign guests
with uncommon warmth and unstinting hospitality.

Yet sixty years after the end of World War Two, it is startling to realize
how *little* Japanese values really have changed and how passive the people remain amid a long and seemingly intractable national malaise. These

perceptions were reinforced not only by my experience of living in Japan and writing about it as a journalist, but also by conversations with Japanese who understood their society far better than I could.

In 1997, I interviewed Shizue Kato, the first woman elected to Japan's parliament, where she championed workers' rights and the environment. In 1937, after Japan had already begun its campaign of colonial conquest, Mrs. Kato had been jailed by the Japanese Imperial Army for advocating birth control in an era when the government sought ever larger families to support its military ambitions. Now, at the twilight of the twentieth century, on the eve of her hundredth birthday, rail-thin and demure, her silver hair pinned up high, Mrs. Kato sat in the parlor of her comfortably modern Tokyo apartment and told me in insistent though dignified tones that Japanese men had not changed their behavior in her lifetime. They remain samurai—only now camouflaged in business suits.

"Even now they are trapped and cannot speak their minds," she told me in the flawless English she had acquired while living in New York during the presidency of Woodrow Wilson. Japanese men "are tangled up in *shigarami*, vines of obligation [like those of a Japanese wisteria] from which they cannot escape. They are bound up by many social relations and obligations." Likewise, she insisted, true democracy has never taken hold in her nation.

"After we were defeated in war, we thought we had to learn democracy and Western culture," she said, as she glanced at the walls and tables around us with their historic photographs and framed letters displaying highlights of her distinguished, if controversial, career. A female secretary stood nearby, pouring tea. "We all appreciated receiving the idea of democracy, but our leaders did not understand what democracy really is.

"I was once asked [during the early 1990s] to speak at a prominent men's university about human rights. They asked me, 'What is this thing they call human rights?' Even in this prominent university they simply did not understand. They did not understand concepts of democracy, or human rights, or privacy—they had not heard of them."

Although her nation constantly borrows foreign concepts, digesting and reprocessing their essential ingredients, these often come out "differ-

ent," somehow genuinely "Japanese," once the repackaging is complete.
A Japanese pizza can be ordered with pineapple and squid. A 1950s GI
bomber jacket or Italian motorbike reproduced in Japan seems more perfect than the original. A Japanese-baked baguette is often lighter and
more flavorful than one found in Paris. Only Japanese could develop
green-tea ice cream, shoehorn a golf driving range into the tiniest city
block, or turn Christmas Eve into a romantic holiday when the nation's
hotels are booked solid by trysting young couples, even though everyone
goes back to work early on Christmas morning. Schoolchildren are
shocked to learn that *Makudonarudo*, the hamburger chain known elsewhere as McDonald's, is not actually a Japanese invention.

In contrast to the West, where competing civilizations buffeted one
another and jostled for ascendancy through phases of conquest, rebellion, and subjugation, Meiji Japan was never compelled to abandon either its homogeneity or its sense of being superior to other Asians, as it
drove its people to master the art of manufacturing rifles or the skill of
operating a steam-powered railroad. Moreover, it did not take up democracy from the West, but preferred instead to appropriate elements of
modern bureaucratic government from the Prussian example as better
suiting its feudal past. In the first half of the twentieth century, Japan remained an autocratic state in which the throne—and later the military—
controlled political parties from behind the scenes. And when the United
States imposed democracy on the Japanese people after World War
Two—much as it is trying to do today on Iraq—they did not enter into it
willingly. After the horrific fire bombings and two atomic attacks that devastated its great cities, the nation was effectively forced to accept the
postwar Constitution General Douglas MacArthur and the American occupiers drafted. The Japanese could not demand what they did not know,
and never engaged in the demonstrations, public protest, struggle, and
confrontation, the painful learning process through which democratic
government is usually forged—as, indeed, later occurred in South Korea
(see Chapter 12). What Japan did, instead, was to emasculate its Imperial system—reducing a godhead into a mere figurehead—and consent to
the reestablishment of a parliamentary democracy that met the demands

and preconceptions of its American conquerors. These changes were carried out swiftly, pragmatically, and without much fuss—and without actually undermining or tinkering with fundamental, underlying beliefs about the nature of the state, its role in society, and its relations to the self.

Beyond the political realm, however, other behaviors I encountered in everyday life also suggested that the Japanese look at the world and their place in it very differently. I often wondered why Japanese motorists seldom move aside when they see the flashing lights or hear the blaring sirens of an ambulance. Or why, when my wife fell while bicycling on a busy side street, not one of the dozens of pedestrians streaming past stopped to inquire whether she might be hurt. Or why so few Japanese seem to be motivated by altruism or civic engagement or believe in donating to charity. According to OECD data, Japan ranked twentieth of twenty-one nations in per capita humanitarian relief aid in 2003.[1]

I felt that to know the rebels who close themselves off from such a society compelled me to examine more closely the ecosystem they are attempting to renounce.

*   *   *

Unlike most of the people in the West who profess belief in a force beyond themselves, the Japanese worship many gods, not one. Modern Japanese find no contradiction in visiting a Shinto shrine at New Year's to bow and pray for health and prosperity; and then hiring a Caucasian preacher to conduct their wedding ceremony in a Christian church for the status it conveys; and finally being cremated in a Buddhist temple as saffron-robed monks chant sutras in Sanskrit amid wafting incense. In this pragmatic menu of beliefs, Japanese learn to pick à la carte, to choose what they need, when they need it, much as they might place their orders for individual morsels at a sushi bar. By implication, even moral values are situational. Taiichi Sakaiya—economist, former Cabinet minister, and renowned social thinker—says this relativist belief system allows Japanese to go through life without ever developing either a conviction about absolute, inviolable, or divine teachings, or a fixed "road map" of ethical principles. "What's morally right today is what a majority of Japanese people say is right today," he told me, when I asked him to define Japanese ethics. "Of course, if tomorrow the majority changes its mind, then the same behavior becomes immoral and wrong."[2] A Japanese must cast his gaze outside, not within, to discern right and wrong.

Perhaps never did a nation's ethical outlook change more radically than in 1945, when this nation's subjects, sworn to destroy the American and British devils, heard an Imperial proclamation beseeching them to "endure the unendurable." After a night or two of relieving its sorrows with cheap liquor, Japan immediately readied itself for a "democratic restructuring" from the top down, even if this slogan meant, in practical reality, that militarists now donned the morning coat of democracy and politicians earnestly proclaimed "liberalism" as a replacement for their fulsome wartime sloganeering.[3]

Sakaiya notes that Christians and Muslims, who rely on "god's teachings" or "holy texts" to discern right from wrong, hold fundamental beliefs that are not subject to debate, and cannot be swayed by any utilitarian, "cost-benefit" analysis. In this sense, the Western view of "freedom" is—if taken seriously (as it too often is not)—limited by the absolutist teaching of their religions. The Japanese construct is more relative, humanistic, and practical: "virtue" is whatever a person with power in a given situation or at a specific time thinks is "good." And since the most powerful person is usually in the majority, Sakaiya notes, this good conforms to what is good for others. What is good for those who have power over the company's employees becomes that which is also good for the company.[4]

In Tokugawa Japan (1600–1868), Christian practice was rigorously suppressed because it seemed to threaten the hierarchy of the shogunate. But even during the Meiji period of accelerated modernization—the period after 1863 when the disciplined importation of Western learning and civilization was emphasized and the slogan "rich country, strong army" encapsulated the national mood—a de facto ban on Christian practice remained in place, so as not to undermine the authority of a theocratic state only recently reestablished. Lest anyone question the legitimacy of this new Imperial regime created nearly overnight, the Meiji throne invoked the imagined purity of antiquity even as it sought to create a modern state free of the chains of "backward" feudalism. As the historian Marius B. Jansen has noted, a nation that entered the 1860s as perhaps the world's last truly feudal state had, within thirty years, been recast as one of the world's most centralized regimes.[5]

So single-minded were the Japanese in their zeal to master the technological, to modernize, and to catch up with the Great Powers that they never bothered to absorb either the philosophical or the religious underpinnings of what they were appropriating from the West: its foundation of individuation, inquiry, and risk-taking. Over a century, Japan proved expert at importing and replicating technologies from abroad, but routinely ignored the philosophical methods other cultures relied upon in order to nurture such advances. The Japanese learned that copying a master's product exactly is the most efficient way to acquire new skills, much as it later copied Renaults and Austin automobiles to help create its Toyotas and Nissans, and "reverse engineered" electronics parts from overseas first to build transistor radios and later to create its television industry. Likewise, it could adopt specific features from foreign religions and economic systems, while leaving behind the potentially threatening ideology of personal empowerment. Kant and Hegel never arrived on Japan's shores.

Thus, in a very real sense, Japan mounted a bullet train, and traveled at breakneck speed from feudalism to industrialization, to war and then reconstruction, without ever experiencing the Enlightenment. In other words, neither the power of the individual separate from the state, nor a self separate from society, nor the validity of an individual conscience separate from group sensibilities, ever gained a toehold.

The sociologist Max Weber has famously suggested that at the root of the Protestant ethic of frugality and industriousness was the sense of work as an individual's "calling." As industrialism developed in the West, along the lines of Judeo-Christian traditions, European burghers believed that their thrift and industriousness and the capitalist drive to amass great wealth also expressed their sense of moral duty to a single god, who had invested in each human being a unique spark of ingenuity and creativity. Working together with others instead of merely for one's self, Martin Luther said, expresses a form of Christian charity by allowing man to express his individual spirit.

Yet Japanese persisted, since feudal times, in seeing hard labor as an expression not of self or even of selflessness, but of pitiless self-denial.[6] Hard work—so Buddhist doctrines, as reinterpreted by the seventeenth-century scholar Baigan Ishida, instruct—causes man to abandon his ego and lose himself just as assuredly as does the emptiness produced through hours of Zen meditation. Even today, the extreme, sometimes fanatical attention to detail Japanese demonstrate in their craftsmanship pays homage to this ideal because it is the labor itself, not efficiency, that matters. Indeed, this special aspect of the conscientious Japanese "manufacturing ethic" is one that consumers around the globe have come to admire. The reverse side of a weld, the inside sleeve of a kimono, or the fine grain of a wood beam that, once it is used to frame a house, will be invisible to its owner, remains critically important to the Japanese craftsman and his customer. It is one admirable quality the West has come to expect from Japan, even if it does not always subscribe to it. A revered Japanese artisan spends decades copying his predecessors. Even for the gifted master, work tends to deny self instead of enhancing it, and no monotheistic paradigm offers an alternate route toward setting oneself apart from the collective or for expressing a healthy sense of "uniqueness" separate from others.

The only religious practice indigenous to Japan, the animist Shinto, holds that rocks, trees, bodies of water, and animals are all *kami*, or gods, worthy of human reverence. Each year, residents in individual neighborhoods hold a *matsuri*, or festival, to pay homage to their local *kamisama*. They dance and parade wildly in the streets, put on loincloths, drink beer, and carry a heavy portable shrine, or *omikoshi*, on their shoulders to humor and entertain the *kami*. A properly amused *kami* brings prosperity to the community.

Whatever religious influences Japan imported from outside were quietly reformulated to better conform to local standards. When Confucianism arrived from China, for instance, the Japanese obliterated the ideal of a "mandate of heaven," the notion that an emperor's reign could be cut short by ethical or moral failure. While Confucian precepts of industriousness, filial piety, and discipline took hold in Japan, the Emperor himself remained divine and above reproach. The fact that those who served him actually ruled—that the Emperor was often little more than a figurehead acquiescing to actions devised and executed at lower levels—ensured that political intrigue remained ever-present in the Imperial Court. But it also validated the immense influence of *amae*—the parent-child attachment—and undermined any suggestion that those at the very top of the political pyramid could be held accountable for their actions.

Japanese decide right from wrong by relying on context—on "everyone's opinion," as Sakaiya put it to me—for guidance. The hierarchical nature of the social architecture, the need to maintain group harmony, and the fear of standing out only make the tendency to acquiesce more powerful. "Individual conscience never became a significant fact" in describing freedom within Japan, concluded Masao Maruyama, Japan's most important postwar historian.[7]

Over drinks one day near his office, my friend Akira once told me about an incident that he thought perfectly captured routinely unethical Japanese conduct. In an international golf tournament shown on satellite TV, he had watched a Japanese player hit the ball into the rough. Then, much to Akira's surprise, the golfer reached into his bag to retrieve a giant driver, a two-wood—the wrong club for digging a ball out of tall grasses. The golfer didn't want the club to whack at the ball, however. Instead he used the club's broad face as a hammer to beat down the grass surrounding his lie. "He wasn't directly accused of cheating," Akira said, "but it isn't the proper way to play." He hated the scene because the golfer showed no appreciation for the honor of the game and the spirit of "fair play" as other golfers understood it. "He just wanted to bend the rules so he could win," said Akira, one of a tiny handful of Japanese Christians. It distresses him that many Japanese approach business practices the same way. He compared the Japanese golfer's attitude to an anecdote he had heard about the American golfer Tom Kite. Kite had become arrogant after one tournament, and his golf teacher scolded him. "It's not *what* you are, it's *who* you are that matters," the instructor had told Kite. To Akira, this was the difference between life in Japan and in the West. Certainly recent U.S. history is blemished by many examples of corporate leaders who used unethical conduct to bolster their pay packages. But Akira was convinced that most Japanese would not find the golfer's bending of the rule objectionable, or that a Japanese CEO would be similarly punished for his dishonest conduct.

However grossly they may ignore it in practice, Westerners today retain a belief in a transcendental power outside and above the commonplace, which has over the centuries provided a viable compass whereby a nation's people may judge the behavior of its leaders and others and exact accountability. At base, we profess a belief in moral leadership. In Japan, however, the boundary between sacred and profane, self and nature, society and self, and even, especially, between right and wrong are murky. In conversations with Japanese historians, sociologists, psychiatrists, and other social thinkers, I was struck by how often they highlighted the absence of monotheism in Japanese culture as an important element distinguishing their society from a Western one. In turn, the American theologian Thomas Kasulis believes that Japanese morality must be unfathomable to Westerners: "We find in the Japanese account no marked emphasis on any of the following: the individual [soul] as the primary unit of spiritual, moral, and political meaning; the notion of a set of universal principles applying to all humankind as the ideal of behavior; the idea of a legalistic, contractual relationship among persons or between a people and their God; the idea of a divine plan worked out in natural and human history to which we feel responsible; or the hierarchy of rationality as what sets off the human from other animals."[8]

The absence of universal principles and of a contractual, consensual relationship among a people may explain the relative passivity of civil society in contemporary Japan. Because Japanese are not taught that they have a duty to help those outside their own kin, they seldom exercise altruism. The homeless men and women camping rough in Tokyo's Ueno

Park are usually fed hot soup by Korean Christians, not by native Japanese. This may be the reason motorists don't make way for an ambulance. It also suggests why Japanese can be so honorable and trustworthy in their personal dealings with "honored customers" or people they know, while their nation is rife with shocking corporate dishonesty. While Americans may cheat to enrich themselves, it is said, Japanese usually steal for their companies.

Some optimists claim that, with the growing disillusionment with big government and big business, recent legal changes to bolster nongovernment organizations in Japan will ultimately help a robust civil society emerge, one which can transform the nation. It will take years for this to happen, however. In the meantime, civil society remains all but powerless against either the conformist, group-oriented, and hierarchical nature of Japanese society or the autopilot tendencies of its unrepentant government machinery.

*   *   *

Japanese and Westerners also "see" the world differently. When it comes to cognition—literally, how individuals process bits of information in order to perceive the world around them—Japanese look at the world through eyes that actually function differently, that are culturally primed to look at different things, and this variation can powerfully influence behavior. We know that cultures differ in the way they define hazard, opportunity, novelty, risk, gratification, and loss. One can attribute coming down with a common cold, for example, variously to witchcraft, germs, God's will, planetary alignments, or one's own moral failings. Hayao Kawai, one of Japan's most prominent Jungian therapists, suggests that, when evaluating others, Japanese employ "field-oriented thinking" while Westerners use an "individual ethic." Based on their Judeo-Christian tradition, he told me, Western societies rely on a "paternal" ethic, in which each person is evaluated according to his or her own talents and abilities. Japan, however, more resembles a "maternal" society, in which all children are accepted whether they are good or bad, and all are treated equally, as long as they do not renounce the family.

In the West, he notes in an article, if you apologize for a mistake, you are admitting fault and will accept responsibility to compensate the injured. But in Japan, when a wrongdoer bows and apologizes to his victim, the act immediately creates "common ground" between the two. The victim is not allowed to request compensation, as it might destroy that common ground. Whether the act was good or evil is not part of the equation, Kawai says; belonging to the same social field is the bigger concern. "As long as you are a member of the field, you will somehow be rescued . . . But once you are out of the field, then you will become a total stranger, and those people in the field cannot do anything for the stranger."[9]

On a continuum differentiating individualism from collectivism, no societies seem farther apart than the American and the Japanese. An American worldview centralizes the personal—attaining personal goals, establishing uniqueness, and asserting personal control and self-reliance—while deemphasizing the responsibilities or constraints the larger society might impose. The Japanese culture, however, emphasizes self-discipline and restraint of internal attributes that might interfere with the cohesion of the group. It tends to rely on the influence of groups in binding and mutually obligating individuals, all in the name of group harmony. A vast body of research in cultural psychology shows that while Americans tend to emphasize the importance of a positive self-image and seek to develop self-esteem, Japanese tend to be self-critical, and focus on ways they might work persistently in order to "improve" themselves and meet the expectations of others. (The term "self-esteem" does not exist in Japanese.) In addition, research comparing American and Japanese college students shows that American participants more readily recall situations where they influence the world around them, while Japanese mostly remember modifying their behavior to suit a situation. Likewise, Americans commonly report feeling more effective when *influencing* a situation, while Japanese take greater satisfaction from the connectedness they feel when *adjusting* to fit in.[10]

The influence of Confucian thought in shaping this view of self—and of the importance in maintaining one's role in the harmonious operation of a larger hierarchy—seems obvious when viewed within the Japanese context. Since the interdependent Japanese tend to acquiesce, not argue, the Japanese self appears relatively malleable. To meet its obligations, the group expects you to adjust rather than remain separate and autonomous. The boundary between self and society or between self and others inevitably dissolves.[11]

As the Japanese constantly need to ascertain context in order to establish their own identity, this fixation can also diminish their ability to detach objects from their background—to shift focus, that is, from context to abstraction. Indeed, Richard E. Nisbett, a social psychologist at the University of Michigan, has shown that Japanese literally see the world differently from the way Westerners do. "Human cognition is not everywhere the same," his experiments demonstrate.

Westerners emphasize analytical thought, an intellectual tradition derived from the Greeks. They tend to separate an object from its context, to focus on the attributes of an object in order to categorize it, and to create rules that explain the behavior of various categories of object. They tend to employ formal rules of logic, to avoid contradiction, and to deconstruct structure from context.

The Asian intellectual approach, however, tends to be holistic, to connect the whole to its parts. It orients itself to appreciate the field, or context, in which an object exists; carefully notes the relationship between focal object and background; and prefers to explain and predict events on the basis of these relationships. It easily accepts contradiction, striving to discern a "middle way" between dialectical poles. These differences between the analytic and the holistic, between abstract and contextual thinking can actually be observed as they affect a person's or a group's cognitive and perceptual behaviors.[12]

In one fascinating experiment, college students in Kyoto and Ann Arbor were presented with identical animated vignettes of underwater scenes. In each scene, large and colorful fish moved in front of a complicated background of ferns, shells, frogs, bubbles, and sand placed amid the flowing waters of an aquarium. When researchers asked the students to describe what they saw, the Japanese were twice as likely to describe the background first, rather than the objects in the foreground, while the Americans were far more likely to describe the most salient objects first.

The researchers then manipulated the background to see whether this changed context would affect participants' abilities to recognize specific animals. Indeed, Japanese students made substantially more errors when animals were presented against a novel new background, while American responses were unaffected. Nisbett suggests that while Japanese literally see *more* of the world—they report more about a background context than their American counterparts do—they find it more difficult to *detach* an individual object from its surroundings.

In another study, Japanese and American students were given identical cameras and asked to photograph their best friend. The Americans tended to shoot extreme close-ups, zooming in to ensure that the face occupies the vast majority of the photographic field. The Japanese, by contrast, stepped back from the subject, and snapped pictures in which their friend occupied far less space in the frame relative to the background.

Such contrasting physical images neatly illustrate competing concepts of self. In America, a person exists alone, relatively indifferent to, or not necessarily affected by, his surroundings. In Japan, it is nearly impossible to portray a person cut off from his context. You might argue that in Japan, an individual shorn of his tangling vines of context, without a business card or a group to belong to, ceases to exist. This perception, expressed repeatedly in Japanese society, raises a nagging existential question. Does a *hikikomori* continue to exist if he remains in his room, cutting off all relations with the world outside his doorway and refusing to accommodate himself to a world he renounces?

*   *   *

Trust is a crucial component of "social capital," the ingredient that helps make a society efficient, productive, and responsive to innovation and new ideas. The importance of social capital was first proposed by

Robert D. Putnam, now a Harvard professor, who wondered why northern Italians were wealthier than their southern cousins. His pioneering research showed that the ability of the northerners to develop trusting relations with strangers led to their affluence; and that civic engagement, rather than patronage, motivated its citizens. Northern Italians did not become civic-minded after becoming wealthy, Putnam says. On the contrary, civic engagement is what helped create their wealth. In civic-minded communities, residents "trust one another to act fairly and obey the law. Leaders in these communities are relatively honest and committed to equality. Social and political networks are organized horizontally, not hierarchically. These 'civic communities' value solidarity, civic participation, and integrity. And here democracy works."

In districts of southern Italy such as Umbria and Sicily, by contrast, social and cultural life remains relatively threadbare. Politics there is somebody else's job to take care of. Laws are made to be broken. Fearing others' lawlessness, citizens demand sterner discipline. "Trapped in these interlocking vicious circles, nearly everyone feels powerless, exploited, and unhappy," Putnam has found. This lack of civic engagement made it harder for southern Italians to form guilds or mutual aid associations that might have led to wider prosperity.

Social capital is important because, as with conventional capital, the more one has, the more one gets. Social capital also tends to be cumulative and self-reinforcing. As you use it to build connections and generate trust, it becomes easier to accumulate more trust, create denser networks, and produce more effective social norms. Unlike normal capital, however, social capital tends to deplete and waste away if not regularly paid out.[13]

Another political scientist, Francis Fukuyama, argues that "trust"—as contrasted to what he calls "familism"—generates wealth. Rich countries exhibit higher levels of social trust than poor ones, he thinks, and Japan's prosperity results from "networks based on moral obligation . . . Something in the Japanese culture makes it very easy for one person to incur a reciprocal obligation over extended periods of time," he writes, without ever defining what this "something" might be. Because it is prosperous, he says, Japan must be a highly trusting society like the United States.[14]

The Japanese networks I encountered each day—the *keiretsu* of bank and manufacturing groups, the factions within the powerful bureaucracy, or the tribal-like *zoku* of special interests within political parties—do not, however, bear out Fukuyama's argument. (Despite his Japanese surname, Fukuyama is an American born in Chicago.) These networks—closed, confined, and exclusive, as they are based on preexisting relationships—are not "trusting." They do not readily accommodate outsiders. They tend to be impenetrable and controlling, not open and sharing. They husband and broker information instead of distributing it, and use their internally created confidences to gain advantage over members of rival groups. Organized into rigid vertical hierarchies, various branches within the same company or ministry often refuse even to share information with one another. For example, the Japanese once hired a French hydrologist's firm to custom-build a water pollution control system, but would not share water samples that disclosed the precise nature of the pollutants the system should be designed to control. Even the contractor was an outsider, not part of the inside "network."

In the West today, information is often "free" and widely dispersed—look at the rise of Internet blogs, and open source software—developments that Japan, with its rigid organizational style, could never embrace. Japan succeeded in an era of vertical integration, when firms could use proprietary architecture to dominate complex systems, but it lost its way in an era of "open" and global standards in which customers, not companies, gain ascendancy. Even today, Japan is only slowly allowing desktop computers and e-mail to saturate the workplace. Japanese are less likely, research shows, to integrate their use of database and information systems than are comparable firms in other advanced nations; and Japanese still rely on interpersonal relations within closed *keiretsu* to organize their normal business activities. Even online transactions in Japan tend to be focused within a business unit, not venture outside it.[15] One reason that eBay, the online auction service, failed in Japan is that the company insisted that, as in America, bidders use credit cards for their payments. But many Japanese simply don't trust electronic payments and prefer to pay with cash and bank transfers.[16]

Since their society is homogeneous and remarkably stable, with little street crime and bank robberies and few murders, you might expect the Japanese to readily trust other Japanese with whom they are not already acquainted. After all, they share such profound racial and cultural bonds. Yet opinion surveys consistently confirm my own observations: that Japanese are generally suspicious not only of foreigners, but also of fellow Japanese they don't know. Americans, who live in a relatively rowdy, mixed-up, rootless nation amid guns and violence, are far more trusting of strangers, in part because they encounter more strangers in their daily lives and must learn how to live in their midst.[17] When asked, for example, whether they could "put their trust in others," or whether "it's always best to maintain one's guard," 47 percent of Americans say other people can be trusted while only 26 percent of Japanese give a similar response. Likewise, when asked whether they believe that other people usually try to be altruistic, or are just looking out for themselves, 47 percent of Americans say strangers tend to want to help while only 19 percent of Japanese concur. It remains something of a surprise that distrust should seem so relatively high in a society notable for its homogeneity and collectivism. Asked whether they agree with the traditional aphorism, "If I see a stranger, I think he is a robber," a sizable majority of Japanese will say they do.

How to explain this paradox? Toshio Yamagishi, a social psychologist at Hokkaido University, has demonstrated in a fascinating series of laboratory experiments that Japan's intensely collectivist society undermines trust and prevents social capital from accumulating.[18]

In situations of social uncertainty, individuals confront competing choices. They can generally trust others, sizing up each individual's character, or form closed exclusive communities to protect themselves from being exploited by strangers. In a society of strong interpersonal relations, people need not develop their own trusting skills. Much as the southern Italians depend on their local Mafia, so do the Japanese rely on their strong networks. The Japanese don't join these groups willingly, as a matter of personal choice. They are forced to join by the highly engineered system of mutual monitoring and sanctioning—social obligations, keeping up face, the "tangling vines of relationships," or *shigarami*, to which Shizue Kato referred. This system can probably be traced to the closed, suspicious culture of control instituted within traditional village society during the Tokugawa period. The newly centralized government divided each village into five-family units of mutual surveillance, or *gonin-gumi*, to assure loyalty and conformity. If any individual within the five-family unit broke the rules, all members were held accountable. This system created strong mutual dependency and trust, but also sowed distrust of those outside the village's boundaries. As an old peasant told the political scientist Daikichi Irokawa in 1949, "Peasants form communities to ensure life will be humane." The peasants "know that mankind is basically crafty and that the individual is weak when isolated from his fellows."[19]

The strong, stable relationships families and corporations form within Japan promote *assurance* within these groups, but they actually undermine *trust* outside them. Where mutual surveillance—not trust—constrains behavior, strangers are not welcomed. When context guides propriety, it is difficult to ascertain whether an outsider shares the same code book. Japanese tend to rely on close personal contacts, instead of formal contracts, to guide behavior and on context, rather than impersonal institutions like government, to equitably negotiate among strangers. As one behavior reinforces the other, they lose the incentive and motivation to develop the social intelligence that would enable them either to distinguish between the trustworthy and the unscrupulous outsider or to explore potential opportunities lying outside their own narrow networks.

These closed networks strongly bind Japanese one to the other, but also blind them from developing trust—even in other Japanese in other confined networks. This blindness prevents most from looking outside the scope of their predefined relationships. In the heterogeneity of America, by contrast, where weak ties among a random cast of strangers predominate, people must, if they are to prosper, learn to open their eyes to discern whether unfamiliar people may be trustworthy, and create flexible, porous networks that can adapt as circumstances change, and take advantage of promising new connections.

In Japanese society, one who abandons a network finds himself ostracized and isolated. Little wonder that Japanese often choose to travel abroad in large groups, or that a Japanese traveling alone in a foreign country is notoriously an easy mark who can be duped or cheated because he is so naïve. (Likewise, it is those who feel they cannot comfortably find a place for themselves in such closed networks who often seek escape by "leaving the field" entirely, and abandon Japan for life abroad. Many of the twenty- and thirty-something Japanese women who troll the fashion shops of Manhattan, Santa Monica, and San Francisco come from this group.)

If a Japanese dares to consider abandoning his network, he knows there is no better one he can turn to for support: once he leaves his old network, he will have become an "outsider," to whom all other potential networks are closed. Thus, in Japan's traditional lifetime employment system, a person who seeks "liberation" from the confines of his old job cannot expect to benefit by becoming a "free agent." It's unlikely that another Japanese firm, wedded to its own closed and restricted network, will offer him work, no matter how distinctive his talents. (In Japan these talented "free agents" often wind up working in foreign-owned firms which encourage individual risk-taking and pay according to merit.) As Yamagishi notes: "The one who deserts a relationship for quick profits will have a harder time in a society in which other relationships are mainly closed to outsiders." Yamagishi goes on to explain how the architecture of Japanese networks both minimizes social uncertainty and makes for security within their bounds. "This sense of security," he says, "is what is often considered 'trust' when characterizing the Japanese scene. However, once such socio-relational bases of security are removed, the Japanese may feel more insecure than Americans do."[20]

Where Americans exhibit *weak* forms of trust among strangers to generate productive and cooperative reciprocity, Japanese seek to reassure one another through enduring ties. They minimize risk through *strong* trust given to those within a narrow *uchi*, or in-group, beyond which trust and risk taking don't readily extend.[21] This explains why "friendship" among Japanese is far less casual than among Americans. In Japan, a friend is a friend for life; and a friendship is like a ledger book, where favors gained and given are regularly tallied, and the object is to even up the accounts before death. A Japanese woman once explained why a Japanese would be reluctant to open a new page on his ledger to accommodate a friendship with an expatriate. "If he asks you how long you intend to live in Japan and you say, 'Ten years,' you think that's a really long time. But to him, a new friendship is not worth taking on if he knows you will move away in a decade."

On a deeper level, opening a closed network in Japan undermines its vital ability to maintain the support and loyalty of those already within it. Thus, when a vacancy arises in a U.S. college, the dean must conduct a wide search, interview a diverse array of candidates, and follow affirmative action criteria to ensure full consideration of such underrepresented groups as minorities and women. The candidates' achievements are thoroughly reviewed, as is their potential to have a lasting impact on the department and on scholarship. If he fails to conduct a sufficiently "open" search, his university, theoretically, could be challenged with a lawsuit. In Japan, however, where academic departments are usually headed by a long-tenured professor who surrounds himself with a flock of sycophantic disciples, only a strong loyalist who is a member of the in-group is likely to be offered a promotion. The candidate's obedience, not his achievements, is likely to be scrutinized. To behave in any other manner, Yamagishi argues, only weakens the chairman's hold on the devotion of his staff. Should he hire someone from outside the network, the network will soon wither away, since its very rationale—protection and mutual support—has been undermined.

The fact that real debate and intellectual exchange are systematically de-emphasized, while loyalty to the senior dean is reinforced, goes far toward explaining both the lack of rigorous intellectual debate within most Japanese universities and the tendency of Japanese researchers to fall behind their foreign counterparts. Since achievement does not necessarily lead to a higher salary or greater recognition, and the young must always defer to their elders, a bright or gifted researcher has little incentive to move to another, more prestigious institution. These closed systems also impair Japan's ability to innovate or conduct cutting-edge research. Although a Japanese invented the arthroscope that makes possible the most advanced knee surgery, Japanese surgeons don't as readily perform the common forms of arthroscopic knee surgery that American sports medicine clinics carry out every day, because the senior surgeons lead surgical teams and they cannot be expected to have learned how to use such innovative new tools. Even if one of the junior members of the team has been trained in the latest technology, it would violate hierarchical relations for him to lead the surgery.

*   *   *

For decades, Japan's closed system of networks successfully reduced transaction costs. In its formative era, members of the Toyota corporate clan did not really need written contracts, performance guarantees, or incentive clauses to function effectively as a compact domestic organization. Corporate governance didn't really matter as much as mutual surveillance. Working together for decades in a closed and harmonious network, the employees of Toyota could maximize efficiency and achieve high growth.

As the global economic system became more complex in the 1990s, however, closed-network clans became increasingly inefficient and unproductive if they overlooked new opportunities being created outside their restricted field of vision. In today's world, firms debug software in India, manufacture in China, do the accounting work in France, and keep a sales force in Boston. In a twenty-first-century economy where capital, design, factors of production, and advanced technology can quickly flow from one nation to another, flexible and geographically dispersed production networks create greater innovation and efficiency than do static, long-term "relationship" contracts. As Toyota became compelled to expand its reach far beyond Japan, it too was forced to overhaul its own corporate governance to keep up. "Openness and transparency, that's the way of the world these days," explained a Toyota spokesman, when asked about Toyota's dramatic changes in internal governance. The vast majority of Japanese business, however, remains far less globally focused than Toyota.

In an era of mass customization and flexible, networked production, business partners in other parts of the globe cannot be quickly accommodated unless close ties with preexisting domestic partners are radically reshaped. In Japan, however, loyalty and mutual obligation often interfere. New opportunities cannot be seized because one company's grandfather made commitments to another firm's grandfather. In time, the costs of missed opportunities eventually overwhelm the savings that closed networks once produced. As the political scientist Takashi Inoguchi notes, "The very success Japan achieved on the basis of relatively closed social capital, reassurance-oriented social capital and binding social capital has started to function negatively in the age of globalization."[22]

America itself had once been an insulated, agrarian, small-town society, but the massive social and economic turbulence that arose in the 1880s compelled adaptation. Amid surging industrialization, rapid urbanization, an influx of immigrants from Europe and Asia, and the mass migration of labor facilitated by the construction of railroads, America eventually created new institutions to mediate relationships formed in a more unstable world. The passage of the Sherman Antitrust Act, the creation of labor unions and joint-stock corporations, and the formation of the Interstate Commerce Commission, for example; all these were institutions created to guarantee the standing of strangers and foster trust in an economy newly transformed by a sudden surge of mobility. In such a world, older, narrow networks of reassurance could no longer function effectively.[23]

Cracking open long-closed networks lies at the heart of the remarkable comeback of Nissan Motor Co. carried out by Carlos Ghosn, its Brazilian-French-Lebanese president. He insisted on using objective measures of cost and efficiency when the carmaker reviewed contracts with even longtime suppliers. In contrast, the relative decline in Japan's competitiveness in areas like software and telecommunications can be attributed to the priority its corporations place on maintaining long-term relations and closed, proprietary standards rather than on forming flexible relations around emerging open standards. Robert Cole of the University of California, Berkeley, has shown that by selecting a closed, proprietary standard for its second-generation digital cellular phones, Japan severely limited the ability of its firms to compete in the rapidly growing global market for handsets. Korean manufacturers such as Samsung, by contrast, chose to adopt open, international standards, and, as a result, became powerful and profitable exporters of sophisticated mobile phones to the United States and Europe.[24]

* * *

The *hikikomori* are, in their lonely darkened rooms, painfully impaled on the points of a psychic triangle. Though desperate to free themselves from their nation's rigid educational, employment, and social patterns, they know that if they choose the risky route of personal "emancipation" and flee into the sunshine, they will be doubly punished. Shunned by the school or work group from which they have withdrawn, they likely may find no other network or group willing to accept them. They feel certain that few strangers will reach out to help them find a new path. And without membership in any group, shorn of social context, these *hikikomori* have precious little identity on which to fall back. Since to most Japanese these detached and disconnected souls are practically invisible, it is highly unlikely that any social service volunteer or school counselor will ever knock at their door.

Statistics also reflect the dreary state of Japan's mental health system. It has the highest number of hospital patients with mental illness in the world. The average stay at a mental institution is also the longest in the world, 406 days. And most of these patients languish in private hospitals, which often scrimp on nursing staffs or use extraneous procedures to pad their bills. While the Medical Service Law stipulates that there be at least one doctor per sixteen patients and at least one nurse per three patients at hospitals for physical diseases, psychiatric institutions are permitted to have forty-eight patients per doctor and six patients per nurse.[25]

Beyond their own difficult condition, the plight of *hikikomori* reflects a psychic impoverishment broadly visible across a wider Japanese spectrum. This can be seen in the drabness of its public buildings, the penury of its housing, the high costs rigorously engineered into everyday life, and the sheer ugliness of the physical environment set down even in its great cities, where neon signs, telephone wires, repulsive concrete apartment blocks and *pachinko* parlors obscure the ancient beauty of its historic landmarks. The sterility of its urban surfaces denotes the crisis of the spirit, and the stubborn hold of the construction state, which insists on tearing down and rebuilding nearly anything and everything. While it is nearly impossible to get through a day in Japan without seeing some reference—in paper, plastic, neon, or chrome—to flowering cherry blossoms, the young sprigs of the pine forests, rushing rivers, snowy mountains, or seaside nature (my favorite icons were always the small plants put up in the underground passages of subway stations)—you can go for many months, even years, without ever seeing the real thing, unspoiled. And should you lace up your hiking boots and boldly venture forth into the outdoors, the experience can be remarkably unpleasant. In parks, loudspeakers continuously assault visitors. Vending machines line nature trails, which have been paved in concrete. Beaches are befouled with plastic bottles and garbage. No public attraction can be reached without your having to navigate through acres of surrounding souvenir shops.

Many public buildings and retail shops suffer from a dreary sameness, while on those extraordinary projects where the architectural work has been specially commissioned to designers, the resulting glass or concrete cubes seldom bear much spatial or emotional relationship to their surroundings. Thus, the cold concrete hulk that emerged from the design competition for Kyoto's new train station bears no connection to the ancient capital of Buddhist temples which surrounds it—but it does offer travelers another neon-lit opportunity to buy handbags and souvenirs.[26] In the countryside, power lines and metal-clad factories routinely obscure the view of mountain range and rice paddy. Little surprise, perhaps, that Japan is a global laggard in developing its tourism industry. Hotels remain spartan, outdated, and overpriced, which helps discourage domestic tourism. A couple is charged twice as much for a room as a single guest, making a romantic weekend getaway a costly undertaking. At a rural inn or *ryokan*, breakfast is typically served at 7 A.M.—or not at all— and the visitor has little say over what dishes he will be served. The price of domestic airline tickets are kept high through regulations and airports are made inconvenient to discourage foreign travel. Foreigners who come for a visit find it hard to enjoy a country where relatively few natives speak passable English, and few signs, maps, or menus are available in Roman script.

Even when Japanese stay hunkered down, close to their own homes, they are confronted by the penury of their national lifestyle. Japan remains a nation of enormous nominal wealth even after fifteen years of malaise, yet it can be shocking to discover how cramped, drafty, poorly constructed, and devoid of style an average Japanese house really is. Often slapped together with second-rate material, designed with little attention to the grace notes of detail because of government regulations, and offering little privacy to its inhabitants, many apartments and homes still resemble the infamous "rabbit hutches" once described by a visiting French diplomat, rather than the warm and inviting refuges of a prosperous people. You can see why many Japanese stay out late every night after work at a restaurant or a club to put off as long as possible being shoehorned into their cramped and unpleasant homes. Even the vast, high-rise public housing projects that crowd the skyline in Seoul typically offer their residents far more space than Japanese are allotted. And Japanese know, from the increasing frequency of their trips overseas, that a closed network of business and political conspirators keeps their prices high and their choices limited because consumer markets are kept from being opened to true competition.

As a result of satellite TV, foreign films, and overseas vacations, young Japanese are waking up to the imbalances and inadequacies so apparent to outsiders in their rich nation. They now see how others live, how young people in other nations tend to take greater control over their lives. But having never been taught or given incentive to think critically, and lacking any social mechanism that would allow them to rebel, all too many of the young—those in their twenties, thirties, and forties, who should be helping Japan readjust and realign its society to the realities of the information age—are, like the *hikikomori*, finding ultimately self-destructive ways to detach from that society. The suicide rate has risen precipitously, while women in growing numbers are saying no to marriage and motherhood. Youth unemployment is stuck at an all-time high. Alcoholism, depression, and divorce are increasing. Violence among teenagers grows more pronounced, and grade school children, some as young as eleven, kill classmates in sudden snaps of rage, known as *kireru*. Colonies of blue plastic tarps, the spontaneous tent cities erected by thousands of homeless, have sprouted like dandelions in Tokyo's biggest parks and are visible along railway embankments and underpasses. Family life is fraying. Faced with such bleak prospects, many young adults hide out in cults that obsess over pursuit of brand-name goods, or retreat into the world of pop culture and cartoons.

I sensed in Kenji and the other *hikikomori* the profound dislocation that many young people of their generation are experiencing in a modern, affluent Japan. Most of these men and women are, like Kenji, imaginative, intelligent, and highly sensitive. Yet each feels that he or she has no safe place to thrive.

8.

THE CULT OF THE BRAND

Sometime before seven on a late-summer Sunday morning in September 2002, I joined a mob that was gathering on the gray-tiled sidewalk of Omotesando, one of Tokyo's most fashionable boulevards. The most zealous of this crowd had started lining up three days earlier, hauling along neatly packaged blue plastic tarpaulins, folding stools, fleece sweaters that could double as pillows, and aluminum thermoses full of strong green tea. Their faith and fortitude shielded them from any self-consciousness as they prepared to bunk down and bide the time with cigarettes, magazine catalogs, and their ubiquitous mobile phones. Others waited only until dawn that day to launch their pilgrimages, hustling onto the first trains from their homes in the distant suburbs, or stumbling out of the smoky rave bars of Shibuya about 5 A.M. after a night of Ecstasy, hard partying, and sweat. I sensed that these latecomers seemed somewhat deflated when they discovered themselves so much farther from the shrine than they had anticipated. Yet they, too, settled in to wait.

To me, this huge, spontaneous, word-of-mouth gathering resembled some surreal religious rite—especially since it was unfolding on Omotesando, a boulevard whose grandeur contrasts so starkly with the dense alleys and dark warrens of modern Tokyo's fascinating sprawl. This broad, tree-lined promenade had been designed as the ceremonial entrance to the vast Shinto shrine honoring the Meiji emperor who, in the late nineteenth century, had ended his nation's long seclusion, and the boulevard was still closed on certain special days for parades and pedestrian strollers. (On one Sunday every March, a few hundred foreigners even stage a St. Patrick's Day parade.) But no public ritual could be more riveting than the one that takes place here each New Year's holiday, or *O-shogatsu*, when more than three million people burst from commuter trains and subways to stream up Omotesando and enter the parklike Meiji Shrine. Treading on the gravel path beneath its ceremonial wooden gate, or *torii*, the worshippers patiently await their turn to stand on the black wooden steps of the shrine to seek ancestral blessing. Hanging in the rafters are clanging bells whose long ropes teenagers and aging grandparents, one by one, grab and tug to gain the gods' full attention. Then, bowing their heads, squeezing their eyes shut, they whisper silent prayers—for wealth and happiness, for a new bank loan perhaps, or for a passing grade on a fiendishly competitive college entrance exam—before solemnly clapping their hands three times. Before departing, they may buy a colorful good-luck amulet, an *omamori*, to protect them against evil.

In this nation of little religious faith and rarely witnessed observance, the throngs who travel to the Meiji Shrine each New Year come out of respect for tradition and a sense, perhaps, that it is better to carry out an old, familiar ritual, meaningful or not, than to tempt the fates. On this humid September Sunday, however, the long processional on the sidewalk seemed to me far more devout and purposeful than the stream of people on *O-shogatsu*. The shrine that these thousands of secretaries, housewives, and haircutters were gathering to visit was Louis Vuitton's flashy new headquarters store, which was opening that morning. This pious flock of supplicants was praying for $700 purses and $2,000 watches.

"I just love Louis Vuitton," Mika Sakamoto gushed, barely able to contain her giddiness over being so close to the brown-and-camel purses that bear the Vuitton logo. This nineteen-year-old high school graduate, who worked in a tanning salon in distant Yamanashi prefecture, told me she had driven down with her mother, leaving the house before midnight, just for this special occasion.

Sakamoto resembled thousands of others in her belief in the power of Vuitton to magically transform her own life and make her feel special. I wanted to know more about her devotion to this brand, and she readily confessed with a hint of pride that she already owned three Vuitton purses, two Vuitton makeup bags, and a monogrammed leather Vuitton carrying case for her filtered cigarettes. Now she wanted two more hand-bags and a watch.

"I figure I'll spend about twenty-one hundred dollars today on new items," Sakamoto said, taking out her tiny calculator to estimate how best to budget her purchases. She especially coveted the commemorative purse Louis Vuitton was selling this one day only to celebrate the open-ing of the French-owned luxury chain's new flagship store.

"It has a tiny insignia in it with today's date inscribed inside, so that makes it very special," Sakamoto confided, having learned this fact from one of the many magazines, as much advertising platforms as editorial sources, that cover in exhaustive, obsessive detail every new offering or alteration in the Vuitton line. She added in a whisper, "I think someday it will be very valuable."

When I asked her how she had acquired her passion for all things Vuitton, Sakamoto nodded toward her mother, who was camped out on the adjacent blanket. Mom, perhaps in her late fifties, was dressed in an expensive designer jacket and what looked to be $500 high heels. At the moment, she was taking some *onigiri* rice ball snacks, wrapped in cello-phane, out of her oversized Vuitton travel bag. "Ever since I was a little girl, my mother has taught me about Louis Vuitton," Sakamoto said, as Mom offered me a snack, too.

The Sakamoto women are hardly unique in their devotion. Re-searchers estimate that one in six Japanese owns some item bearing a Louis Vuitton logo, and the Saison Research Institute recently calculated that 94 percent of all Tokyo women in their twenties have at least one Vuitton product in a drawer of their *tansu* dresser.[1] Year by year, the com-pany's presence has swelled in the retail sector as well as in the national consciousness, and today Vuitton rings up more sales in Japan than in any other nation. This seemingly insatiable appetite for high-end con-sumption by women like Mika and her mom has in turn exerted a pow-erful force on designer houses across the world, eager to cater to this wealthy market. The rapidly changing mix of nearby retailers—as mom-and-pop stationery shops and prosaic purveyors of *senbei* rice crackers and kitchenware were replaced by the titans of Paris, Milan, and Seventh Avenue—testified to the deep inner hunger Japanese were expressing for the artifice of designer goods and the status they promise. It was not un-common to hear tales of sixteen-year-old high school girls engaging in what is euphemistically termed *enjo kosai*, or "compensated dates," with a middle-aged *sarariman* in order to outfit herself with a new Vuitton purse. As I talked to the dozens of eager would-be customers camped in the line—beauticians, waiters, office clerks, and part-time workers—I found that none of them seemed to see any incongruity between the out-landish cost of the goods they clamored for and the nation's stagnant macroeconomic condition or the rising numbers of homeless.

Already by 8:30 A.M. the long queue wound past the luxurious seven-story Aoyama Diamond wedding hall, a building that only recently had been gutted and completely rebuilt. Now, on the ground floor of the gray stone edifice, an elegant Gucci boutique beckoned, a discreet shop fronted by an elongated silver-handled double doorway, where, later in the day, a pair of wiry and virile male greeters in sleek black suits and white gloves would hold the doors open for the pretty young ladies who flocked to browse there. On the other side of the intersection, Prada was erecting a luminous green-glass wedge of architectural significance, while Giorgio Armani had already opened a black-marble boutique along the boulevard near Christian Dior. Dolce & Gabbana was nearby. And gruff workmen—wearing pantaloons and cloth-toed slippers, with towels wrapped around their heads, the quintessential construction crew garb in Japan—were busily at work even on this Sunday morning completing a new retail palace for Versace.

This contagion of new construction vividly reflected the great flood of cash still sloshing through the nation's opaque and often mysterious underground plumbing system, despite painful years of contraction and recession. Some global fashion brands now catered specially to their Japanese customers. Louis Vuitton's revenue in Japan accounted for nearly a third of its total global sales, for example, and no one knew better how crucial Japan was to his company's economic future than Yves Carcelle, Vuitton's chief executive. As this elegant Frenchman with a diplomat's bearing watched from a third-floor window, he felt both triumph and some trepidation as the growing line in the street below threatened to become more than his tiny phalanx of security guards could cope with. He knew his store would be popular; but never, he told me, had he imagined so large a turnout.

Opening a thirty-six-thousand-square-foot, ten-story boutique larger than his own Paris headquarters had always been something of a financial risk, Carcelle knew. Yet with the previous decade's deflation and the consequent erosion of land prices in Tokyo's best neighborhoods, the real estate needed for such a large project had become cheap enough for his company to acquire. In addition, the media attention Vuitton would generate from this opening day extravaganza would echo up and down the archipelago, boosting sales at the nearly four dozen other Louis Vuitton shops scattered across it. Besides, the sheer size of this outpouring—the line would eventually be more than a quarter mile long—dramatically reaffirmed the power of Vuitton's allure.

"This is not just a store," Carcelle told me, pausing for emphasis. "It's a statement."

Yet—aside from the obvious commercial benefit accruing to his company from the crowd now spilling across the sidewalk below his elegant new building, where fine-spun steel mesh separated salons and blond woods burnished the interiors, casting the luminous glow of opulence over his inventory—Carcelle would have difficulty explaining precisely what that "statement" was. What does it mean, I wondered, that so many thousands seemed so entranced, so utterly spellbound and enthralled with his Vuitton brand? This was no knock on the product; undoubtedly, LV products are durable classics that bring some perceived measure of cachet to their owners. Yet why do everyday, lower-middle-class Japanese humiliate themselves by spending hours milling around on a sidewalk on a steamy summer morning just for the chance to buy a purse? What motivates young secretaries, housewives, and even high school students with only marginal incomes to park themselves on a sidewalk for days and lust after what people in most other wealthy nations consider either exclusive products for the elite and privileged or silly, effete nonsense?

There was another incongruity. Conspicuous consumption is supposed to signal the extravagance of the very wealthy and subtly advertise their status. But no French heiress or Italian baroness, Carcelle admitted—his eyes on the long, scruffy queue of office workers and part-timers—would deign to stand in the street for hours just to buy an expensive handbag. It would be downright undignified.

"It's truly unbelievable," he said of the crowd, which now looked to be perhaps twice the size his Japanese staff had predicted. He shrugged. "This kind of scene would only happen in Japan."

* * *

Many things seem to occur "only in Japan"; that is, in their daily lives Japanese do many things that Westerners—and even other Asians—find slightly unusual. Take the many Japanese men who, to while away their long commutes to work, paw through thick *manga*, or comic books, full of sadomasochistic violence without a hint of self-consciousness. Or the way businessmen bow respectfully when they speak to some invisible other on their mobile phones. Or the fact that long beyond infancy, many five- and six-year-old children continue to sleep in the same bed with their parents.

Yet familiar as these other habits had become to me, this Vuitton fixation seemed more than trivial. Indeed, this obsession with appearance, with finding the right costume to wear out in the world seemed a direct expression of the modern Japanese's perilous quest to find identity. Even as I observed these women amid the din of postmodernism rising up from every busy intersection, this culture still remained essentially fixed in a "premodern" world, peopled, as Shizue Kato had counseled me, by samurai and nameless serfs.

Some analysts told me that in their cultish passion for brand-name products, young Japanese were demonstrating their fundamental distrust in traditional institutions. As the Japanese system of social control—

through discipline, hard work, scrimping, and self-denial—began to fray, people's natural impulses began to stir. As the nation grew affluent, young adults especially began to resist the pressure of self-denial and moderation an older system had thrust upon them. They began to develop a visceral hunger to indulge self and to seek some deeper meaning from the world around them. Yet, this search could be easily channeled into a fascination for luxury goods and a fetish for conspicuous consumption.

In addition, the Iron Triangle that had prospered so mightily as a result of this epic period of national self-sacrifice could no longer guarantee the well-being of today's young people, as all around them banks collapsed, renowned companies were forced into bankruptcy, and a once-admired system of government fell into disrepute. Meanwhile, the press of powerful new images, transmitted especially through Hollywood movies and TV shows, was exposing young Japanese to the lives—and ways of life—others enjoyed, especially their American peers. Hedonism was the crucial factor. These foreign lives seemed very different and somehow "happier" or, at least, more self-indulgent. Few twenty-five-year-olds in Japan now expected to have a job for life, as their parents had. Since the future appeared uncertain, they figured it was better to buy things now rather than deny themselves and defer gratification.

If young Japanese now hungered for authentic forms of self-expression, the purveyors of designer brands were more than happy to divert them into their boutiques with slick advertising and savvy marketing campaigns. And if the traditional Japanese system was now falling into disrepute, what else could a young Japanese trust other than a solid foreign brand name like Vuitton?

I thought of how Masao Miyamoto, the Japanese psychiatrist and author, would have loved watching this outlandish scene play out in front of Vuitton. A man who never concerned himself with conventional fashion trends, Miyamoto drove an electric-pink Porsche convertible which would have stood out on any street corner on Manhattan's East Side. He had worked for, and ultimately been banished from, Japan's Health Ministry for his unconventional—that is to say, Western—views, and later died of cancer, which he was certain had resulted from the years of harassment he had endured while working for the Ministry. When I visited him one day about six months before his death to talk about the Japanese obsession with brands, he explained that his countrymen used them like fetishes. Comforting as a child's security blanket, high-status brands like Gucci and Vuitton serve as soporifics to ease and calm a vacant national psyche. "The [Japanese] system has encouraged people not to think for themselves," Miyamoto told me. To the Japanese people who have lost confidence in their government and in themselves after a dismal no-growth decade, a label like Gucci or Prada offers an implicit guarantee of safety and security anywhere in the world. And the more insecure the Japanese people feel in their volatile and unstable world, he told me, the more they'll seek such fetishlike goods to make themselves feel better.

This profound Japanese hunger to attain some superficial form of status, some display of self-worth, also suggests collective inferiority, he said, since the purveyor, not the customer, establishes the fashion, designs the "look," and gets to decide one's "worth." People think that by buying up designer purses they are somehow asserting their own style, he said, laughing. "But if you slavishly buy a brand product, you can deny your personality and take on someone else's. Eventually it's not any reflection of your own personality, but of the brand's."

*   *   *

The search for identity—a quest which seemed to haunt young men like Kenji who sat isolated in their rooms for days on end, assiduously cutting off contact with the outside world—also seemed to be at the root of two other social phenomena visible in Japan: the rise of the *otaku* and the power of the *zoku*. Though *otaku* is, literally, an honorific form of "your household," it is generally used to describe a "geek" or a "nerd"—a fan who becomes obsessed, sometimes dangerously so, with the minutiae of a particular bit of pop culture, like *anime* or *manga*. Some *otaku* become fixated on 1960s-era cartoon shows like *Ultraman* or *Astro Boy* or on more contemporary video games, becoming world-class collectors of memorabilia, pins, and posters dedicated to the objects of their fascination. These "geeks" may organize or participate in conventions and swap meets where they show off their collections, trade pins and cards, and discuss in meticulous detail the depths of their obsessions. Others become *otaku* of rock bands, memorizing every lyric and dressing just like their favorite performer. Once, while attending the Fuji Rock Festival in the mid-1990s, I watched, amused, as about seventy-five *otaku*—mostly men, but a scattering of young women, too—mouthed the words and played air guitar to accompany the performance of an aging and fairly obscure British musician named Ray Davies. Only in Japan, I mumbled to myself. One Nomura Research Institute consultant claims that 2.85 million Japanese live as *otaku*.[2] Another economist estimates *otaku* pump $26 billion each year into the domestic economy.

Otaku behavior, sometimes dark and obsessive and sometimes bordering on *hikikomori*, tends to be very much a male domain, a way for young men to establish some sense of belonging to a "secret society" within their blandly conformist world. On the opposite end of the cultural spectrum lies the mostly female world of *kawaii*, or "cuteness," another means for adolescents to belong to a tribe, or *zoku*, which—however superficially weird and nonconformist—offers its members the comfort and assurance of group cohesion.

Hundreds of such female *zoku* abound in Japan, each with a focus on a different fashion. One *zoku* of young women dye their hair golden blonde, spend hours in tanning parlors to broil their skins a dark bronze, and dab their lips with thick white lipstick to emphasize their pouty mouths. Thus, they are transformed into parodies of the California surfer girl. Though they dub themselves "mountain women," they surely consider themselves *kawaii*. Another *zoku* of high school girls insist on tying their navy blue Polo scarves in exactly the same way, so that the red pony insignia always faces left. A "Hello Kitty" *zoku* of teenage girls madly acquires every scarf, key chain, poster, and cell phone attachment bearing the *kawaii* cartoon likeness of a dot-eyed, expressionless white kitten with no mouth and a pink ribbon often pinned to her hair. Yet another tribe favors clashing DayGlo plaids and cowboy hats. Still others dress up in fluffy white linen over black shirts and bow ties to resemble English maids. Some men also find tribal solace in clothing and accessories: they dress up on the weekends as 1950s-style American "greasers," donning leather jackets, denim jeans, and biker boots and pomading their black hair into ducktails. By Monday morning, they are back in their blue business suits.

This palpable expression of "membership" and the need for "belonging" differs markedly from how Westerners often tend to choose fashion and create a public identity for themselves in a world more accepting of nonconformity. One British jeans manufacturer got the tone just right: in an advertising campaign billboard on Tokyo's commuter trains, the company displayed a leggy Caucasian girl outfitted in denim. Where the English caption challenged: "Dare to be different"—an implicit jab at Levi's, the brand champion—the Japanese implored riders: "Fit in with the group." In the West, a woman or man often chooses from among a wide assortment of fashion possibilities to express their own distinctive self-image, possibilities they can mix and match, according to individual taste and changing sensibilities. In Japan, however, the process seems to work in reverse: a young person claims a persona by first selecting the uniform of the group to which she aspires, and then hopes that her style of dress will determine her affect and how others regard her.[3] This again reflects the self-denial and self-sacrifice that is at the center of creating a context-based identity (as discussed in Chapter 7).

The behavior just described seems, on some levels, to resemble what American tenth graders endure as they navigate the clashing social cliques inside the cafeteria of a large public high school—whether to hang out with the "jocks" or the "preppies" or the "Goths." But in Japan, this perilous navigation process can last well into adulthood and symbolizes on a more profound level the "infantilization" of adult Japanese who have become accustomed to following the demands imposed on them by others and of not asserting a right to choice or self-determination.

According to Masahiro Yamada, a sociologist, materialism matters so much to the modern Japanese because their society long ago discarded most of the nation's spiritual character to make room for Western values and lifestyles, part of the nation's grab-bag strategy of foreign acquisition. To accommodate its desire for modernity, for instance, Japan even moved its New Year's celebration from the period indicated on the Chinese lunar calendar to the West's January 1. "We don't have religion in Japan, so what exist are appearances," Yamada explained. "If you look good, you must be having a good life." Owning a Vuitton clutch offers that assurance and forestalls serious self-reflection. Indeed, many brand-name shoppers seem to agree with Yamada's analysis. "Wearing any kind of brand makes you feel more self-confident," said Mayumi, a twenty-one-year-old dental assistant, who was sporting one of those must-have Vuitton purses, a Bulgari necklace, and a Gucci watch. "It just makes you feel good."[4]

The whole concept of self-esteem in which I, a Westerner, was immersed was rooted in the Judeo-Christian tradition's teaching that each individual is infused with an ineffable spirit of the Creator, Yamada told me. "But in Japan, we don't have self-esteem," Yamada said flatly. "We only have the identity of groups. We have group esteem, not self-esteem. Many people think there is nothing else to life other than to chase money, to live an affluent lifestyle." A few monks might still practice Zen and choose a life of monastic seclusion and contemplation, but Yamada believes that, aside from the zealous pursuit of profits, most of his countrymen have precious little to fall back on when it comes to any larger meaning in life. (Of course many Westerners suffer the same fate.)

Like many other contemporary Japanese intellectuals, Yamada was no fan of George W. Bush and believed that Japan should remain a pacifist, peaceful country. But to many social scientists in Japan, the contemporary American political rhetoric focused on "family values," "personal responsibility," and "morality"—a rhetoric that dates back at least to Ronald Reagan's presidency, but that even Democratic President Bill Clinton felt comfortable endorsing after he emerged from church services on Sunday mornings—sets American society drastically apart from the Japanese. Many Americans well understand that these prayerful invocations of God's love, speeches dripping with ideological connotation, can be taken in one of two ways: either to highlight tolerance of the stranger, compassion for the poor, and justice for the oppressed; or vigorously to promote abstinence and opposition to both gay marriage and abortion. In truth, the American view of religion is muddled, divisive, and too often hypocritical.

Yet from the perspective of Japanese sociologists, demographers, and psychologists with whom I discussed *hikikomori* and other contemporary social maladies, the increasing volume and the emphasis on religion and "religious values" now emanating from American politicians has changed public behavior. They believe it helped account for the slight decline in divorce rates in the United States during the 1990s (by 2000 the divorce rate had dropped to 4.1 per thousand, the lowest since 1972) and the accompanying rise in the U.S. birthrate—key statistical metrics for a shrinking Japanese society in which both marriage and birthrates are in freefall. (Of course one reason for the decline of divorce was that Americans, unlike Japanese, now tended to live together before marriage, while the rising birthrate was attributable to growing numbers of immigrant groups, especially from Latin America, with higher-than-average birthrates.)

Indeed, as Yamada and I talked, he seemed to envy Europeans and Americans for being able to escape from the powerful grasp of materialism through some form of spiritual practice—whether through fundamentalist Christianity or twice-weekly yoga training, it didn't really matter. This private, personal search helps energize the individual and infuse his existence with meaning. Japanese, however, seem to have no such recourse. "In order to fill the void" between worldliness and true inner peace, Yamada said, "all [we Japanese] can do is read *manga*, take trips abroad, or go shopping. It's awful. Shopping becomes an addiction, a tranquilizer."

This mania for acquiring symbols of status seems to emerge from within the culture, and also from the way younger generations had been raised in the past quarter century. Older generations of Japanese had struggled to achieve their success, and found it impertinent or arrogant to display one's material prosperity. Preferring discretion, they learned never to flaunt their wealth. Today's young Japanese are still being socialized to think they are all essentially identical—all stolidly middle-class, dark-haired, compliant, and conservative. As in the past, they are being trained to fit in with their peers, not to strike out on their own. But now, for the first time, Japanese live in a generally wealthy world, and some families have demonstrably more wealth than others. In many of these upper-class households, the parents are consumed with their busy working lives, and seldom find time to share with their children. Instead, parents today routinely give their children large amounts of money to make up for the lack of affection and attention, or because they feel they have no other emotional connection to them.

In less wealthy homes, however, the attraction of brand-names is also powerful and seductive. The slowing economy and the exodus of blue-collar factory jobs was reducing the possibility for the kind of social mobility Japan's system once seemed to promise. These days it seems less likely that children of modest means could grow up to attain high-paying professional careers, unless they perform exceptionally well on college entrance exams. Yet if the well-paying, secure factory or service job is probably no longer attainable, at least the trappings of prosperity are, because, as Yamada suggested, if you clutch that Vuitton bag on your arm, you must be successful.

So the frenzy and froth of Omotesando can be understood not simply as a moment's shopping indulgence, but as more of a modern initiation rite. A woman who buys a Vuitton handbag enters a high-status *zoku* and gains a new form of identification.

When the doors opened just before 11 A.M. that Sunday, more than four thousand customers were waiting to crowd inside. By the end of this single shopping day, Carcelle would have reason to feel exceedingly pleased. Louis Vuitton would break all of its own retail records, selling more than $1.2 million in handbags, watches, luggage, and other accessories in a frenzied seven-hour sales orgy, a figure that astounded even that purveyor of luxury products. Never had the brand seemed so magnetic.

* * *

It has been said that Japanese have great difficulty truly understanding themselves because they have not yet learned to understand the other, the *gaijin* outsider. Likewise, in their ardent pursuit of modernity, most Japanese have not, as I have said, really appreciated and cultivated its true spirit: they have not asserted themselves as autonomous individuals in opposition to group demands. Mostly, modern Japanese have been forced to live, at best, as furtive individualists who mask themselves in outlandish clothes or dye their hair pink during a school vacation, but rush to the hairdresser before returning to work or the classroom in the same blue uniform and dark hair as their peers. In the deep ambiguity between their strong need for self-expression and the comfortable assurance that group membership offers, they often grab wildly for random artifacts from the store shelves, just as these avid women shoppers scramble for their Vuitton belts and purses. Rather than feeling authentic, these artificial poses usually come off, even at their outrageous outer limits, only as measured forms of a sanctioned sort of nonconformity. Once properly reprocessed, it reemerges as the uniform of its own new *zoku*; a new badge or staged "fashion" that becomes accepted as yet another form of conformity to be displayed in glamour magazines and peddled in boutique windows. This made the cycles of fashion and the half-life of certain "looks" in Japan exceedingly short; shorter even than fashion trends in the United States. Teenagers often paraded around Omotesando in what looked like homemade outfits, hoping to catch the attention of the fashion photographers who hung out at the busiest intersections and posed the most promising for a quick photo shoot. A week later, their pictures might be in a magazine, and a two-week mini-trend would be launched, in which others would copy and repurpose the look.

In a postmodern capitalist world, young adults in affluent nations the world over probably wonder how they might seek out the genuine and the true; it is a quest that seems particularly daunting for today's young Japanese.

More than a decade ago, in the early 1990s, commentators in Japan began to describe a "new human species," or *shinjinrui*, that is, teens who know nothing of the wartime devastation visited on their parents and grandparents, who have known only peace and affluence; who have little interest in corporate loyalty or lifetime employment; and who spend money and enjoy life rather than scrimping, saving, and humbling themselves persistently each day at their workplace. These new young adults, the older generation fretted, had no political perspective, no dynamism, and little energy, and seemed to stare indifferently at the nation's growing mound of troubles.

After a few years, the talk of a "new species" melted away, as that new generation disappeared, much as its predecessors had, into the churning wheels of the economy (although sometimes on a subway train I'd spy a thirty-something *sarariman* or secretary holding a guidebook or a travel brochure, and dreaming—I liked to think—of climbing a mountain in Nepal or trekking through Africa).

What I came to see as the truly "new species" in Japan actually appeared later. The *hikikomori* and other men and women courageous enough—or desperate enough—to be the sole member of a unique tribe as they chose to withdraw from their collective society. However extreme their social isolation may seem, it is being ratified by others of their generation who have found different—and, for some, even more drastic— "exit strategies" to escape the pressures of contemporary Japan. After 150 years of subjugating the individual spirit to boost collective goals, cracks are appearing in the national psyche.

9.

Kiyoko, at age twenty-eight, exemplifies a Japanese career woman of the early twenty-first century. Well-mannered and demure with lustrous tea-brown hair and piercing, pearl-shaped eyes, this marketing executive for Toyota graduated from a top college, speaks a serviceable, if not flawless, English, and seeks a life that extends beyond marriage and motherhood. As she imagines herself as dutiful, hard-working, and impeccably polite, she hardly seems like a troublemaker, some angry social radical.

Yet Kiyoko is but one of many Japanese women of prime childbearing age who adamantly refuse to marry and bear children. Like the thousands of *hikikomori*, this new generation of ambitious women is choosing to meander through an extended adolescence, spurning matrimony to dwell in their parents' home, often into their thirties and forties. Japan's popular press has come to label women like Kiyoko, who are neither independent nor living with a partner, as *parasaito*, or "parasite single." The term was coined by the sociologist Masahiro Yamada in 1999 to describe women who shop avidly, travel abroad on fancy vacations, and prefer to "live for the moment" rather than marry and start a family. Nearly 90 percent of Japanese women in their late twenties and 60 percent in their late thirties are estimated to be *parasaito*; according to the Health Ministry's estimate, 2.5 million women aged twenty-five to thirty-nine live with their parents, nearly 20 percent of all women in this age range.

"I don't think that every woman in Japan thinks she doesn't want to have a baby," Kiyoko told me one night as we munched on slices of pizza at a lively pub near her office. "But the Japanese system is not fully prepared for both men and women to work while having children. It's the woman who raises the child. Like other women, I would have to choose between my career or my baby, and the reality is most women now are choosing careers."

On a Sunday afternoon stroll in Tokyo nowadays, you are far more likely to see young women walking dogs than pushing a baby carriage. Shrinking maternity wards and abandoned kindergarten classrooms across the nation testify to the pitiless impact of the baby boycott. In 2003, the total fertility rate of Japanese women fell to a record 1.29, down from 1.32 the previous year; and the number of total births fell for the twenty-fourth consecutive year. America's fertility rate, by contrast, stands at 2.1, boosted in no small measure by a swell of Hispanic immigration.[1]

Demographics define destiny. Already in 2005 Japan's population peaked out and began a long, unstoppable descent that forecasters predict will continue for the next thirty years. By 2020 the nation will be the grayest among the world's developed nations. By 2025, nearly one in every nine Japanese will be over the age of eighty, and nearly half the population will be over sixty-five. In this same period, according to a Cabinet Office estimate, Japan's working population—defined as those between ages fifteen and sixty-four—will drop by 15 percent, or some 12 million. Never, in fact, has a nation gotten so old, so quickly. Although the population of the elderly in Japan accounted for only 7 percent of the total population in 1970, it doubled to 14.1 percent in only twenty-four years. It took 61 years for the elderly population to double in Italy, 85 years in Sweden, and 115 years in France.[2] This rapidly shrinking population will slice an estimated 2 percent from future economic output, and Japan will enter a "zero growth" era, when average annual growth is not likely to exceed 0.3 percent. If this decline in the youth population and in family creation continues unchecked, and Japanese continue to enjoy long life expectancy because of their relatively healthy diet of fish and rice, who will pay the pensions and rising medical bills for the swelling ranks of the elderly? Over time, Japan will make South Florida look like a youth hostel.[3]

Perhaps never before have women so systematically defected from motherhood in order to claim some degree of social and economic independence. "We are witnessing a structural change of Japanese women," acknowledged Mariko Bando, herself a working mother, who in 2002 served as director-general of the Cabinet's office on gender equity for Prime Minister Junichiro Koizumi. Her job was to help level the playing field for women. "We are struggling to change the culture, but it is very difficult."

*   *   *

These days Kiyoko prefers returning home each evening to the same small bedroom she had as a child, just a few feet from her parents' room. The comforts of a home-cooked breakfast and the dolls she grew up with are more appealing than having to spend at least $1,300 a month for her own place.

"I go shopping, I go out to dinner, I enjoy musicals, and like to go out with my friends," Kiyoko said, toying absently with a diamond pendant when I asked how she spends her free time. Kiyoko prefers to savor her financial and social independence without having to answer to a husband—though offhandedly she told me that she might like to be a mother someday, if she ever meets the right guy.

Kiyoko studied for a year at the University of Wisconsin during college and took her first job after university graduation at NHK, the prestigious government-owned TV and radio network, hoping to make it her career. She soon learned that her American training and experience was more of a detriment than an advantage, because her language ability was superior to that of many of her bosses. "There were only a few people there who spoke any English, but they wouldn't pay me for my knowledge. I didn't feel appreciated," she said.

After two years, she moved on to Toyota, whose international marketing campaigns she hopes some day to lead. Today she earns enough to shop regularly at Prada and Louis Vuitton and to take regular vacations in Paris and Hong Kong. Her parents effectively subsidize her living costs, aside from the few hundred dollars she pays them each month as "rent."

Up until the 1970s, before the rise of the service and information society, a woman like Kiyoko had to marry just to survive. Her schooling and work training focused on her acquiring the skills needed to please a proper mate, including cooking and household management. By joining a man's household, or *ie*, and taking his family's name, a woman secured identity for herself in Japan's complex social hierarchy and also effectively guaranteed her economic future. Marriage was about duty, not love, and the vast majority of marriages were arranged by parents or intermediaries. As in most cultures, an aging single woman confronted poverty, isolation, and uncertainty.

Also, in the decades just before World War Two, when Japanese society was far more agrarian, men and women commonly worked side by side in the fields and farms, planting rice and growing vegetables. But after the industrial collapse caused by defeat in war, there were fewer factory jobs available and women workers were consigned to low-prestige jobs with little hope of attaining professional stature. A full-blown baby boom, which started in 1947, also drew women back into the nursery.

A woman who worked in a white-collar field became an O.L., as the Japanese call it—an office lady—who poured tea and performed clerical or menial chores. In a factory, she did repetitive chores or operated a textile machine. Society expected her to marry by her mid-twenties, get pregnant, and quit to raise her children. Throughout the 1950s and 1960s, and even into the late 1970s, a woman who didn't marry by age twenty-five was commonly ridiculed as "Christmas cake," the confection no customer wants to purchase on December 26. For thirty years after the war, the average age for a woman's first marriage was rigidly fixed at 24.5 years, according to Japanese census data.

The gender and sexual revolutions that rewrote social codes across the Western world have yet to convulse Japan, however. Just as Kant never arrived on Japan's shores, the feminist ideas of Betty Friedan and Gloria Steinem never got much airtime here, either. Most Japanese men—even those with a college diploma—do not help with child-rearing or domestic chores, and believe that a wife should naturally forfeit her career for family. To them, feminism barely registers. Men and women still inhabit different tiers of the work pyramid and occupy vastly separated social spaces, and both gender discrimination and sexual harassment remain rampant. As a rule, men get higher pay and more responsibility each year; women are put on a "mommy track," expected to quit when they become pregnant, and are referred to as "the girls," even if they are in their forties or fifties.

What awoke many contemporary Japanese women to Western notions of individualism and feminism was a rising swell of national prosperity and the dawning of the information and service economy to supplant the industrial workplace. New kinds of jobs gave women more incentives to pursue an advanced education and to find a white-collar career. Higher salaries, the declining costs of air travel, and greater household prosperity offered women more chances to travel or study abroad. The infiltration of Hollywood cinema also exposed young Japanese to Western-style feminism, and by the early 1990s, foreign-owned firms eager to establish new offices in Japan were only too happy to exploit an underutilized asset—the female workforce—and gave Japanese women better chances for good jobs than domestic firms did. As their life choices multiplied before their eyes, many women came to believe that they could do better for themselves emotionally as well as economically by pursuing a career and staying single.

"It used to be difficult for a woman to be independent and have a decent job for her whole life. A woman got married in order to survive because the man supported her," Kiyoko told me. "But now women can have jobs—it's still not so easy to have a career as a woman of course. Nonetheless, women are saying, 'I'd rather be by myself and do what I want to do, rather than marry somebody I don't want.' Women want to live their lives without depending on a man. Women have changed, but social mores really haven't."

Today, only 11 percent of women believe marriage will prove beneficial financially, surveys show. "The smart women, the savvy ones, are choosing not to marry in order to live a better life," said Rieko Suzuki, a researcher at the Dentsu Institute for Human Studies, a think tank affiliated with Japan's largest advertising and marketing firm. She has written a series of books and articles analyzing the collapse of the nation's birthrate from a feminist perspective.

Today, the mean age of a Japanese woman at first marriage is 27.8 years, fully three years older than in 1975. The number of never-married women is also soaring. In 2000, 54 percent of twenty-five- to twenty-nine-year-old Japanese women had never been brides—double the figure of 1980. In addition, nearly four in ten working women between the ages of thirty and thirty-four have never married. (In America, by contrast, just over 20 percent of all women in this age group have never wed.) The percentage of Japanese women never married at age fifty has doubled in the past forty years. The longer a woman waits before she weds, of course, the fewer children she is likely to produce.

*   *   *

Aside from achieving some independence, Japanese women have other reasons for their "womb strike," for deciding to forgo marriage and motherhood: the feudal attitudes that still govern marriage and family life, the crippling economic costs of child-rearing, and a pervasive pessimism endemic in the nation.

In modern Japanese marriage, the law demands that one party, usually the bride, abandon her maiden name and any claim to her own household, or *ie*, to join the groom's household. Hiroko Mizushima, a member of the national parliament, has been divorced at least six times since she first married Satoshi Hasegawa in 1992 and bore him two children. Because her husband agreed to join Mizushima's legal household but to keep his own name, the couple must formally divorce every time his driver's license or passport expires, he relocates his business address, or needs any other official document from a government agency. The divorce may be only a paper transaction, but—the couple complains—it is time-consuming and needless.

"This is an issue of individual liberty, not just a women's issue," said

Mizushima, a clinical psychiatrist as well as a Diet member. She has been battling, so far unsuccessfully, to change the marriage statute. Conservative members of the ruling Liberal Democratic Party fiercely oppose any change. "If parents and children have different surnames, it will harm the unity of the family and will lead to the corruption of society," argues Takaichi Sanae, one LDP antagonist.

When a woman forsakes her own family name for marriage, she also picks up a host of onerous new obligations. If the husband is the *ie*'s oldest son—the son who, by law, will inherit the household's property and business interests—custom dictates that the new bride care for her in-laws as they age, since elderly Japanese rarely enter nursing homes when no longer self-sufficient. Women often joke that they want to marry a wealthy, handsome man whose parents are already dead.

Marriage doesn't just force a woman to abandon her job. It also consigns her to the utter loneliness of being a homebound mother, since fathers typically don't return home before ten or eleven on weeknights. "For a woman, having a baby, having a full-time job, and doing housework is like committing suicide," Suzuki, the researcher, said. "Unless the grandmother is around to help with child-rearing, it is absolutely impossible to have a baby and a career." Even if day care were easy to come by, the Japanese don't believe in using babysitters from outside the family.

Some women told me that without a commitment from their husbands to share child-rearing, babies are out. "My husband says he simply would not take paternity leave if we had a baby," said Mika, who works in the programming department of a Tokyo-based television company. "So that settled it for me. It means we're simply not going to have children."

Although many women yearn to have children, they view Japan as a society so inimical to working women and so hostile to modern ways of child-rearing that they simply won't raise a baby there. "If we get pregnant, we're moving to Australia," declared Yuki, twenty-nine, whose Japanese husband obtained his law degree in Melbourne. "I could never raise my child in a society as rigid as Japan. So we've agreed, if we get pregnant, [the baby] is going to be raised outside."

Also, many women say they see few inducements to abandoning a career for motherhood when education and day-care costs are prohibitively expensive. "Really, I think it's quite rational not to have children," Suzuki told me. Recently married herself, Suzuki said that she wasn't planning to have children. "Having a baby is risky," she explained. "Economically, you can't work. The educational fees are so expensive, and there is no guarantee that kids will succeed—look at all the old Japanese firms that are going out of business." She even questioned the motives of many women who do choose motherhood. "In Japan you don't really expect kids to be independent. You want your kid to go to a good school and a good university," in order to broadcast to others what a good parent you were. "It's as if," she said, "I want to add another brand to my Hermès or Vuitton collection, to have a child who went to Tokyo University," the nation's most prestigious.

The fierce competition to enter the nation's most influential high schools and universities—despite the nation's declining birthrate—also discourages women from motherhood. In what used to be seen as an egalitarian society, child-rearing has taken on some of the uglier aspects of class-based competitive sport. Not unlike well-to-do parents in Manhattan or San Francisco, every Japanese mother who wants her son to attend the best school does all she can to boost her child's chances. Many four- and five-year-old Japanese children now trundle off each afternoon to *juku*, or "cram school," to practice for rigorous entrance examinations for *elementary* school. One study estimated that low-income families (those earning less than 4 million yen each year, or approximately $36,500) devote more than half the family budget on education, while wealthy families spend 22 percent of their annual income on schooling fees.

The battle for spots in places like the "feeder" primary school affiliated with Waseda University is like that for an upper-tier Manhattan preschool. Parents of successful applicants are asked to donate 3.5 million yen, some $32,000, on top of the $45,000 in annual enrollment and fees, to secure their child's place in the school. One newspaper reported that more than 1,200 applicants sought ninety places in the private grade school, knowing that a spot would guarantee admission to Waseda's university program a dozen years later. The boom in private grade schools can also be attributed to growing distrust of the nation's public education system, which has begun, since 2002, to implement five-day schooling instead of the traditional six, while shrinking the core curriculum. In 2003, cram school attendance hit record levels, a dramatic comeback from the late 1990s, when many seemed on the brink of closing as both the youth population and the number of college applications declined. As the birthrate declines, however, more and more children become the beneficiaries of the "six pocket" syndrome, where parents, grandparents, and perhaps even uncles and aunts contribute to a single child's education.[4] Although women say they hate the psychological pressure this system imposes on a child, they feel they have no choice but to go along: if the child fails to get accepted to a good high school and a good college, how can he hope to succeed in a slow-growth world where there will be fewer guaranteed jobs for those without advanced skills and critical thinking ability—precisely the skills many of Japan's schools don't teach?

It isn't just school fees that add up. Piano lessons can cost $100 an hour. A Japanese mother who wishes to return to work finds it hard to secure day care for her child, and one who is forced to work late like her male counterparts will likely find it difficult to get a babysitter, unless her mother or mother-in-law lives nearby. A government survey estimates that it takes 16 percent of a household's total living expenses to raise a single child, and 20 percent if the child is in junior high.[5] Mikiko Fujiwara, who used to work as a banker in Tokyo before escaping to London, bluntly explained the birth decline to a seminar of Japanese bureaucrats. "Raising a kid these days is so expensive it forces you to choose between having a baby or having a summer house in the mountains or a late-model Mercedes."[6]

The amount of income a woman is forced to forgo by leaving her job to become a mother is termed by economists as the "opportunity cost" of child-rearing. Because more women now work, and the salaries they receive in full-time work has gone up, the "opportunity cost" associated with motherhood has also climbed. A 2004 white paper by Japan's Cabinet Office estimated that a woman who enters the workforce at age twenty-two, leaves at twenty-eight to have children, and comes back to work full-time six years later would forgo an estimated $847,000 in undiscounted income by the time she retires at age sixty. If the woman returns to only part-time labor after having children, the lost income would total nearly $2.4 million.

These economic disincentives to motherhood are even stitched into the fabric of the nation's tax and welfare systems. A married woman who returns to work after having a baby can effectively earn only about 1 million yen per year (just under $10,000) before she has to pay separate taxes on her income. If she earns more than 1.4 million yen, she can no longer be included in her husband's pension benefits, but has to start making her own individual contributions. These rules tend to consign mothers to part-time labor when they return to the workforce, and employers take full advantage. They create job categories suitable only for mid-career part-timers. While women activists argue that rewriting these outdated tax and pension rules might offer women greater incentives to marry, bear children, and return to full-time work, business groups say that they'd be unable to survive tough times if they could no longer rely on a cheap female workforce to help them compete against the Chinese. So there's a large gap between what a woman might earn in a full-time job and what she can earn as a part-timer with a child.

Aside from all these factors, profound pessimism may well contribute significantly to the nation's shrinking population. According to the government's own survey data, 62 percent of women without children believe that raising them would be too expensive and arduous; one in five say Japanese society today is not a good place for raising children. A separate survey of international students showed that only 34 percent of young Japanese adults believe that the twenty-first century offers them hope—compared with 86 percent in the United States, 71 percent in South Korea, and 64 percent in France. Only 9 percent of the Japanese say they are satisfied with society in general—probably a realistic view, but by far the lowest percentage among nations surveyed.[7] Similarly, a global poll on values conducted by the Pew Foundation showed that Japanese are the most pessimistic compared with respondents in other wealthy nations. One career woman, Mika Nemoto, told me she adores children: "But there's no way I'd raise a child in Japan. This is not a place where you can be interested in raising a family. Children are an obstacle." (Some economists believe that, across the industrialized world, the "preference" expressed by young adults for children is declining. If so, Japan is leading the way.)

Yamada, the sociologist, says the hopelessness that infects many young Japanese today results from the growing gap in expectation between those who believe their work can lead to success and those who know that no matter how hard they labor, they will never get ahead. During the era of Japan's high economic growth, most people felt sure that their efforts would yield rewards; that even a modest high school graduate, if he was male, could join a company right out of school, work reasonably hard, and be assured he could enjoy a decent life and relative material prosperity. However, in the "new economy" of the global age in which information services dominate, only a core group of specialized workers and professionals—males and a few select females—can expect success, while lesser-skilled workers have little hope of achieving the "good life," no matter how hard they exert themselves. Today "a college degree is no longer a guarantee of steady, respectable employment," he notes. Why not live for the moment, then, if the traditional formula of persistence and patience won't pay off in today's world?[8]

One day, talking to Kiyoko in a French bistro, I asked her to describe how young adults feel about their nation. "We strove, but our generation never saw the summit, so it's very difficult to have much hope," she said. "It's been the character of Japanese women to be dependent," she said, looking suddenly forlorn as she sipped a glass of burgundy. "We have been educated to be perfect and humble. But now when you look around at what is going on in Japan, you feel like where we once might have had a chance to see the top of the mountain, the summit, now we can only go downhill . . ."

With us were some of her other female friends—all sophisticated, attractive, and defiantly unmarried—whom she'd brought along for me to meet. Her friend Shizuko, who works in a trading company and is thirty-one, said that adults like her have little trust in Japanese institutions and their hidebound corporate cultures. "Why do you think so many of us want to work for foreign-owned firms?" she asked. "We don't like to be constantly hitting our heads against the glass ceiling."

It turns out that neither love nor duty succeed in overcoming the resistance so evident among young women today to marriage and motherhood. What ultimately leads many to the altar is pregnancy.

In Japan, out-of-wedlock birth and single motherhood are as shameful today as they were in Nathaniel Hawthorne's vision of Puritan New England. Unwed mothers account for only 1.9 percent of births today, while in Sweden, 55 percent of mothers are unmarried. Even in the predominately Catholic country of Spain, 18 percent of all children are born to unmarried women. "It's almost the last taboo in our society," Suzuki, the Dentsu researcher, explained. "Even though today fourteen- or fifteen-year-old girls engage in *enjo kosai* ["compensated dating," a euphemism for prostitution], we have a double standard about giving birth to a child when unmarried. As long as you don't have an illegitimate child, you can do whatever you want, whether it's *enjo kosai*, divorce, or becoming a parasite single."

So when an unmarried woman does become pregnant, her choices boil down to abortion or marriage. In 2000, 26 percent of the nation's first births were attributed to women already pregnant before marriage, double the figure of 1980. Among women aged twenty to twenty-four, moreover, 58 percent of first-born babies were conceived before marriage, compared with just 20 percent in 1980. These data suggest not only that women are having sex at an earlier age, but also that unintended pregnancy is often the prime motivation for finally tying the knot, since single motherhood remains a forbidden option. "Without pregnancy a woman has no reason to marry," explained Reiko Ohkawa, head of the gynecological department of a hospital in suburban Chiba prefecture. "Especially for my women patients, marriage is no longer considered attractive."

Furthermore, a government survey showed that 37 percent of single women said that having a baby is the most important reason to wed, ahead of "comfort and companionship" and far ahead of social advantage. At the same time, only 3 percent of married women said that they didn't want any children at all.

*   *   *

Since new birth control techniques and changing social values have also slowed reproductive rates in Italy, Spain, and other European nations in the last two decades, the reluctance of Japanese women to have babies may seem to reflect some broader, international consensus. Yet again, young Japanese behave differently than their peers.

Take cohabitation. In Spain and France, young adults also confront the high cost of housing, making it more difficult for them to "spread their wings" and venture out on their own to create independent households. To cope, an estimated 53 percent of young French and 12 percent of young Spaniards, for instance, live together before marriage; less than 2 percent of Japanese tell researchers they cohabit.[9] Moreover, a vast majority of Japanese tell government researchers they believe that people should marry before they live together, while in Western nations, cohabitation is often viewed as the "try out" phase that naturally leads a couple to marriage. Like their European counterparts, contemporary Japanese have become sexually active at earlier ages, but they are unlike Europeans in that they tend to still live with their parents, getting away on occasion to gaudy "love hotels" with faux French or Statue of Liberty motifs. As marriage becomes less of a prerequisite for sex, and the institution of marriage less desirable as a choice for adult life, young Japanese tend to "live apart together," says the demographer Miho Iwasawa, who has studied these patterns.[10] While young adults may maintain monogamous relationships, they choose to live separately, often with their parents, thus transforming once legal ties, through marriage, into less formal bonds. Iwasawa's work suggests that combining "love" with "companionship" either is not considered feasible or is not terribly important to young Japanese.

Another key contrast with modern Western societies is that in Japan, the higher a woman's salary, the *less* likely she is to marry. In Sweden and the United States, a woman's tendency to cohabit and subsequently marry *rises* as she attains a higher salary. The demographer Hiromi Ono, who has compiled these data, says that an educated woman doesn't marry in Japan because, with gender alone tending to define one's social role, society still won't allow her to have both a child and a high-powered career.[11] Other census data not only corroborate Ono's findings but underline a gaping mismatch in the Japanese marriage market, where it can prove difficult for a highly educated woman to find a suitable mate. Today, 12 percent of all female university graduates above the age of fifty who live in metropolitan Tokyo have never married. The largest category of never-married males, by contrast, is those who never got beyond a junior high school education; these men tend to seek "traditional" stay-at-home wives. The problem for educated women is that they want a "liberated" husband who will share the burdens of raising a child and allow them both to work outside the home, while the majority of highly educated men say they want a "traditional," stay-at-home wife.

Kiyoko often crashes against this divergence in values when she has a date with a prospective marriage partner. "I meet men with decent jobs, who are my age or a little older, and they say things like 'I want my wife to be at home all the time' or 'I can become a real man when I can feed my wife and my baby,' and you just know the gap between us is so, so big," Kiyoko told me, shaking her head. "The men are so conservative, and their attitudes really don't seem to be changing much." Men only seem to accept equality when the dinner bill comes, she joked. "You'd be surprised how often we go dutch."

The role of religion in mediating family values and determining contraceptive practices also distinguishes Japan from Europe. In the West, the various Christian churches once wielded powerful social control over reproduction and family formation, steering young adults toward marriage, denouncing premarital sex, and, in the case of the Catholic Church, opposing contraception and abortion. As such church influence declined, casual sex increased, and the widespread use of the Pill warded off unwanted pregnancy. Many Italian women live with their boyfriends before marriage, and a growing number, more than 10 percent, have children out of wedlock. Even in conservative, Catholic Italy, young women generally use the Pill to control their fertility.

In Japan, however, there is neither moral taboo against, nor political opposition to, abortion. It has been accepted in society since feudal times and remains, along with the condom, the most popular form of contraception along with the "rhythm method." (About 340,000 abortions are reported each year in Japan, about 30 percent the number of births.) Yet the Pill itself was legalized only in 1999 after a vigorous nine-year campaign waged by foreign drugmakers, and today fewer than 5 percent of Japanese women rely on it. Doctors warn their female patients that oral contraceptives are "unnatural" and pose health dangers. "We've all been told the Pill has dangerous side effects," Shizuko explained. Instead, Japanese doctors enthusiastically recommend abortion, because the procedure earns them larger profits from the national health care system than does dispensing the Pill.

Foreign-owned pharmaceutical firms have gone so far as to open chic coffee houses in Tokyo's upscale neighborhoods to offer women information in a stress-free environment about the low-dose Pill's modest health risks and obvious benefits. "It's easier for a Japanese woman to come out and say she's had an abortion than to say she's on the Pill," said the gynecologist Tomoko Saotome, one activist who had pushed for the Pill's approval.[12]

While it took nine years for the male-dominated Health Ministry to approve the low-dose Pill, Viagra was put on the "fast track" to legalization and introduced just six months after Pfizer asked for permission. "It's a double standard," Yoriko Ashino, deputy executive director of the Family Planning Federation of Japan, which had been crusading for the Pill, complained to me. Yasuhide Furusawa, a Health Ministry official, acknowledged that the most serious stumbling blocks to legalizing the Pill were "social concerns"—not medical ones. "There is a significant concern that permitting use of the Pill will accelerate the spread of HIV," and encourage sexual promiscuity, he told me in an interview.

Since the Pill cannot be blamed for Japan's shrinking birthrate, feudal values loom larger. Makoto Atoh, director-general of the National Institute of Population and Social Security Research, which compiles the nation's demographic data, shrugged. "In Japan, women don't have their own fertility control methods. They must still depend on men."

* * *

More than two-thirds of women aged twenty-five to thirty-four who have a regular sex partner still live with their parents.[13] These are Japan's most robust consumers, the well-dressed flocks who crowd the specialty boutiques and patiently wait their turn in line to enter the houses of high fashion. They pay little or no rent, don't need cars in big-city Japan, and don't have college loans to pay off because the bills have been paid by their parents. While their consumption patterns benefit Gucci, Prada, and other high-status foreign designers, they wreak significant long-term damage on the domestic Japanese economy. These *parasaitos* spend their disposable income on clothing, the kind of diamond necklace Kiyoko wore, and vacations, not on apartments or refrigerators or babies. According to the sociologist Yamada, these women, with their womb strike and refusal to marry, represent—along with the *hikikomori*—the "social and psychological deadlock" contemporary Japan confronts.

"In traditional Japanese society, economic dependency was always a virtue," he explained one humid September afternoon as we sat in his tiny office, crowded with books, file folders, and research papers, on the campus of Tokyo Gakugei University in one of the capital's vast suburbs. But with Japan's current economic dislocation, "these dependency virtues don't work anymore," he continued. Old formulas no longer produce prosperity, "yet our young people still believe that you can obtain an affluent lifestyle without making any effort. If you are living with your parents, have spending money for your life, can see your boyfriend or girlfriend whenever you want, then it's a paradise, isn't it?" Since the future seems fragile, "they escape into a culture of hedonism, shopping, and foreign travel. You feel like you are at a dead-end as a nation when people have all they want at present, and really have few prospects for the future." In Yamada's view, the falling birthrate has become a rational response to this national paralysis.

He likened the parasite singles to the dodgy loans piling up in Japanese banks. For just as delay compounds the expense of cleaning up bad debts, the cost of shrinking demographics also grows more acute over time. "Instead of taking risks now, these parasites just postpone them indefinitely into the future," he said. "They think that Prince Charming will come along, just as the banks think the economy will someday turn around. But what happens if there's no prince?"

10.

MARRIAGE IN A HOMOSOCIAL SOCIETY

A stranger who peeked inside the mail slots in my Tokyo apartment building would be forgiven for thinking it belonged in front of some sleazy sex arcade. Stuffed between the form letters and utility bills, he'd find dozens of flyers advertising massage clubs, dating services, "telephone clubs," and sex "salons." Usually, these handbills, a dozen or more each week, were adorned with pictures of doe-eyed Japanese girls clad in bikinis, wrapped in towels, or wearing nothing at all. A helpful footnote usually specified each girl's bra size.

Wandering through Tokyo's Kabukicho or some other "pink" neighborhood in one of Japan's big cities, you would be right in thinking that the Japanese are captivated by "soaplands," where a scantily-clad girl helps you bathe; by "image clubs," where young girls in sailor suits give lap dances; or by *"no pan shabu shabu"* restaurants, where waitresses without panties stand on platforms above your table and reach down to deliver your order of boiling beef and frosty cold beer. Limitless sexual fantasy seems to be on offer everywhere.

Japanese, it has been estimated, spend as much in the illicit sex trade as the nation does on its defense budget, and tens of thousands of Thai and Filipino girls are imported to Japan each year on "entertainment" visas to help Japanese men escape the stresses of their joyless lives as *sarari-men*.[1] Japan's *mizu shobai*, or "water world," has existed for centuries, and Japanese males often indulge in elaborate sex tours to China, Thailand, and other Asian nations—tours that sometimes stir fierce local protest.

The fact is, however, that these neon-gilded establishments exist precisely because Japanese find it so difficult to establish casual social relations in situations where money doesn't change hands. Data show that men and women live separate lives, have sex less often than those in other nations, and have little relaxed contact with the opposite sex.[2] Of the few places where men and women can freely mingle without a commercial transaction being involved, most seem to be through casual social "clubs" established for weekend hiking or the occasional ski trip. School ties or friends from the office are other important ways young people use to connect.

Because Japanese find themselves bound tight in relatively inflexible networks, however, most young people find it remarkably difficult to form casual connections and meet members of the opposite sex outside of work or the classroom. Women like thirty-five-year-old Yuriko desperately want to marry and start a family, but can't find a husband. "I'd really like to be someone's partner," she told me one afternoon over tea, "but I really don't have much opportunity to meet people."

I met her in the handsome city of Kanazawa, on the northwest Sea of Japan, where I had gone to see how marriage and coupling play out in a smaller, if still cosmopolitan city of 450,000, as opposed to the anomic environment of Tokyo.

Yuriko studied tea ceremony and flower arranging—in part, to make herself more appealing to a potential suitor. Comfortable in both Western clothes and the traditional kimono, she lives with her parents, works in their small floral business, and finds little chance in her daily life to encounter an eligible man. "Most of the people I meet in the office are already married, and the single men seem so helpless. They really seem like parasites that are completely dependent on their mothers," she said. (Different from the *hikikomori*, another large segment of young Japanese men hold down steady jobs, but prefer to have their mothers cook and clean for them—not unlike so-called mama's boys in Italy or the United States.)

Yuriko has thick, long hair, a broad nose, and delicate, narrow eyes. As she talked, she grew increasingly emotional. "Sometimes I feel despondent about being alone," she said. "But I don't really think it's my fault. Maybe it's because I live in a small town, but it's hard to meet the right person." Only a few days earlier, Yuriko said, she had met four of her high school girlfriends for a social dinner, and only one of the five had married. "I myself can't believe I am in this situation," she said. "Since I was a child I knew people who were getting married and having babies, and I always assumed I'd be one of them. Why are we still single? I don't really know. Where did we lose the chance to become mothers?"

In the 1960s and 1970s, Yuriko would have been "set up" with a man through the feudal system of arranged marriage. Rules governing *omiai* were formalized in the Edo Period (1600–1868), when serfs had to live under the strict laws imposed by the shogunate and enforced by the samurai. Peasants lived in close-knit village communities under constant surveillance, making it difficult for potential lovers to establish relationships. The samurai themselves also required matchmakers in their male-dominated world, in which homosexuality was common and it was difficult to meet suitable women. A matchmaker was needed to ensure that a warrior was introduced to a potential partner of appropriate social standing, a woman who would neither embarrass the household nor taint the samurai's strict code of honor.

In the traditional social structure of Japan, marriage was nothing less than a corporate merger involving two family empires, like a deal between Time Inc. and Warner Brothers, engineered to ensure the continuity and success of the *ie* household. The prospective bride and groom had little say over whom they would wed. Love had almost no bearing on a matrimonial contract. Duty, status, perpetuating the family "line," and maintaining property were priorities for the clan, and an individual's romantic desires hardly mattered.

These feudal attitudes toward marriage persisted well into the modern era. As late as 1966, while American mores were being turned upside down by the sexual revolution and the women's rights movement, there were still more arranged marriages in Japan than ones fashioned by volition and love. As recently as 1982, three in ten marriages were arranged, government statistics show. By 2002, however, "love marriages" predominated, accounting for 89 percent of all weddings, while just 8 percent were arranged.

The emancipation of young couples to make their own marital choices has become common throughout the cultures of the modern West. As Western notions of love infiltrated Japan through movies and TV, young Japanese naturally demanded the autonomy to be free to select their own life partners. They proved, however, somewhat ill equipped for the transition. For one thing, as the psychologist Hayao Kawai believes, Japanese grasped only the most superficial aspects of Western love; many could not understand how love might emanate from individualism and individual self-expression. Westerners, he said to me, "naturally express feeling. They say things like 'I love you.' But in Japan, if I say to my wife, 'I love you,' she would become very skeptical. She might think I'm nuts. The Japanese way is that if we just sit down together, that's enough. Often, we talk with silence [a concept known in Japan as *haragei*, literally "belly talk," a sense of "listening to the silence"]. If I actually articulate something in words, it will be doubted."

Shigesato Takahashi, chief demographer for the National Institute of Population and Social Security Research, has examined reams of census data and believes the decline of matchmaking is the single most important cause for Japan's population crisis. Without leisure time, widely dispersed social networks, and family intermediaries, young Japanese simply have no way to find suitable partners, he says.

"These days," Takahashi told me, "it is very difficult to find a girlfriend or a relationship that will ultimately end up in marriage"—because work, and the requisite after-work bonding, consumes too much time. "If you look at our data, many young single people just don't have any friends of the opposite sex. Sexual activity in Japan hasn't really changed that much, but there is more sexual activity without marriage, and therefore less household formation."

A man who seems constantly buried in the reams of statistical spreadsheets stacked neatly in binders around his office, Takahashi works for a division of Japan's Ministry of Health, Labor and Welfare, which conducts periodic face-to-face interviews with nearly ten thousand Japanese singles. His survey teams not only gather data about marriage and family structure, but also ask important attitudinal questions, repeated over decades, to chronicle the changing nature of friendship, social expectation, and living patterns.

His statistics depict young Japanese as distressingly isolated and lonely. More than half of unmarried Japanese men between the ages of eighteen and thirty-four report having no sexual relationships, friendships, or even casual companionship with a woman. This astonishing fact emerged in a 2002 survey that posed the simple question, "Do you have any friends of the opposite sex?" Among unmarried women in the same age bracket of young adults, 40 percent said they had no casual male companion or intimate partner. In addition, nearly 35 percent of Japanese women and 30 percent of men between the ages of twenty-five and twenty-nine told the survey they had never had a sexual experience.[3] These data echo a far less scientific survey conducted by the condom maker Durex in 2001, which concluded that Japanese ranked last among 28 countries in the frequency of sex: the average Japanese had sex just 36 times a year, while Americans ranked number one, reporting that they had sex 124 times annually. This finding was also effectively corroborated by Pfizer, the manufacturer of Viagra, which found it sold less of its erectile dysfunction treatment in Japan than initially expected—only two-thirds of sales forecasts—because Japanese engage in relatively little sex. Similarly, the vast extent of sexlessness in Japan was uncovered in a 2004 Health Ministry survey that concluded that 20 percent of marriages had lacked physical intimacy for one year or more, while almost one-third of married couples had not had sex for at least a month.[4]

Takahashi's survey also asks singles to give their reasons for not choosing to marry. While 34 percent of unmarried men between the ages of twenty-five and thirty-four said they "didn't feel a need" to marry, 44 percent admitted that "they couldn't meet the appropriate partner." Nearly half of unmarried women in this age group acknowledged that, like Kiyoko, they, too, could not find Mr. Right.

The marriage brokerage system once guaranteed that eligible brides and grooms would be paired off, much as the "convoy system" within the economic system once ensured that strong banks or manufacturers pro-tected weaker ones. Strong networks comprised of stable, long-term so-cial relationships identified those families with potential brides and used matchmakers to link these females with suitable men. Often, attractive women were recruited to join a company just so that eligible men might meet and marry them. Even in the 1970s and early 1980s, leading cor-porations and government agencies sponsored matchmaking events to fix up their male employees with suitable brides.

"This 'convoy system' for bachelors protected everybody," Takahashi told me, because it ensured that everyone got married, and that the pop-ulation was replenished. "Until quite recently there was no strong need to go out and find someone on your own. Someone at your office would introduce you to a woman, and the problem would be taken care of."

As a once-rigid marriage system falls into disuse, however, young adults encounter great difficulty meeting others, much less finding ap-propriate mates. They lack a wide network of casual acquaintances, the skills to acquire them, and the casual forms of social trust needed to maintain such a network. The new, more "open" marriage market creates more competition to find an attractive partner, Takahashi said, while the rate of failure is climbing for those deemed unappealing. "An attractive person may marry sooner, but a less attractive partner may find it more difficult to meet or marry." Unwittingly, perhaps, Takahashi cited the re-inforcing nature of social network theory: "Those who are socially active remain socially active, but those who aren't active stay inactive." As fun-damental changes take place in the way men and women relate to one another, he characterizes this transition from a "closed" market to a "free market" as being chaotic and incomplete.

Since no woman today can be forced to get married against her will, the matchmaking process has become significantly less intrusive. Often women are set up for "arranged dates," but these can seem like torture, Yuriko told me. One thirty-seven-year-old man admitted to her that, though he lived only five minutes from his office, "I'm late every day un-less my mother wakes me up." Another told her that he stayed home every night watching TV while eating dinner. "If that is the extent of his social life, what's the point of getting married?" she scoffed. "You are bet-ter off to keep working and have your freedom.

"Sure, I'd like to have a baby and be somebody's partner," she went on, "but right now I'm guess I'm happier just living with Mom and Dad."

Yuriko did not readily admit it, but friends later told me that her mas-ter's degree usually scared away potential suitors. Men in this conserva-tive city tend to shy away from women with an education or a salary higher than their own.

Hirooyo, now thirty-seven, had been on nearly forty "arranged dates" over the past decade, before finally meeting her prospective husband, a computer technician. "At least half of the arranged meetings were with doctors," she told me. "My parents were so eager for me to go to these meetings, but I always wondered what on earth I would talk about."

The atmosphere she described was stifling. No sooner would she be ushered into a small hotel room to meet the prospective groom and his parents, than a matchmaker would begin pressuring the two to become engaged. "They tell you that you have a month to decide [whether to marry], and you feel as if the matchmaker is mostly focused on getting a fee for a successful match." Companionship does not come easily under this microscope. Nor does love seem to enter the equation.

Still, the social pressure to wed is palpable. "People will meet you in the street and say, 'Oh, you haven't changed your name yet?'" Hirooyo said. "They make you feel uncomfortable when you're not yet married."

She was now finally engaged to a man she had met in a coffee shop, but she admitted that she really didn't know her fiancé well. She told me they had never traveled outside of town together for a weekend trip or been to a "love hotel" to have sex. She did not say it outright, and I dared not ask the question in front of others, but I came away with the impres-sion that she was still a virgin at thirty-seven. "In this town, it's impossi-ble to go to a love hotel because you're so afraid of other people's eyes" and the shame of being discovered, she confided. "Usually we just drive around or have a meal together. He seems nice and reliable."

Twenty-nine-year-old Rie Masodome had escaped to Kanazawa from Kagoshima, one of Japan's most fiercely conservative prefectures, because she wanted to live together with her Australian boyfriend. "Everybody in my town knows everybody else. They all know who is married and who is divorced, and there's a really bad image of living together with a man outside of marriage," she told me. In Melbourne, where she had met her boyfriend, Andrew, "everyone spends at least two years living together before getting married. Since we couldn't do that in my hometown, we moved here, where nobody really knows me."

* * *

The inability of men to attract women—with the resulting decline in population—seems positively heartbreaking in aging rural Japan. Though most young people no longer want to work the fields, preferring the neon lights and anonymous freedoms of big-city life, tradition dictates that the eldest son or *chonan* stay attached to the ground he will someday inherit. Few women want to marry such men, however. They want to get away from the harshness of rural life, and they don't want to care for and feed a new set of in-laws.

"Last year, we had only 127 babies in this town," said the marriage broker Setsuko Takano, whose tiny village of Shirataka most of its young women have abandoned for urban life. A small, sturdy woman, she doubles as the village's local tailor. "At that rate, we'd have to close all the schools soon. The very existence of the town itself is facing a crisis."

Takano told me that most women want to work these days and don't want to stay in the village. "They study and get educated," she said. The town's eldest sons, however, "spend their time drinking, watching TV, and playing *pachinko*," the Japanese form of pinball, which amounts to legalized gambling. Many of these single men are completely dominated by their mothers, Takano confided. "Honestly speaking, the men themselves are not eye-catching," she said, shaking her head with disgust. "They're not attractive, and they don't know much about what's going on in the world."

To cope with its rapidly aging population, Shirataka and dozens of other hamlets throughout Yamagata prefecture, in Japan's rugged and wintry north, encourage families to spend more than $25,000 each to import brides from China, South Korea, Thailand, and the Philippines to wed the *chonan*. In 1997 alone, the Justice Ministry issued 274,000 residency visas for foreign spouses, an increase of 30 percent in five years. Today about 4.5 percent of all marriages are "mixed"—between Japanese and non-Japanese spouses. The hope is that the foreign woman will replace the local girls who simply can't be dragged to the altar, and create a stable marriage.

That only a few of these marriages may actually end up happy seems somewhat beside the point. Psychiatrists who counsel mail-order brides told me that many of these new wives complain of being little more than housekeepers for their aging mothers-in-law. "I often think of getting a divorce," said Jocelyn Izumino, aged twenty-nine, who had come to Japan from the Philippines eight years earlier and has two children. "My in-laws think I am an ideal bride, but really I am nothing more than a housekeeper."

Seven people spanning four generations lived in the Izumino farmhouse when I visited her in 1999. She was expected to care for and feed all of them while also holding down a full-time factory job building parts for Nissan. "I clean and I cook," Izumino told me, speaking in the Japanese she mastered after arriving here as a twenty-one-year-old college student. "In the Philippines, we have maids who do what I do." Each day, she wakes up at 5 A.M. to cook breakfast and prepare lunch boxes for the entire family before trudging off to her job. "If I didn't have babies, definitely I would leave. I love my husband, but I can't get along with my in-laws," Izumino told me.

Another woman, Irene—a slim, brown-haired Filipina with a weak smile, a faraway gaze, and a designer purse—spent two hours describing to me her brokered marriage to a Japanese farmer twice her age, a union that produced two children.

"My in-laws accept me," the thirty-year-old bride insisted, as her six-year-old daughter, her youngest child, amused herself in the corner with a Nintendo Gameboy. "They are happy to have my support. None of the other Filipinas who've moved to my town to marry have suffered a divorce."

But when she left, the psychiatrist Norihiko Kuwayama, who runs a hotline for imported brides, revealed the unhappy truth. After thirteen years of marriage, "this couple is a speechless pair," he told me. "They have no family life. Every night, Irene works in a bar selling drinks and waiting on customers," as a hostess, "and I worry about . . . the children."

At one point, Irene went back to the Philippines and left one of her children there when she returned to the Japanese countryside. "The husband didn't seem to care," Kuwayama said. "We were all a bit surprised that she decided to come back here."

The tiny village of Nishimera on the southern island of Kyushu has developed a remarkably different way to boost its population. Instead of bringing in matchmakers or foreign brides, it built two blocks of "singles' apartments" and—promising them total privacy—invited unmarried people between the ages of eighteen and forty to live there. Through having the security of their own private residence, the young adults who came to the village found ways to meet one another casually and create their own social networks. Coupling spontaneously took hold. "You get to hang out with everyone when there are events and other things taking place," one recent bridegroom explained. "It's important to have a space where you can take things easy."[5]

*　　*　　*

If you take a weekend stroll through Ebisu Garden Place, or any of a dozen other modern Tokyo shopping centers, you will see what the anthropologists who label Japan's society "homosocial" really mean. You will find shops and cafés filled with smartly dressed women, eating Italian *panini*, sorting through Fendi scarves, or lining up for a matinee performance at the movie theater. But—unlike the scene in a typical American suburban shopping mall on a Saturday afternoon—you will see almost no men. Of the people visible, 90 percent will be women, with only a handful of couples. Rarer still would be a man and woman strolling together with their child.

Where is Dad? He is either at home sleeping, recovering from a stressful week at work and the after-work "drinking meetings" that are inseparable from his duties; or at the golf course, playing with his bosses or entertaining clients. Statistical surveys show that "sleeping" consistently ranks as the most popular weekend pastime of Japanese men. According to family counselors, most Japanese fathers devote little attention to their children.

Even adolescence can be shaped and distorted by such gender separation. Men and women often attend separate schools, and Japanese teenagers have notably less time than American children for casual play or to socialize with others because they have to set aside time to study for their high school or university entrance exams. "A male student suppresses his desire to go out with girls in order to get into university," Takahashi said. "When people study so hard, it's hard for them to meet up with others." In the push to attain high academic achievement, people often fail to acquire important social skills. Yet despite the constant emphasis on study and cram school, Japanese students are actually falling behind. Recent tests of fifteen-years-olds show that among the thirty OECD nations, Japan rates no better than average in reading; since 2000, Japan has fallen from first to sixth in math.

In adulthood, work *is* the family for most men, and they are also far more likely to spend time outside work with colleagues—not necessarily because they want to, but because it is part of getting ahead. Data show that men who don't join company outings, or refuse to socialize regularly with work colleagues, more often fail to win coveted promotions. In his landmark study of a Japanese bank, the sociologist Thomas Rohlen described how men and women associated almost exclusively with other members of the firm, mostly those in the same age bracket.[6] So intense was the pressure to conform and create a family-like social network that employees were expected both to marry at the same age and to raise precisely the same number of children. Of course, few women hold executive-level jobs within the firm.

Gender segregation persists outside work. At night most of Tokyo's estimated 80,000 restaurants are packed with clients—men drinking and dining with other men, women with other women. Some restaurant guides even publish demographic indices of customers, so diners can choose those "special" restaurants that cater to couples looking for a romantic evening, not just to *sararimen* bonding over grilled chicken yakitori and cold beer.

The well-defined split of gender roles was orchestrated by corporations, endorsed by educators, and reinforced by bureaucrats—a way for the powerful Iron Triangle to impose itself into the nation's social spaces during Japan's industrial catch-up. This served to boost social efficiency and reassure working men that their home life would be stable in their absence. "The so-called corporate warrior, even of the blue collar ranks, was able and willing to make his professional commitment at work because his wife was secure in a homemaker's role, [then] defined as a modern, scientific contributor to building a new Japan," one sociologist explained.[7] Long after the period of "catch-up" ended, however, the relatively inflexible division between genders remains intact.

* * *

Big-city professional women who want to escape from the cage of Japanese values sometimes just pick up and leave. Kazue Ishihara, thirty-seven and single, had once been obsessed with getting married. "I thought I must have a husband. Otherwise, I'll be so worried about my future," recalled the trim, well-dressed sales executive for a computer company, who speaks excellent English. She had grown up in Nagoya, the central Japanese city where Toyota is based, the daughter of a business executive. "My parents always warned me. They said if a woman gets an education, she'll have trouble finding a man."

In her mid-twenties and still living at her parents' home, Ishihara had registered with a marriage broker to find a partner. She paid between $100 and $200 each time to be fixed up on five separate "dates" with eligible men, "but it was so incredibly boring. The guys were so unappealing and very conservative. I thought, 'This is no good. These men will never accept my independent character. They will never let me work, or have my own opinions.'"

Frustrated, she turned to the support of girlfriends. Together they organized so-called *go-kon*, parties where five eligible men are invited to meet five women friends for an informal dinner at a restaurant. "It was pretty superficial," she told me. "You had some fun times, I guess, but it wasn't very interesting and nobody really caught my fancy." Women often complain that these parties only proved how boorish and inept men could be. It was not uncommon at a party like this for a man's opening question to be, "What color panties are you wearing?" women told me.

Finally, she gave up on Japan completely and accepted a job offer in Singapore. "I was tired of waiting for marriage. I figured it was a waste of time. Better to get on with my career, and I thought working abroad would help."

Ishihara stayed for three years before returning a transformed woman. She no longer agonized over whether she needed to find a husband. She attributed her radical change of attitude to her discovery of Christian faith during an emotional crisis. "Now when I see a problem, I realize God will give me strength to do what's required," she said. "When I didn't have that faith, it was easy to feel devastated because I was alone. When I see other parasite singles now, I feel the pain they suffer because I was just like that. But now I have my own family, because of my faith and my Church."

Surprisingly, the demographer Takahashi, who bases his conclusions about Japan's social trends on hard, statistical evidence, not on intuition or blind faith, took seriously the transformative power associated with her religious conversion when I told him about Ishihara's spiritual journey. He, too, believes that fixed social values and an absence of religious sentiment have influenced the rapid decline in family formation and population in modern Japan. As a counterexample, he points to the United States, a society that veered to the right in the 1980s and 1990s as conservative politicians began to use the rhetoric of "family values" and "morality" to further their own agendas, including tax credits for working mothers and ending the "marriage penalty" in the tax code. Although liberals in America could scoff at these initiatives as hypocritical and politically motivated, offering only lip service to the notion of public morality, Takahashi felt, as a Japanese demographer, that the data bore it out: attendance at church services went up, divorce rates headed down, and the political clout associated with Christian fundamentalists rose markedly, especially after the electoral victory of George W. Bush in 2000.[8]

Japan, by contrast, having focused solely on achieving economic well-being after World War Two, tended to sacrifice even family relationships to achieve corporate success. Now, after years of recession, "many people have started to realize that the way of life centered just on making money is wrong. We still live in a society in which having a partner or a child is not easy, and data show young people want to be happy 'seeking themselves.'

"In America, an individual still stands before God and tries to play a role in society," Takahashi said, looking up from his desk and waxing philosophical. "A Japanese individualist is far more of an egoist, someone who keeps to himself or herself and has no relationship with others. They tend to be more egocentric and self-reliant, and that ends up causing more problems for our society." As the psychiatrist Takeo Doi had proposed, a Japanese person who put herself and her own self-fulfillment ahead of communal virtues was likely to find herself condemned.

So the *parasaito* woman who feels that she cannot abide the constraints of married life, and the woman who, though willing to put a spouse and a child above her own independence, still cannot find an appropriate mate, constitute an unhappy pair of bookends in a society undergoing social as well as economic upheaval. Yet many women are also sympathetic to the miserable plight of Japanese males who are also confined to traditional roles: through the rituals and requirements of the workplace, the need to defer to their senior managers and bosses, and the demand that they wait patiently for their turn to have a voice in determining corporate decisions. At least as women they have the freedom not to work—or to spend their salaries on material pleasures.

Mariko Bando, the government's leading spokeswoman for gender equity, agreed that the population decline reflects a crisis of national values. She recounted that when she attended Tokyo University, there was only one female student for every thirty males, and that most of her women classmates were forced to abandon promising careers for motherhood.

"The employment system has to be changed," she told me as we sat in a large office directly across the street from the prime minister's official residence. "Even today the circumstances are not supportive for a woman to have a job and family so they chose either, or." Despite new laws guaranteeing more equality in the workplace, two-thirds of all women quit their first jobs, she said. "It's not a question of policies or countermeasures. It's a question of values toward marriage, family, or children. Japanese women are losing their dreams to have a happy married life, and that's the real crisis for women."

In contrast to her youth, when Japan was focused on catching up, today's young adults lack vitality and energy, she told me. Japan's *hikikomori* suffer the same deficits, she said. She suggested that theirs might be an organic response to prosperity—that young people are too coddled and spoiled to seize the moment. "In the West you take the risks and you pay the costs. But we in Japan are too timid to sacrifice or pay the cost for change. So we postpone the tough decisions."

She looked away from her desk, toward the shiny glass building with darkened windows where the prime minister works. "We keep postponing catastrophe because we don't have the courage to change," she sighed. "Like those troubled boys, we must go out from our protected homes and encounter the serious, difficult real world.

"If I was a freelance critic, I would say, 'We must restructure the society, ask the old people to give more opportunity to the younger, frustrated people, and take the risks of accepting challenges and having new dreams' . . . But I am a cabinet member . . ."

Her voiced trailed away, sorrowfully. As only one official in a huge government bureaucracy, she was well aware how little weight her single voice would carry.

11.

Hajimu Asada ended his life just the way many of his neighbors expected, and probably demanded: dangling from a tree, a noose tight around his neck. In his suicide note, he apologized. "We have caused a great deal of inconvenience, and we are very sorry."

Asada, sixty-seven, and his wife, Chisako, sixty-four, were found swinging back-to-back near one of the chicken coops on their giant poultry farm near Himeji, in western Japan, early on a wintry March Monday in 2004. They had been dead for several hours when discovered by a female employee arriving for work.

Asada was no petty criminal. The owner of a giant poultry processor with six separate operations, he had covered up an epidemic of highly contagious avian flu that decimated the flocks in one plant. Even as thousands of chickens were coughing up blood and dying, his company continued to sell live eggs and poultry to unsuspecting consumers. The outbreak was at least one week old when, alerted by an anonymous tip, prefectural officials inspected the plant, found the dead birds, and quickly quarantined the premises. In the days that followed, snarling yellow bulldozers buried thousands of chickens in a giant earthen pit, while the influenza virus spread to other nearby farms and to wild birds in the area, triggering a nationwide panic.

Hours before taking his life, Asada, the white-haired chairman of the company that bore his name and which he founded in 1957, held his second news conference. Bowing low before the cameras, as if to the nation itself, he expressed his "deep apologies for causing concern and trouble." His sudden exit, however, spared him the further indignity of having to face the people his dishonesty had injured, to repair the damage, or to be jailed. That burden would be shouldered by, among others, his surviving son, who subsequently was arrested.

Kazuhiro Keitoku, by contrast, had done no wrong. The fifty-six-year-old former vice manager of a bank, Keitoku chose to become principal of a Hiroshima elementary school in March 2002 in the hope that his decades of managerial experience would help rejuvenate the school and improve student life. He was given but two days' training before taking up his new post.

A gentle man with a wide oval face and oversized metal glasses, Keitoku greeted many of the seven hundred pupils each day as they trudged up the steep hill to enter the school's front gate. He reviewed homework assignments, sometimes staying at his desk until late at night. He even proposed to take the students mountain climbing on a fine day so they could experience nature beyond the confines of their classroom. His proposals were fiercely resisted by the district's teacher's union, which said the hectic five-day-a-week school calendar allowed no time for frivolous expeditions; he soon found himself wedged between a national government insistent that young students raise the national flag and sing the national anthem to instill patriotism, and a left-wing teacher's union unalterably opposed to such flamboyant reminders of Japan's wartime past. As Keitoku once confessed to a member of the school's PTA, "I had an image of school that was about forty years out of date. Now I have realized that there's a gap between the ideal and the reality."

On a quiet Sunday morning in March 2003, less than a year after taking the job, Keitoku helped teachers and PTA officials plant a flower garden on the school grounds, then walked back into the building, attached a rope to the handrail of a staircase, and hanged himself. "I'm sorry that I've caused trouble for many people because I, an incapable person, was appointed principal," read the note police found in his desk drawer.

Months later, education officials admitted that Keitoku had been bullied by teachers and by parents dissatisfied with his approach, and that the principal had been hospitalized briefly for depression about a month after taking the job. Adding to the stress, officials refused to name a successor to replace Keitoku's more experienced vice principal after the other man was hospitalized for stress. Altogether they seemed to do little to help the rookie principal gain his sea legs.

The principal's suicide reverberated throughout the city. Less than four months later, on July 4, the deputy head of the local school board also killed himself. Shokichi Yamaoka, fifty-five, was found in the backseat of his car in a wooded area, his legs stretched out, a rope made of fabric fastened around his neck and tied to the handgrip above the passenger window. He was the man who had listened to Keitoku's concerns but failed to replace the vice principal. Later, the widows of both men asked the local government for compensation, saying stress, overwork, and fatigue had triggered their husbands' premature deaths.

Work stress had nothing to do, however, with the suicide of Yohei, a twenty-eight-year-old part-time deliveryman for a sushi restaurant, who surfed the Internet to find companions to die with. Checking Web sites with names like "Underground Suicide" to seek introductions and download detailed instructions, he met up for the first time with two other young men just hours before their last act. Together, the three strangers drove to a quiet mountain pass six hours north of Tokyo. There in the alpine solitude, they downed handfuls of sleeping pills and lit a charcoal brazier inside the car, where they slipped into sleep and died from carbon monoxide poisoning.

These are just three of at least thirty-two young adults who used the Internet to plan their own group suicides in 2003. "There was no discussion of why he was doing it, just an indication that maybe he was tired of living," Yohei's father, a security guard, later told a local journalist.[1]

*   *   *

In these first years of the twenty-first century, Japan, a prosperous country whose citizens eat well, dress meticulously, and have countless opportunities to seek pleasure and amusement, is suffering a plague of suicides among its men. Some, like Asada, kill themselves out of shame; others, like the school principal Keitoku, out of resignation and regret; still others, like the young drifters who meet over the Web, feel so disconnected from the rest of society that suicide seems the only way to wrest meaning from their loneliness.

In a nation where even uttering the word "depression" remains taboo, and where almost all advanced antidepressant medications like Prozac and Zoloft remain illegal and unavailable, more than 660 Japanese commit suicide every single week—ninety-four persons per day, according to the National Police Agency. In 2003, the number of Japanese who committed suicide rose 7 percent from the previous year, to a record 34,427.[2]

"Suicide is the biggest health care issue facing Japan," Yukio Saito, one of the nation's leading suicide counselors told me. The government, however, has consistently refused to make any similar admissions, resisting nearly as much as it has tried to deny the existence of that other group who also blot out the sun—the *hikikomori*.

Every February, the Fuji-Yoshida police station in Yamanashi prefecture conducts a grim ritual. Officers collect bodies and calculate the number of suicides committed in the Aokigahara woods, a dark and sprawling forest around the base of Mount Fuji popular among those seeking to end their lives. In their annual sweep in late 2003, authorities recovered a record seventy-eight bodies, twenty more than the year before and five more than the previous high set in 1998. Another eighty-three people were taken into protective custody before they could commit the act, the police said.

Most Japanese coolly accept these deaths as normal, even righteous. Unlike Westerners, who tend to view suicide as an irrational submission to despair or have a religious taboo against it, the suicide act in Japan often represents the ultimate ritualistic expression of self-sacrifice to the collective, of fulfilling a perceived duty to the larger society. In Japan, committing suicide can also have the salutary effect of cleansing a family's name. Once you die, the thinking goes, neighbors will stop saying bad things about you.

In the West, many experts believe that suicide is preventable through early medical or psychiatric intervention. Another view, made popular by the sociologist Emile Durkheim, suggests that deeper forces within society, rather than any individual crisis, provoke suicide. Durkheim believed that suicide occurs with greatest frequency in situations of acute or chronic disturbance of the social order, and that high suicide rates measure some acid eating away at its fabric. Whichever philosophy you embrace—that the trigger for suicide is uniquely personal or broadly societal—this swell of self-destruction suggests some deep inner disturbance among the Japanese people. The fear, insecurity, and aimlessness that ultimately lead to suicide are exacerbated by the absence both of open networks of general trust, where individuals can freely express their distress, and of transcendent ethical values that give real meaning to work, and to life itself.

No other country as prosperous suffers such a high rate of suicide. Three times as many people die by suicide in Japan as die in automobile accidents. Global statistics compiled by the World Health Organization estimate the suicide rate for Japanese men at 36.5 per 100,000, about double the comparable rate for American males (17.6 per 100,000) or for South Koreans (18.8). The only nations that report higher rates are former Soviet republics, such as Estonia, Slovenia, Ukraine, and Belarus, where vodka and gunplay commingle amid political and economic chaos. The rate is also high in Hungary, where suicide is linked with drunkenness. Japanese certainly drink as much as, if not more, than others, but have no access to handguns, which are strictly banned. Yet no other member of the "rich man's club" of the Organization of Economic Cooperation and Development reports suicide levels even close to Japan's,[3] though the Finns—the dour, unsmiling, and repressed people, often labeled the "Japanese of Europe"—have a male suicide rate that, at 34.6 per 100,000, is also high. When women are included, Japan's total suicide rate is 25.1 per 100,000, because far fewer Japanese females choose to take their own lives.

The decade-long rise in suicide, which reflects the nation's economic turmoil, has prompted social critics as well as psychiatrists to declare a national emergency. "The country is at war," declared Hiroyuki Itsuki, one of Japan's best-selling authors, who admits in one of his most popular works that he twice considered killing himself. "This is a national crisis, a crisis of the heart. People view their lives too lightly. Japanese do not respect their own lives and so do not respect each other. The suicide rate is high because people do not have God in their hearts."[4]

Hanging and jumping in front of a commuter train are the most common forms of Japanese self-annihilation—Westerners often prefer drug overdoses—but the Internet suicide trend, first detected in 2003, is perhaps the most disturbing new phenomenon. Victims of these Internet suicide pacts "are lost and confused," the Tokyo psychiatrist Rika Kayama said. "The long-held direction and goals of Japanese society are collapsing around them. Japanese adults used to be able to say to their children that if you try very hard at school or at work, you'll see the reward. But adults can no longer say that, because in many ways it is no longer true." Another psychiatrist suggested young Japanese had little understanding of the reality death imposes. "They think it's an extension of a game in cyberworld," he said.

Not only does suicide in Japan carry little of the religious stigma associated with it in the West, but some forms, like *seppuku*, ritual disembowelment with a short sword, were glorified in the samurai period as a means of expressing fealty to one's master. Even in the twentieth century, some of the nation's most important novelists and writers—men like Osamu Dazai, Yukio Mishima, and Yasunari Kawabata—killed themselves while still at the height of their literary powers. No other advanced industrial nation seems so resigned to such a high rate of suicide among its people. "Japanese today do not know who they are," says Itsuki. "If asked to identify themselves, they can only give a job title or a company name."[5]

The character of suicide victims has changed markedly. Thirty years ago, when the country was growing smartly, the very young and the very old were the most likely to take their own lives. Today, those over sixty still constitute the highest number of suicide victims, mainly because elderly women decide they no longer want to be a "burden" on their families or suffer declining health. Suicide among youths twenty and under has actually declined sharply.

Instead, those now most at risk come from Japan's postwar "baby boom" generation—men in their forties and fifties—the vital center of any society. Suicide rates have doubled in this group. Today they account for one in three suicides, or more than eleven thousand in 2003 alone. Police estimate that 25 percent of all suicide victims took their lives because of "economic or livelihood problems." More than half were committed by the jobless.

Yukio Saito launched the nation's first telephone hotline to counsel those pondering suicide more than thirty years ago, in 1971. His *Inochi no Denwa* service, housed in offices above his Tokyo rectory, logs more than twenty-six thousand phone calls each year from troubled Japanese desperate to find a sympathetic ear. A courtly, soft-spoken Lutheran minister who likes to don woolen vests in winter and would not seem out of place in a shingled New England parish hall, Saito told me his hotline acts like a barometer measuring national anxiety. In the early days, one in every four clients was a teenager. Now, it is "middle-aged men who are besieged," he says. Calls often come from wives worried about their husbands, men whose guaranteed jobs are no longer secure, whose homes usually are worth much less than what they originally paid as land prices tumble, and whose prospects for a stress-free retirement now seem jeopardized.

"In Japan, people are lonely and isolated these days," Saito said, "and people can't find others who can listen to them."

A middle-aged man has no way of working through the frustrations he endures in his office life, Saito told me, and that is a major cause of emotional distress. In a culture where men don't know and have never been taught how to open up emotionally and communicate with others, they have learned instead that silence is golden, and *gaman*, or endurance, prized. "When father comes home, he just wants his rice bowl," Saito told me. "A Japanese man believes that the beauty of being a man is to be silent. Naturally, he doesn't complain about work at the office, because he risks being fired. He doesn't complain about his poor relationship with his children when he comes home. He has been taught to be silent and patient, so he just sits in silence and drinks his beer."

Saito sees a close parallel between the *hikikomori* phenomenon and the epidemic of suicide: teens are escaping the pressure of entrance exams and school bullying, while their fathers are escaping comparable anguish in the office. Neither father nor son can openly express his fears or frustrations. "The father rarely appears in the house. He is always running away from his responsibilities, saying, 'I am too busy,'" Saito said. "When he comes home, he doesn't communicate." This reluctance to open up exacerbates the tendency to suicide. "It isn't just the *hikikomori*," Saito said, somberly. "As a people, we Japanese are socially withdrawn."

*　　*　　*

Men become desperate enough to end their lives for other reasons, too. Life insurance companies actually give them incentive. They usually pay out premiums to the families of suicide deaths. In the United States, evidence of suicide usually voids any insurance payout, but Japan's Supreme Court in 2004 supported the family of a company president who hanged himself after designating his firm as the beneficiary.[6] Some insurers now stipulate that death benefits will not be paid in the first twelve months after a policy is signed.

Suicide victims also find in death a reverence and comfort that have usually eluded them in life. So important is work in shaping a man's identity that when a company confronts some difficulty or scandal, managers are expected to apologize—as Hajimu Asada did—with their lives, according to Tomotake Yamazaki, a workplace counselor and therapist. "People view dying as a consequence of their shame as a virtuous act," he told me. "It's a way of taking responsibility for causing trouble. Politicians and businessmen act the same way. Dying is better than living in shame."

Yamazaki helps large computer and information technology firms design programs to help employees cope with depression and anxiety. He is also a member of a special Health Ministry committee that was impaneled to study workplace stress. At fifty-six, he identifies with Japanese "boomers" unnerved by the nation's long slowdown. "To the corporate warrior, dying seems a natural act," Yamazaki said late one evening, as we sat in his clinic in Tokyo's Shibuya district, where Western-styled Muzak is piped into the conference rooms to calm the shattered nerves of his clients. "Many people think it's easier to commit suicide than to continue living" because of the urgent need to keep up appearances and never admit failure.

The very characteristics that make Japanese such devoted workers—punctiliousness, selfless obedience, a serious commitment to their labor, and a strong sense of responsibility and mutual dependence—now make them prime candidates for depression, or worse. These men rarely say no to a boss's outrageous demands or seek counseling for sleeplessness.

Rapid technological change, an accelerating pace of work, and the threat of corporate mergers and layoffs continuously buffet these middle-aged workers Yamazaki counsels each day. Mergers can prove especially stressful. Middle managers who have always worked in a single, rigid system find it difficult to adapt when separate firms combine; former rivals often refuse to work with one another after a consolidation. It is rare for such cultural clashes to become visible, but such a classic case became public in April 2002 after three large Tokyo banks merged to form Mizuho Bank, the world's largest. Each refused to permit one central group to mesh together the software needed to allow the new firm to integrate three discrete sets of database and account information. So on its very first day of business as a newly integrated bank, hundreds of thousands of customers found that their ATM cards wouldn't work and millions of automatic payments were misrouted. The snafus created weeks of commercial chaos and corporate embarrassment.[7] A merger also creates fear that some staff members will be let go, so the *sarariman* who once felt sure of having a job for life now feels a desperate need to prove his usefulness.

As companies cut workers, those who remain have to work harder just to keep up, and some have difficulty embracing the new technologies be-

ing introduced to boost efficiency. Computers, faxes, and e-mail accelerate the pace of office life, generating yet more stress and anxiety. "These
middle-aged managers in their forties and fifties aren't used to computers, and it is very difficult for them to ask younger people for help . . . It's
a matter of pride," Yamazaki said. "The younger workers don't volunteer
to help their bosses, either. This becomes another major trigger for depression."

A decade ago, perhaps 40 percent of the workforce suffered from
stress, Yamazaki reckons. "Now it's more like 70 percent." He told me
that one in every four Japanese workers is depressed, overworked, or on
the verge of a classic mental breakdown. "A decade ago, we didn't talk
about depression in our corporate training seminars," Yamazaki said. "We
taught managers how to motivate. Now we have to teach corporate managers how to keep their workers alive."

Stress "was just accepted," when Japan was booming, he said. "No one
really paid attention." But after the economy turned deeply sluggish, "the
problem of stress became far more visible. The subliminal forces, if you
like, came to the surface . . . Medical costs grew higher as soon as economic growth began to fade away." Formal epidemiological surveys also
show a strong correlation between economic stress and suicide, especially among middle-aged males.[8] Yamazaki's own panel found that suicide rates rise significantly within a firm during the year after the ratio of
operating-profit-per-employee falls.

Others studies document the depths of Japanese depression. One released in October 2002 estimates that 60 percent of female employees
and 50 percent of males in small and medium-sized companies suffer
some depression, while 16 percent of females and 11 percent of males
said they suffer from moderate or severe depression. Another study
estimated that 64,000 people per day consulted specialists or were hospitalized for mood disorder in 1999, double the rate recorded in 1993—
whether it was because more people were depressed, or because more
recognized the symptoms, isn't clear. And children can be affected, too.
A study by researchers at Hokkaido University found that one in four
Japanese junior high school students is depressed, more than their coun-

terparts in the United States or Europe. Said one teacher, "Children are worn-out dishrags."

The World Health Organization estimates that Japan is second only to the United States in its number of depressed people, but Japan has only ten thousand psychiatrists for a nation of 120 million. More than any other nation, Japan warehouses its mentally ill patients in hospitals, usually private, profit-making facilities, rather than find ways to place them back into society. The average stay at mental institutions is also the longest in the world, 406 days.[9]

Yamazaki believes the growing incidence of depression and suicide demonstrates that Japan now faces a decisive turning point as it moves from being "a mother-centered society," in which everyone was protected and supported, to what he calls "a father-centered society," where individualism and individual initiative matters far more. "These days, if you don't have your own individual strength, you cannot survive." In trying to accommodate this transition, men, he says, experience far more stress than women.

As severe as depression seems to be, workers tend to avoid seeking help because they fear being punished for admitting their symptoms. Some are kept from promotion, shunned, or even tossed out of their jobs for seeking help. The vast majority of employees don't dare be seen entering or leaving the "counseling rooms" Yamazaki helps the companies set up. No wonder the Health Ministry estimates that only 25 percent of those who feel they have experienced bouts of depression actually seek medical treatment. Of those officially recognized as having died from work-related stress, some 70 percent never consulted a doctor or counselor before taking their lives.[10]

No matter how worn down they may be, most Japanese male workers will not even take the vacation days to which they are legally entitled. For even after contributing eighty hours or more of unpaid overtime in a month, taking a single day's vacation could jeopardize an employee's career. "If you take vacation, you will lose your job," Yamazaki told me. "That may not literally be true, but that is the fear most workers express." An employee's absence gives others a chance to steal his work because a typical Japanese company doesn't clearly define individual responsibilities or create transparent reporting structures: "There is intense competition in the firm. With times so difficult, your colleagues may pull your legs out from under you." This obsessive devotion to work may explain why the government has built so many national holidays into the calendar—nearly one each month, which ensure that offices are forced to shut down at least occasionally.

Of course, the ultimate corporate sacrifice—death on the job—is also prototypically Japanese. The word *karoshi* was coined to describe death from overwork. Symptoms can include heart attack, stroke, or cerebral hemorrhage. In fiscal 2002, a record 317 cases of death from overwork were formally recognized by the national worker's compensation system, in addition to a record forty-three *karoshi*-related suicides.

Naturally, such fatigue and overwork contribute to family dysfunction. Because young fathers come home late most every night, they seldom see their young children, a form of psychological abandonment many children recall with bitterness as they grow older—especially women, whose urge to develop closer emotional ties with their fathers is thwarted by their continual absence. Weekends aren't much better, with "sleeping"—according to opinion polls—consistently surpassing even golf as a Japanese male's single most popular weekend pastime, an activity which displaces family shopping trips or outings to the park. It is nearly inconceivable to imagine a modern Japanese father leaving work early to watch his son's soccer or Little League baseball game.

Among married couples, physical contact is so infrequent that some of Japan's leading homebuilders now report that more than one in three custom homes is built with separate bedrooms for husband and wife. "It's hard for Americans to believe," said Takao Sano of Mitsui Homes, one of the nation's largest homebuilders. "But forty percent of our customers ask us to separate the bedrooms." Often the couple is in their late forties, Sano said, and usually the wife asks for her own room.

"They say they don't want to bother each other," Sano went on. "Or the wife says she goes to bed early while the husband likes to stay up late" or only returns from work after midnight. What starts as a convenience often becomes routine. Responding to increased demand, the company now provides three different floor plans that offer separate bedrooms for each spouse. The firm's own surveys also show that 94 percent of couples over the age of sixty don't sleep together in the same room.

Natsuki Nagata, a researcher on sex and marriage, says couples rarely talk about their feelings or sexual longings, and often refuse to realize that theirs is a troubled relationship. In a society where husbands often don't come home from work, families don't eat together, and young students stay late at cram schools, "sexless couplehood is becoming a new model of modern life," she told me. "Maybe the traditional family just doesn't work anymore." Psychiatrist Teruo Abe, a pioneer in the field of Japanese sexuality, told one newspaper he counseled 165 sexless patients during 2004, nearly nine times the number he saw in 1993.[11]

*　　*　　*

Americans today work far more than most Europeans, and official labor statistics suggest that the long days the Japanese put in are not exceptional: 1,970 hours per year in the manufacturing industries, for instance, or slightly fewer than the 1,986 hours logged by comparable American workers each year. These statistics do not, however, reflect the unpaid or "service" overtime Japanese workers are forced to perform. One survey by Japan's trade unions shows that half of all union members perform unpaid overtime, and the unions claim government could create more than 1.5 million new jobs if it rigorously enforced its own overtime rules. Excess overtime is even more of an acute problem in white-collar professions, where working late is considered a badge of pride, a sign of how essential that worker really is to the organization.

In Kasumigaseki, the seat of the bureaucracy in Tokyo, workers routinely roll out cots for a few hours of sleep during the busiest times of the year, as when budgets are being finalized, instead of going home. In my office building, workers at an architectural design studio routinely worked until three or four in the morning five or six nights a week. "Being exhausted is considered a virtue," the psychiatrist Masao Miyamoto told me, because Japanese accept the masochistic nature of their society. It is hardly unusual to find workers sleeping on the job or napping at their desks in mid-afternoon to compensate for sleep deprivation.

Plenty of anecdotal evidence exists, moreover, to suggest that Japanese stay late at their desk because they lack for attractive alternatives, compared to Europeans, who relish their thirty-five-hour work weeks and six-week vacations. "Japanese accept that foreigners can take vacations and that we can not," Miyamoto said. Japanese also seem resigned to living in cramped apartments that are not conducive to relaxation, and to the high costs associated with tourism and travel.

The reluctance of Japanese white-collar workers to leave their desks before nightfall, whether or not there is work to complete, has become the standard explanation for Japan's reluctance to switch to daylight saving time. Pushing back sundown and setting the clock ahead in summer gives Westerners more time for outdoor leisure after work and saves energy. In Japan, an implicit fear suggests that a time change will chain office workers to their desks until 10 P.M. or later, since no employee will dare leave while the sun shines.

Miyamoto traces the history of Japan's "overwork psychosis" to the Tokugawa period, when each provincial warlord was commanded to appear in Edo, the capital, every second year, along with a vast entourage of advisers, samurai, horsemen, and other members of his court. The grandiose yet obsessively precise protocols surrounding these official pilgrimages demanded that officials visit other lords along their route, present each vassal with elaborate gifts, attend formal banquets, and perform other ceremonial duties. Provincial leaders competed with one another in order to display their wealth and lordly authority. Yet preparing for and then completing these arduous biennial expeditions became so time-consuming that potential rivals never had sufficient energy to plot a coup.

Miyamoto's radical view—that overwork was consciously engineered into the Japanese system to displace or discourage resistance—was too extreme for most workplace counselors, who simply suggest that Japanese have been socialized to emphasize working over "being." Tsukasa Mizusawa, who treats burn-out victims and alcoholics in his own treat-

ment center, faulted Japan's "codependent society." Workers loyally sacrifice themselves for their companies, and families routinely accept that
the male adult will not play the full part in family life expected in other
societies. "In Japan, unless you have a real sense of being enmeshed with
others, dependent on others, then you cannot feel secure. We're still a
country where it's difficult for each person to live for himself," Mizusawa
said. "That has been the foundation of our society. That makes us codependent in a way that Americans raised in a culture of independence
have great difficulty understanding." If some Americans tend to put their
families above all else, many Japanese put their bosses ahead of all
others.

*　　*　　*

Burn-out, alcoholism, depression, and suicide can be strongly linked to
common causes, yet Mizusawa says that most Japanese refuse to see
them as related. They prefer to insist that each phenomenon is nothing
more than a failure of individual will, rather than any reflection of wider
social dysfunction. "They think it's a lack of effort or of ability. They don't
say, 'Oh, he has an alcohol sickness' . . . They just say, 'He drinks too
much' or 'He's relieving the stress from work.' There is a lot of prejudice
and misunderstanding."

When Mizusawa translated into Japanese *Happiness Is a Choice*, a
book about depression written by two American physicians, he altered
the title to read *If You Stop Being Depressed, You'll Be Happy*. By putting
the title into active voice, he wanted readers to understand that they
had the power to transform their own lives. "Telling people they don't
have to be depressed, that they can choose to do something about it is
terribly important. You have to give people the option—that they actually
can do something to feel better." According to Mizusawa, Japanese tend
to be passive anyway, and depressives often refuse help because they
have low self-esteem and worry more about others than themselves. De-
risively terming this trait "psychological castration," Miyamoto said, "The
sarariman knows he cannot challenge because he is afraid. All he can do

is say, Okay, *shikata ga nai*, there's nothing to be done. Helpless, helpless like a little baby—that is the kind of stance he takes. He hopes that somebody will somehow come along who is going to take care of him. To me, it's a very infantile position."

When I reported Miyamoto's view to Mizusawa, he expressed more sympathy for the *sarariman*'s confined life. "If the father goes to a psychiatric clinic for treatment of depression, do you really think his daughter will not encounter any problems before marriage?" Mizusawa asked, referring to the likelihood that the parents of a potential husband might hire a private investigator to "check up" on the potential in-laws. "Yes, there may be some prejudice in the United States when it comes to depression, but compared to Japan it is much less severe."

Fear is also abetted by ignorance. Tetsuya, forty-two, told me he had literally never heard the word *utsubyo*, or "depression," until he was diagnosed with it seven months before. A graduate of the prestigious Keio University and a sales manager for one of Japan's best trading houses, he became anxious and sleepless after being transferred from an outside sales job to a strategic management group, where his bosses were fifteen years older.

"I remember that he just couldn't sleep," Yuriko, his wife, recalled.

I met the couple one night in an unusual encounter Yamazaki arranged on my behalf so that I could hear a patient describe the stress he commonly endures. "We always take one week off for summer vacation, but he could not stop thinking about having to go back to work the following Monday. He was very unhappy. He was anxious. His appetite slacked off. And he would wake up at four or five o'clock in the morning. His eyes would open, but he could not drag himself out of bed." Lying on the futon next to his on the tatami-mat floor of their Yokohoma apartment, Yuriko could sense her husband's growing apprehension.

Tetsuya refused to acknowledge any problem, however, and for months would not bring himself to see a doctor. "I can honestly tell you that the only reason I went to see a doctor is that I thought it would make Yuriko happy," he said. "She just kept insisting."

When the doctor diagnosed Tetsuya's depression, "I really couldn't understand what he was talking about," Tetsuya told me. "I thought that I was being lazy or listless. I blamed myself for being a loafer. I walked out of the clinic and, I'll honestly tell you, I thought, How dare this guy listen to what I said . . . and then diagnose me as depressed?"

The doctor immediately put Tetsuya on Paxil, the first of the new generation of selective serotonin reuptake inhibitor (SSRI) antidepressants to be made legal in Japan. But Tetsuya kept insisting to everyone that he would continue going to work.

The breaking point came during a four-day business trip to Osaka, when Tetsuya called his wife four or five times a day wondering why he was on the trip and what exactly he was supposed to do. One evening, Tetsuya called and told his wife he was going to rent a car and go drinking with an old friend from college.

"I thought, Going out drinking by car? That made me very worried," Yuriko remembered. She thought her husband might be thinking of suicide, and tried to call family friends in Osaka, but found no one around. She kept calling Tetsuya's cell phone every fifteen minutes, but no one answered. She thought of calling the police in Osaka to launch a manhunt.

Finally at 3:30 in the morning, Tetsuya answered his cell phone, explaining to his wife that the friend had passed out in the car. When Tetsuya returned, Yuriko insisted he take time off and see a therapist.

Yamazaki, who knew the human resources manager in Tetsuya's company, recalled his first meeting with Tetsuya. "When I asked him, 'How are you?' he said, 'Good or bad, I don't really understand my condition, I don't really understand what it means, good or bad.' He said, 'I don't want to take a rest.'

" 'Why?' "

" 'Because I'm lazy, I'm loafing. I don't want to be lazy so I don't want to take off.'"

"No matter how hard I explained about depression, he didn't understand," the therapist said. "Finally, I told him, 'You are tired. Anyone can get tired. You should take a rest.'"

In the end, Tetsuya agreed to take an extended break, but wondered why everyone insisted he stay away from work. Every Monday he said to his wife, "I'll stay off just this week, but go back next week"—only to decide the following Monday to take yet more time off. He finally returned after six months leave—to find that he had been transferred back to the sales department. Although Tetsuya's managers never said anything directly, they were reluctant to promise him new accounts, and Tetsuya felt that they doubted that he could perform adequately.

Though his company's sales offices span the globe, few people in the headquarters actually understood the nature of Tetsuya's illness. "Even in the human resources department, people don't have a clue," he said. "They don't know what depression is or how to judge it. People come by and slap you on the shoulder and say, 'Gambaro' [keep trying, or persevere], but I could feel these people had absolutely no idea what I was going through. Nobody talks about it. Most managers feel you have depression because you aren't tough enough to gut things out."

He had taken a valuable lesson from his break, Tetsuya told me. "When you think of life as if you are walking a tightrope, as long as you are walking, no matter how slowly, you can see ahead and keep a pace, and view the distant horizon. But as soon as you stop and look down, you see the bottom and get frightened. When that happens, you end up having to look at your own life . . .

"Many people don't even have a chance to stop and look at their lives with some perspective," Tetsuya said. "At least I got that chance."

*   *   *

This reluctance of most Japanese even to discuss depression—and how it might be overcome—makes it more difficult to combat the illness. Just as efforts to treat AIDS in Africa collide against brick walls of denial, manufacturers of Paxil faced similar challenges after their drug was legalized for sale in Japan in November 2000. How could they market a drug to treat an estimated 6 million sufferers of a disease no one talks about?

It is a sign of the times that now in Japan people can say that their heart, or kokoro, has come down with a cold. In its effort to introduce the

Western notion of depression, the drug industry uses this euphemism to replace the word *utsubyo,* which had been used in mental hospitals to describe intense manic-depressive disorder as well as to describe less intense, Western-style forms of depression. "In this country, depression hasn't been appropriately recognized," explained Koji Nakagawa, who headed the effort to introduce Paxil into the Japanese market. "The biggest difference between selling this drug in Japan and in other countries was the attitude of the patients."

Like Prozac, the SSRI Paxil improves the flow of serotonin, a chemical thought to help control mood, through the brain. GlaxoSmithKline, the pharmaceutical giant, invested more than a decade in clinical trials to prove the efficacy of this new class of antidepressant among Japanese patients, but Nakagawa admits marketing was also crucial. "Japanese patients have a strong sense of stigma about depression. They reject the notion that a patient should go to a psychiatric doctor for treatment of their depression," he said. Some two-thirds of 1,500 people the company surveyed said that they "definitely" would not want others to know they were feeling depressed, while more than half, 56 percent, thought that seeking a physician's help for depression was "very unusual."

"There's a great deal of prejudice," Nakagawa continued. "Most people think that if you go to a psychiatric counselor you are really mentally disturbed." Such attitudes were once common in the United States, before the country was transformed into a "Prozac nation," where housewives and celebrities openly proclaim their devotion to antidepressants, and where chemical treatments rather than "talk therapy" have become standard. Moreover, in the Japanese culture, sadness, silence, and suffering are considered inevitable: Japanese love to view cherry blossoms because of their evanescence; and few Japanese fables, the clinical psychologist Hayao Kawai notes, have happy endings.[12]

Still reluctant to write the word *utsubyo* on a patient's chart, doctors sometimes describe an illness as "autonomic imbalance" or a "menopausal disorder." Even when they do specify *utsubyo,* many patients refuse to accept the diagnosis, fearing they will be fired or lose status in their company. Many Japanese now engage in "doctor shopping," bouncing from pharmacologist to acupuncturist to Chinese herb dispensary, hoping to find one who can relieve their crushing mental fatigue.

Faced with these realities, GlaxoSmithKline launched the sort of public service–style campaign it might have hoped government would undertake: a direct-to-consumer advertising fusillade on television and in national newspapers. It is easy to criticize the drugmakers for their use of such sophisticated advertising techniques to peddle pills. But the necessity for some sort of public conversation about depression and suicide is all too obvious on rail and subway platforms in Tokyo: guardrails have been put up on some lines to prevent men from jumping on the tracks in front of trains and disrupting rush hour; on other platforms, giant mirrors have been installed so that a potential jumper must first look at himself before leaping.

The GSK ads showed average Japanese—a student, a businessman, a housewife, a retiree—describing their fatigue or inability to sleep, backache, or feelings of anxiety, and suggested that there was treatment to overcome these symptoms. The ads directed potential patients to a toll-free hotline and a Web site, www.utsu.jp, where they could find further information or reference to a physician. The ads and the Web site offered only the tiniest hint that a pharmaceutical company was sponsoring them. "We are trying to lower the bar, in terms of getting people to go to a doctor to seek help and to try and clear away the negative image toward this disease," Nakagawa said. "Our goal is to change minds and change the image of this disease, and give sufferers hope that they can be treated."

In spite of the nation's long reluctance to discuss depression, the response to the drugmaker's campaign was dramatic. Within days of the launch, thousands of adults were calling the GSK depression hotline. The Web site also registered lots of hits. In its first full year on the Japanese market, sales of Paxil reached 12 billion yen, or $96.5 million, in 2001; and by 2003 sales increased to $298 million, or nearly equivalent, on a per capita basis, to American sales.[13]

GSK's approach fits neatly into the sales culture of the Japanese medical establishment, which likes to load up patients with medications.

Doctors are free to sell drugs directly to their patients and earn big prof-its this way. Drug companies conduct hundreds of seminars across the country to describe the uses and benefits of their drugs, and the drug in-dustry's sales force is a constant presence in doctors' offices. The pay-ment schedule of the national health insurance system also aids drugmakers since a psychiatrist gets no more reimbursement for a fifty-minute counseling session with a patient than for a quick, three-minute drive-by to fill a prescription.

The medical establishment remains remarkably resistant to calls for expanded counseling services and psychotherapy. Unlike the United States, where clinical social workers and psychologists as well as psy-chiatrists receive state licenses, the Japanese government does not officially recognize nonphysicians in the mental health field. To get reim-bursement for patient care, a clinical psychologist must work "under the supervision" of a licensed M.D. and usually is required to give that physi-cian a percentage of his fees, an arrangement many psychologists find de-meaning. Until the late 1990s, a clinical psychologist did not even need a college degree to practice; now he requires only an undergraduate de-gree, and reimbursement schedules remain meager. Some clinical psy-chologists, like Yuichi Hattori, find it easier to work outside the insurance system, while others have little choice but to accept their second-class status.

"We need many, many clinical psychologists in Japan. We are behind because of the medical doctors," said Hayao Kawai, president of the As-sociation of Japanese Clinical Psychology and one of the nation's most in-fluential therapists. "The medical doctors have a great deal of money, very strong contact with politicians and the ruling party, and they are strongly opposed to psychologists. They don't want to lose any of their patients."

*   *   *

There is no more pervasive sense of denial in Japanese culture than around the issue of alcoholism. A night of drinking often seems the most popular national pastime for men, along with playing *pachinko* and watching TV. And binge drinking is widely accepted as "stress relief" after a hard day at the office.

There is no better place to get a feel for the drunken, boisterous mobs that populate Tokyo after dark than in the sprawling Shinjuku station around midnight, when tens of thousands of commuters, goggle-eyed and plastered, stagger onto the platforms to catch the last rides home to distant suburbs.

Near one stairwell, a well-dressed woman vomits in front of a vending machine. At another entrance, a fifty-something *sarariman* in a trench coat keels over and collapses on the steps leading up to the railway platform. A drunken colleague flails wildly, trying to help him up. About seventy-five thousand passengers—the size of a sold-out NFL football stadium—swarm this station's twenty-four platforms shortly before service ends at 12:45 A.M., and officials of the Japan Railway estimate that at least 60 percent are drunk.

"During the holidays, it's more like eighty percent," Hideki Okazaki, a vice manager for East Japan Railway told me. "It's one of the major problems we face." Once a day, on average, a trainman is kicked or assaulted by an abusive drunk; and during the holiday season before January 1, when Japanese attend nightly *bonenkai* parties to "forget the year," the railroad puts on extra security guards. One railway, the Keio line, actually introduced "women only" railcars for late-night trains, in order to keep drunken men from groping or sexually assaulting female passengers.

"Every night I work here I'm scared," said one police officer posted inside the station as a raucous mob poured through the turnstiles, the din reverberating along distant concourses. These nighttime mêlées are at odds with the traditional image of Japanese as introverted, meek, and nearly silent. Alcohol seems to induce a personality transplant, allowing a man's angry "inner" soul to surface. In truth, drunken violence is actually rare, and nearly everyone gets home safely in the end.

Japan at night resembles a college fraternity house in which booze remains a key social lubricant, especially for adults. Cementing relationships over a bottle of saké is always considered appropriate. Less tongue-tied and inhibited then, Japanese can speak their *honne*, or true feelings, yet still be able to resort to *tatemae*, their public "face," to deny those same feelings when sober the next day.

Only in Japan is it customary for someone to pour a drink for his companion rather than for himself, a ritual that tends to emphasize the social aspects of drinking, says Shinji Shimizu, who teaches at Nara Women's University and specializes in alcoholism. Men, he said, are unable to establish a relationship, much less argue or apologize, without drinking. "What matters is not the alcohol, but the human relationships," which is why Japanese pay so much notice to how much and how fast their companions imbibe.[14]

Whether in the fashionable neighborhood of Setagaya, or in an older neighborhood like Kanda, it is common to see red-faced drunks in expensive suits careening down the street late at night swinging their briefcases and giggling. On subways and suburban-bound trains, their jelly limbs sway uncontrollably as they droop from the overhead straps. In the streets around Shinjuku, young people who miss the last trains curl up in heaps of newspapers to sleep off their binges. Others check into "capsule hotels" where they sleep in narrow pods.

There is, however, little hard data on alcoholism, as if the medical community does not want to quantify what everyone knows. A 2001 nutrition survey by the Health Ministry estimated there were over two million alcoholics in Japan. Previously, the ministry had published official figures showing that only 17,100 suffered from the disease.[15] While alcohol consumption is decreasing in most of the rest of the industrial world, it is still rising in Japan. Over the past three decades, per capita alcohol consumption has risen 20 percent in Japan, according to OECD statistics, while it has fallen in Italy, France, Canada, and the United States. Only in the United Kingdom has the rate of alcohol consumption grown more quickly than in Japan.[16] Japanese today drink about as much on average as Americans do, but because many more Japanese women are teetotalers, some studies estimate that Japanese men in their fifties actually drink more than twice as much as their white American contemporaries.

Mizusawa, who specializes in alcohol addiction, said that Japanese "just don't regard alcohol as a drug. We doctors and social workers are very concerned, but society isn't really very interested. Denial is very strong."

Corporate America has launched aggressive measures to reduce drug and alcohol abuse among employees, fearing workplace injuries and declining productivity. Mothers Against Drunk Driving campaigned to raise the legal drinking age and increase penalties for drunk driving. Treatment centers like the Betty Ford Center help patients conquer their alcohol dependency. In Japan, by contrast, bosses often force their subordinates to drink, while vending machines sell beer and saké to teenagers. Beverage companies have also developed new beverages that combine fruit juices, carbonated water, and *shochu*, a distilled alcohol similar to vodka, to appeal to young drinkers and women, much like the premixed margaritas that American firms have developed and that are available at convenience stores.

Japan's embrace of alcohol dates to feudal times, Mizusawa said. "Only the super-rich and those of high status could make and drink saké" in that era, since one needed a coveted allotment of rice to brew the liquor. "To have a chance to drink saké was a rare honor, and you could never refuse a glass when it was offered."

Likewise, in contemporary Japan, "to refuse to accept saké from someone, especially from your boss, is a terrible insult," he continued. "If you don't accept a drink from your boss, it can really damage your career. The boss will say, 'How dare you not accept my saké?' Often he just keeps pouring," to test his subordinates' endurance.

Japanese face a genetic handicap, too. Lacking a particular enzyme, many don't metabolize their liquor as well as Caucasians do, and become inebriated far more quickly. They often get flush-faced. "Only sixty percent of Japanese can drink as much as Western races," Mizusawa said. "Somewhere between thirty and forty percent actually get sick from drinking. They drink, throw up, and drink again."

In recent years, a new term has crept into the Japanese language: *akuru-hara*, or alcohol harassment, which describes a company worker being forced to get drunk even though drinking makes him sick. Thirty-six percent of those surveyed by the Health Ministry said they had been forced to drink more than they wanted.

Koji, a twenty-seven-year-old engineer at Toshiba, the electronics giant, described a weekend trip he took with colleagues to Kyoto, a corporate junket to enhance group solidarity. "As soon as we arrived at the train station, they started feeding us beer and saké, whether we wanted to drink or not. We were drunk all day in Kyoto, and a younger worker like me is not supposed to refuse the boss's offer to drink. The only way to avoid drinking was to pretend to fall asleep in the middle of the evening drinking party," Koji recalled.

"Next morning, first thing, there was beer and saké set out at each breakfast table. I just couldn't get away from this. I couldn't refuse it . . . and what really stings is that I had to help pay for this trip out of my own salary. Whether I like it or not, it's almost a duty to attend, and it's not pleasant at all."

Complaints of alcohol harassment are rising in the corporate world, but intervention is sometimes difficult. "People just don't accept the reality that we have a problem with drinking," Mizusawa said. Few companies want to acknowledge a drinking problem in their midst. "They're afraid it will hurt their reputation.

"I don't love America," he said one afternoon, discussing the bruised corporate psyche of Japanese males, "but one of the reasons I admire the U.S. is that people there are flexible. When someone has a problem, as long as he's responsible and tries to make an effort to get cured, people applaud him. The American way of thinking is that you'll be accepted as long as you try. If he expresses a will to survive, society supports him as a survivor.

"In Japan, what happens? A person who is a hostage in war and survives feels shame. He'd rather die by his own hand than face the shame of being a survivor. It is very difficult to overcome a disease and be accepted. You can't just go home and return to your life. It won't happen. Our society says, 'Don't make a mistake. Don't take a risk. Don't take responsibility. Just go along with the others and procrastinate.' That's the culture."

There is some hopeful evidence that change is slowly occurring. In 2002, the Education Ministry announced that it would begin to teach about alcohol abuse. An Osaka District Court ruled that, in a hit-and-run accident where a teenage boy was killed, a fifty-two-year-old man was partially responsible for that death because he had urged the driver, a thirty-three-year-old subordinate, to get drunk. Also, liquor stores and vending machine owners are starting to block sales of alcohol and beer to underage customers. Still, according to Mizusawa, it will take many, many years for Japanese thinking to change.

"I never have to worry that I will lose my job," he said.

12.

On a bitterly cold, gunship-gray morning in January 1998, as snow flurries dusted the streets of downtown Seoul, Ahn Kye Sun stood outside the Housing & Commercial Bank along with hundreds of other Koreans bundled up in down jackets, woolen scarves, and knit caps. She was waiting to trade in her gold jewelry and help save her nation.

Fighting back tears, the sixty-one-year-old housewife handed over several rings and a small gold turtle—this last a sixtieth birthday present from her children. In exchange, she received a fistful of *won*, the nation's volatile paper currency, whose value had suddenly plummeted in international markets. "I just hope it can be of help to our country," she said of her tiny gesture. "Whatever little gold I have is all I've got, but I don't care. I've lived my life and I'm not too poor," she reflected. "Now it's time to give something back," she told a local correspondent.

Across the nation, a reverse gold rush was in full swing. Just one month prior, South Korea, not long before considered one of the world's wealthiest nations, had been forced to its knees to beg for a $58 billion bailout from the International Monetary Fund to stave off financial ruin. Humiliated by financial mismanagement, excess corporate borrowing, and a run on its currency carried out by cunning overseas speculators, citizens around the country were now mobilizing. Baseball stars turned in their trophies, school teachers sold off their gold keys. Top CEOs and private citizens found their way to department stores, crowded church basements, and banks to give up their gold and silver.

By melting the gold into bars and selling it abroad, Koreans hoped to fortify the value of their own paper currency and help the government accelerate repayment of the IMF loan. In just the first forty-eight hours of its campaign to "Collect Gold for the Love of Korea," the Housing Bank amassed more than 3,900 pounds of gold from more than 40,000 people. Korean churches also took up the banner. "We are urging our four million Church members to donate or sell their gold," said Pastor Kim Young-jo, a spokesman for the National Council of Churches.[1]

Within three weeks, the movement collected more than one billion dollars' worth of gold—some ninety tons—from more than 1.5 million ordinary Koreans. Within three months, a new, democratically elected president launched a major overhaul of South Korea's economic system, taking the first step to dismantle the closed, mercantilist, "developmental model," which, like Japan's, had earlier propelled its sprint to prosperity. Yet when faced with crisis, the administration of incoming President Kim Dae-jung's new government, very much unlike Japan, moved quickly to reverse thirty years of dogma. It encouraged foreigners to buy into the local economy and urged consumers to spend, not save. Kim acted swiftly to reduce the grasp of the nation's largest family-run conglomerates, known as *chaebol*, and forced highly indebted firms to declare bankruptcy and shut down. Kim's government also moved aggressively to sell off and recycle the assets held by failed banks as it imposed new labor laws to give companies more leeway to fire redundant workers.

These startling changes of policy yielded impressive results, quickly. In 2002, just four years after starting its radical transformation, South Korea fully paid off its IMF obligation. A domestic consumer sector long suppressed by government fiat was thriving—to the point where excessive credit card debt, not a surplus of savings, now posed the greatest challenge. Foreign investors now owned significant stakes in Korean banks and industries—and more than 40 percent of the equity market—compelling local firms to become more globally competitive. Once again the nation was recording strong GDP growth—averaging better than 7 percent annually. Flat panel TV sets, cellular telephones, and automobiles manufactured by South Korean firms began to win over consumers in the United States, Europe, and China long accustomed to buying Japanese. After suffering a near-death experience, the nation had miraculously revived itself. "When forced to do it differently, and break away from the Japanese model, the Koreans did it with gusto," I was told by James Rooney, a prominent business consultant in Seoul and eyewitness to this revolution.

I found—as did others of my colleagues who lived in Japan and traveled regularly to Seoul to report and write about this tumultuous period— the pace and scope of the reforms astounding. In a few short years, South Korea had boldly and decisively implemented the sort of sweeping reforms that Japan had consistently rejected as if resolutely choosing to shut out the sun.

No two Asian nations share such similar economic systems, social organizations, and cultural values as do Japan and South Korea. Both demand the hard work, discipline, and respect for elders they inherited from China's Confucianism. Both encourage organic "insider" networks bound by blood, school, regional, or social ties to share information, maintain economic control, and reduce transaction costs. Both rely on fiercely competitive educational systems and emphasize entrance examinations and testing. Relatively isolated and racially homogeneous, both look upon outsiders with suspicion. Both were cloistered for centuries from the Western world and its influences until that world inexorably intruded—first on Japan in 1853, with Commodore Perry's arrival; then on Korea, whose status as the "Hermit Kingdom" ended in the 1880s with the Japanese incursion, the arrival of Christian missionaries, and forced colonization shortly after the consolidation of Meiji power.

Latecomers to modernization and intensely xenophobic, both nations relied on strong state power to inculcate industrial might. Both developed coherent, coordinated strategies to stoke export-led growth. Both created strong state systems to guide investment decisions, set prices, protect cartels, and stabilize markets. Close cooperation between government and large corporate networks managed both economies in ways that boldly challenged the Anglo-Saxon convention that "arms length" transactions conducted by "free markets" are the most efficient way to organize an economy. In South Korea, as in Japan, the government orchestrated business activities more than it regulated them, because it believed that bureaucrats and corporate leaders should work hand in hand with politicians to deliver growth.

Both nations also implemented policies to keep foreigners at bay and used complex nontariff barriers—rigorous inspection procedures or mysterious distribution roadblocks—to block foreign goods. Both disdained any foreign involvement in the domestic economy.

In truth, South Korea had appropriated wholesale from Tokyo most of its ideas on how to create an advanced industrial economy during the administration of strongman Park Chung-hee, who led the nation from 1961 to 1979 and orchestrated its rapid modernization. For despite a frequently expressed antipathy for the Japanese, who had carried out a brutal, thirty-five-year colonial occupation of their country, Koreans routinely acknowledge their intellectual debt to Japan. The same innovative export-driven development model Japan pioneered helped an impoverished, resource-poor South Korea. Having lost half of its territory in the Korean War in 1954, it nevertheless emerged in the 1980s and 1990s as a "little tiger" of economic growth.

Similar these nations were in many ways, yet—when jolted by economic crisis—their paths dramatically diverged. In a strange and unexpected way, South Korea represented the elusive yardstick I was seeking to measure the elements missing from modern Japanese society.

*　　*　　*

As a resident of Japan who visited South Korea frequently, I found the social environment of the two nations starkly different. To walk through the streets of Seoul after some months in the confinement of Japan is to suck down pure oxygen, the people seeming much more communicative and expressive. Koreans are entrepreneurial risk-takers, while Japanese try to protect against risk. Koreans seem to accept individual responsibility for failure; Japanese try to shirk it. Korean citizens regularly take to the streets in protest to demand better corporate governance and greater accountability. Japanese civil society—the political space between government and the commercial world—remains dormant by contrast, co-opted and compromised by government subsidy. Patriotism and a sense of duty to their country have animated mass citizen movements in South Korea; in Japan, normal patriotic gestures and emotions—even the raising of the *Hinomaru*, or national flag, the red sun on its stark white field, or singing *Kimigayo*, the national anthem—are deemed shocking and controversial. I couldn't imagine that the same Japanese who could spend hours lingering in a line to buy a Louis Vuitton purse would ever line up in front of a bank branch on a frosty day to donate their gold and valuables for the sake of their country.

Nor does South Korean society exhibit the obvious signs of social fatigue so evident in Japan. I suspect that this absence, too, has something to do with the nation's eagerness to embrace rapid and effective change. South Korea exhibits few of Japan's social symptoms—the high level of male suicide, the rapidly shrinking population, the record-low birthrate, and the mysterious syndrome known as *hikikomori*; only the former's declining birthrate reflects Korean women's embrace of elements of Western feminism. The suicide rate is half Japan's.

Though I inquired frequently, Korean doctors reported no incidence of *hikikomori* among their patients. Among the community of psychiatrists in South Korea, only Si Hyung-lee, who practices at Samsung Hospital in Seoul, said that, while he had diagnosed a few hundred cases of what he described as "introverted social loners," he estimated that of these there were no more than twenty-five hundred in South Korea. These loners suffer symptoms far less aggressive than the socially withdrawn in Japan and do not, for instance, attack their parents. Another comparison is telling: virtually all the "loners," or *wittori*, identified in South Korea use the ubiquitous broadband Internet connections available in South Korea to exchange e-mail with friends, surf the Web, or "chat" in virtual chat rooms. By contrast, less than 10 percent of Japanese *hikikomori* use personal computers or the Internet, according to Dr. Tamaki Saito, the Japanese clinician who treats many such patients.[2] In addition, an estimated 70 percent of the Korean *wittori* maintain dialogue with their parents, while most *hikikomori* cut their ties. I could find no other public health agencies or psychiatrists who reported evidence of Japanese-style *hikikomori* in South Korea, and besides, a South Korean can seclude himself in his room only until his eighteenth birthday. Then, like all other South Korean men, he faces compulsory military duty.

Indeed, far from the social fatigue exhibited by most Japanese, who passively accept their fate and mutter *shikata ga nai* ("It can't be helped") whenever trouble looms, a lively and irrepressible new generation of South Koreans readily took to the streets in the last decades of the twentieth century to demand political accountability. They marched in protest, languished in prison, launched hunger strikes, and died in the streets to demand a democratic political process and an end to military rule. They dragged change from the bottom up, as demonstrated by the elections of the insurgent presidents Kim Dae-jung in 1997 and Roh Moo-hyun in 2002.

In addition, these exuberant young adults formed cutting-edge entrepreneurial companies, explored new frontiers of broadband connectivity, and pioneered new uses for devices like cellular telephones. Young Koreans seem empowered, personally and politically. Somehow these Koreans had developed looser forms of social networks and a greater sense of individualism and general trust than the Japanese.

While the entrenched elderly still held sway in Japan, a youth revolution had taken firm hold over Seoul. In 2003, South Korea even reported having achieved the world's highest penetration of broadband Internet access—nineteen per every hundred people, significantly higher than Japan's rate of four per hundred or than America's of 5.6. What Koreans called the "386" generation—those born in the 1960s, who studied in universities in the 1980s and were the first to use computers based on the 386 semiconductor chip popularized by Intel Corporation—had become the most influential in contemporary society. The victory of a progressive former labor lawyer like Roh in South Korea's presidential elections in December 2002—when the vote was clearly split along generational as well as ideological lines—was attributable to the energy and organizing drive of this younger generation and its outsized influence. In less than two decades, South Korea had rejected military dictatorship and built one of Asia's most dynamic and democratic societies despite the presence of Stalinist North Korea and its million-man army just a thirty-minute drive from downtown Seoul.[3]

*   *   *

Never was evidence of the stark contrast in national behavior—and competing attitudes toward trust—more on display than in the sweltering summer of 2002, when I watched as Japan and Korea cohosted the World Cup soccer tournament.

Little surprise that both nations used the games as the pretext for an orgy of new construction, spending millions to build new soccer stadiums and other public projects. Yet the Koreans seemed to focus their efforts just as much on the human side of the competition, not just on creating infrastructure. Foreigners visiting Seoul discovered to their delight that their Korean hosts used every excuse possible to meet and celebrate the tournament with the diverse array of soccer fans arriving from abroad, even organizing Korean cheering squads for teams unable to send large delegations of their own nationals to the tourney. Japanese citizens, by contrast, were constantly warned about the danger foreigners posed. Outsiders were usually portrayed as brawling roughnecks and drunken hooligans, rendered *fuuriganzu* in Japanese. Newspapers repeatedly carried stark warnings about the violent behavior to be expected of European soccer fans, and police were instructed to break up any spontaneous gathering of more than ten people on the street. As Koreans welcomed visitors from around the globe with open arms, in Japan local inns, hotels, and restaurants in many of the cities where World Cup matches were scheduled actually shut their doors rather than cater to potential foreign customers, so fearful were they of criminal mischief and violence—incidents of which never materialized.

Once the tournament got under way in the steamy Asian summer, thousands of young Koreans began to gather spontaneously in the streets to watch the matches on gigantic TV monitors and cheer on their "Red

Devils." They sponsored parties for tourists, practiced speaking foreign languages, and toasted their nation's vibrant rebirth after the IMF crisis. As the intensity of the games grew, the celebratory vibe of the outdoor parties took on a life of their own. Eventually, more than one million people, young and old alike, were converging on Seoul's City Hall plaza, the traditional site of noisy political protests, to wave red flags, drink beer, and cheer on their team.[4] "Dreams will come true!" became the Korean team's slogan; the fact that the plucky South Koreans made it to the final round of the tournament, with the help of a daring coach named Guus Hiddink imported from the Netherlands, only seemed to reaffirm the nation's new attitude of self-confidence and pride. No longer was South Korea just a poor "developing" nation; it was a prideful, wired, assertive, and influential leader that had boldly taken its place on the world stage, competing favorably against the world's best. The electric mood demonstrated to even apolitical young Koreans that the energy of their numbers could bring them influence and power.

"In the past, Korean young people never got together for big social gatherings," Jwajin Yun, then a twenty-two-year-old senior at Yonsei University, told me. "There were no rallies or group events. But as the excitement of the World Cup brought us together in the streets, as you saw millions of people jamming together to support our team, we began to realize we're really Korean. Together, we can make our own identity." Added her friend, Esther Yoon, another Yonsei senior, "It made us understand we young people have power, even power to change our society!"

Japan, by contrast, was deadly still. There were no street demonstrations. Police tried to break up any spontaneous parties. And the Japanese team crashed out before the semifinals.

*　　*　　*

Only a few months later, the groundswell of youthful Korean empowerment and vitality moved beyond the sports arena and proved decisive in helping Roh claim his presidential victory. Armies of young "netizens," wielding cell phones and employing sophisticated Web sites, systematically canvassed their friends and pushed them to the polls just in time to secure the liberal labor lawyer's narrow victory over his conservative, establishment opponent. And less than two years afterward, in a historic parliamentary election held in April 2004, a new party created to support Roh even captured control of the National Assembly, winning 152 seats out of 299 and for the first time breaking the conservatives' stranglehold on South Korea's legislature. "Koreans wanted a change in their country's corruption-scarred and conservative-controlled politics," the *Korea Herald* newspaper proclaimed after the results were tallied. The old ruling party "failed to adjust to the nation's rapidly shifting political culture."[5] This was a kind of generational revolution that not only had never taken place in Japan but that the Japanese had systematically repressed.

Facing an economic train wreck in late 1997, South Korea accepted the need to fundamentally retool and open its markets, while Japan— wracked by economic turmoil, plummeting self-confidence, and rising debts after the collapse of its bubble economy—continued to drag its feet. Desperate for foreign help to overcome crisis, South Koreans eventually acknowledged and took responsibility for resolving many of their structural shortcomings. Japanese preferred to obfuscate and deny and maintain their isolation. Koreans initiated bold reforms to clean up their corporate sector and rewrite government policy, using IMF pressure to force trade liberalization and domestic deregulation that might otherwise have been thwarted. The Japanese demurred. Korean leaders closed banks, reorganized conglomerates, and accepted the painful spike in unemployment these measures would cause, while enforcing new rules to boost corporate accountability and disclosure. Japanese policymakers, by contrast, bumbled along a path of incremental and half-baked change, as if a little extra shot of government spending or currency manipulation could solve any economic challenge. As one economics commentator concluded in 2002 as President Kim's term was expiring, "Since the 1997–98 Asian crisis, Seoul accomplished [in five years] what Japan hasn't in twelve."[6]

If Korea's crisis was sudden and sharp, Japan—after its bubble economy burst—entered a longer period of rolling blackouts, slow or negative

growth, relentless economic deterioration, and rising domestic indebted-
ness. Nonetheless, only a handful of banks, brokerages, and factories
shut down; nor were many workers tossed into the streets; blessings perhaps, but ones that indefinitely postponed a necessary retooling. In five
years of service, Prime Minister Koizumi's signal achievement was to win
approval for the eventual dismantling of the Japanese postal savings system. If South Korea was waylaid by a sudden puncture, Japan's slow,
gradual decline was more like the air slowly leaking from a tire, and gave
society's dominant institutions ample excuse to postpone pulling off the
road. Moreover, Japan's long hostility to foreign investment had kept financial institutions and corporations almost entirely in domestic hands,
so that when a company collapsed, its creditors and debtors usually were
all Japanese. As a result, even multibillion-dollar negotiations over debt
repayment often seemed to resemble little more than tribal squabbles
bound by tacit social codes, and thus got nowhere.

In South Korea, however, in the early 1990s, some initial and at times
halfhearted movements to enter global financial markets had given foreign investors a toehold in its domestic economy. This process, begun under President Kim Young-sam, gained greater momentum after South
Korea entered the Organization of Economic Cooperation and Development, the multilateral organization representing the world's wealthiest
nations. As South Korea supported a "globalization" effort that offered
chaebol like Hyundai and Daewoo greater opportunities to do business in
Eastern Europe, foreigners reciprocated, and slowly began to seek investments in Korean companies. Holding even a small slice of the nation's
debts when Korea faltered, these outsiders claimed their rightful place at
the negotiating table when default loomed.

Differences in political structure, though subtle, were no less significant. South Korea is governed by a president, a chief executive who can
put his own personal stamp on decisive political action. Indeed, only a
few weeks after his election in December 1997 and two months before
actually taking office, President-elect Kim summoned the heads of Korea's top five conglomerates to his office and hammered out their consent
to a five-point compact requiring major reform of their opaque accounting

and corporate practices. In Japan, on the other hand, a prime minister heads his party before he leads his nation, and often finds himself constrained by a parliamentary system in which he must wrest consensus from his own party leadership. This compels him to compensate factions and the narrow special interests to whom they are beholden—construction companies, doctors, mom-and-pop retailers, and postmasters. This system limits individual leadership and helps explain why the tenure of most Japanese prime ministers is brief: since November 1987, Japan has had eleven.[7] (As an untraditional maverick Koizumi was the exception to the rule.)

Furthermore, the very bedrock of each nation's democracy was formed by different tectonic processes. In 1987, South Koreans fought in the streets against military rule in order to gain their political freedom, while democracy was imposed on Japan by U.S. occupation forces after its defeat in World War Two. These differences make for very different contemporary politics. In Japan, for fifty years since 1955, one party, the Liberal Democrats, has ruled the nation—except for a brief parenthesis in 1993—damping down occasional fires of opposition in a heavy blanket of patronage spending or thickets of bureaucratic regulation. After the bloody Korean war, South Korea suffered under the weight of U.S.-backed military dictatorship through the 1960s and 1970s. At the same time, the country's rapid economic growth encouraged the rise of an educated middle class, many of whom traveled to the United States to obtain advanced degrees; these people began to demand the same sort of participatory democracy they observed in the United States and Europe. In this sense, America's foreign policy worked at planting democratic seeds. South Korea's bid for greater international recognition, manifested by the nation's hosting of the 1988 Summer Olympics, finally forced the government to alter the constitution and permit presidential elections—though until the end of the Cold War, Korea's anti-Communist military and intelligence services remained dominant political players.

When, in December 1997, in the midst of the economic crisis, the human rights activist Kim Dae-jung was elected president by a razor-thin margin, he became the first opposition political figure ever to lead his nation. More than just an average party hack, Kim was a former political prisoner, whom Korean Central Intelligence agents had kidnapped in August 1973 from a Tokyo hotel and military generals later jailed for two years on charges of treason. That a man like this could assume power through orderly, peaceful means, and that South Korea's once-powerful military could accept his victory, demonstrated how dramatically South Korea had changed in only two decades. A deeply committed Catholic, Kim personified the struggle to advance liberty and human rights. He remained deeply indebted to the support he had received from foreigners during his long political exile, and was especially grateful to a U.S. government that had explicitly warned Seoul not to "eliminate" him after the kidnapping; he was convinced that only U.S. intervention had spared his life. He did not need to be convinced that his nation would benefit significantly by opening itself wide to the outside world, and he saw the economic crisis as a way to reduce the influence of Korea's biggest conglomerates and encourage entrepreneurial Koreans to become important new players in a globalizing economy.

In Japan, however, the heavy influence of corporate, bureaucratic, and political interests usually kept potential opponents at bay. Only an internecine feud within the ruling LDP gave opposition leaders a brief hold on the prime minister's post in 1993 in the guise of the ex-LDP politician Motohiro Hosokawa, who briefly led an unstable, eight-party coalition government, but who was forced from office in less than a year. Even after a charismatic, self-styled maverick reformer, Junichiro Koizumi, became prime minister in April 2000 in an LDP vote, not a popular one, he soon found himself stymied in trying to implement a series of even modest policy reforms. Even within his own ruling party, he was an outsider who had difficulty delivering on his pledge to reshape Japan through fundamental structural transformation and by shrinking government. Koizumi did shrink fiscal spending and bolster executive power. But he failed in his bid to radically recast his nation through deregulation and decentralization.

In January 2003, just a month after South Korea's President Roh's razor-thin victory, I witnessed a stark display of the two nations' contrasting attitudes toward economic reform at a conference in Tokyo convened by the Research Institute of Economy, Trade and Industry, a division of Japan's trade ministry, to discuss the global movement to reform corporate governance and improve accountability.

Amid accounting fraud and investor scandals involving Enron and WorldCom in the United States and the grocery chain Ahold in the Netherlands, and a series of bribery and corruption scandals plaguing Japan itself, the ministry asked experts to assess how corporations were changing practices to make themselves more accountable, now that shareholder activism was rising.

Yotaro Kobayashi—the dignified gray-haired chairman of Fuji-Xerox, and then head of the national organization of major Japanese corporations, the Keizai Doyukai—was first to the lectern. He candidly acknowledged that, by tradition, Japanese firms never clearly define where corporate responsibility or accountability lies. Japanese executives run their companies like giant families organized for the benefit of their employees, managers, and society at large, not for that of shareholders outside the *ie*, or household. Some academics term this "stakeholder" capitalism, to distinguish it from the "shareholder" capitalism of the West. In a Japanese company, Kobayashi admitted, "nobody is really accountable. In substance, cooperation among the board itself means, therefore, that it is quite difficult for companies to be quick to change. That is one reason we are losing international competitiveness," he added.

Kobayashi didn't need to mention to his audience that Japan's traditional "main bank" network, which uses personnel and cross-shareholding ties to assert control, and makes it difficult, if not impossible, for any pressure to be exerted from outside this network to improve profitability, was a major culprit in Japan's underperformance. Only slowly, after more than a decade of accumulating red ink and rising debts, were corporations finally beginning to "unwind" their cross-shareholdings, de-leverage their balance sheets, and reduce their hiring of new workers. A few, like Sony Corporation, started to shrink the size of their corporate boards. Yet since shareholders possess almost no rights in Japan, hostile takeovers to unlock wealth "hidden" in a firm's balance sheet remain nearly impossible to execute. Usually, 75 percent of listed companies hold their annual meetings on the very same day, to keep shareholder attendance to the bare minimum. Corporate officers worry more about the presence at these meetings of corporate gangsters, known as *sokaiya*, who seek pay-offs to refrain from asking embarrassing questions and causing executives to "lose face," than about any demands from pension fund investors for higher returns. Though amendments to the Japanese commercial code now permit large corporations to adopt American-style corporate governance structures, only about 40 percent of large companies surveyed by *Nikkei Shimbun*, the nation's leading business daily, have chosen to use them.

In other parts of the world, companies have been forced to accept independent outside directors to monitor corporate behavior closely and to protect shareholders if they hope to woo significant foreign investment. Asked whether Japanese firms were now ready to accept similar reforms, Kobayashi, in traditional Japanese style, demurred. "This is a subject of great debate," he said, "and our views are not yet mature. This is one of the issues we have to tackle."

Kobayashi was immediately followed at the podium by Jang Hasang, a leader of the movement to reform corporate governance in Seoul and a business school professor at Korea University. Dr. Jang had studied finance at the Wharton School and taught for three years at the University of Houston. As he proceeded to review the dramatic pace of corporate, financial, labor, and public-sector reform in South Korea since the 1997 IMF crisis, his remarks crystallized the vast difference in philosophical approaches. "We used to blame China and Japan for our difficulties," Jang told his Japanese hosts, who seemed stunned by his candor. "Then, when the IMF crisis came to our shores, we at first blamed the IMF. But now we have looked in the mirror and found that it was our own fault. Now we say it is our crisis, we blame ourselves and the corporate structure we copied from Japan, and realize that it must be overhauled to meet the challenges of a new century."

In the six years since its crisis, South Korea had taken decisive and irreversible steps to transform its social and economic architecture. Jang described how the Korean system was becoming more transparent and accountable. Large corporations now had to install independent outside directors. Cross-ownership of shares among large corporations had been banned. Restrictions on foreign ownership were abandoned, and the rights of minority shareholders had been enhanced. Now even small shareholders could file class-action lawsuits if they believed stock prices or accounting principles had been manipulated. Not too many years ago, he said, Japan and Korea seemed rather similar, "but they have become more and more different in the past twenty years," as a result of Korea's long struggle to achieve democracy and the rising influence of the 386 generation of social and political activists.

The early evidence even suggested that improved corporate governance was yielding superior economic performance. Firms with better governance delivered better returns in the Korean stock market, according to statistics compiled with the help of Stanford University experts. Over time, Professor Jang argued, this strong correlation between good corporate governance and superior market performance would convince lagging firms to join the global trend toward greater disclosure and more transparent management. Already these reforms were encouraging foreign investors to buy up larger stakes in Seoul's blue chip firms, like Samsung Electronics; this buying surge in turn had boosted the overall performance of the Korean bourse. In April 2004, foreigners owned 60 percent of the shares of Samsung Electronics, 47 percent of Hyundai Motor Company, and 43 percent of all shares of companies traded on the Korea Stock Exchange.[8]

Jang's demonstration of the economic payoffs reforms could yield seemed to matter little to the Japanese corporate executives scattered in the audience. Most seemed unwilling to make tough choices even when their own firms were gasping for life. American management consultants frequently complained that, when their Japanese clients were faced with choices that, while difficult, might ultimately ensure survival of their firm, few could pull the trigger. For example, Kanebo, Ltd.—a hoary, 117-year-old cosmetics and pharmaceutical giant, with 14,000 employees and 500 billion yen in annual sales—was taken over by the Japanese government in March 2004 because its board of directors could never shut its debt-ridden textile and housing divisions, even though its better-known and profit-generating cosmetics division was flourishing. Kanebo operated a synthetic-fiber plant employing more than four hundred workers in rural Yamaguchi prefecture; yet, even though it had long ago stopped contributing profits, the board could not make the decision to close the plant in order to save the company. "Both creditor banks and labor unions had lost much of their influence on Japan's overall corporate scene in the 1990s, but Kanebo was torn between the demands from the two camps and corporate governance by shareholders failed to function adequately," the *Nikkei Shimbun* concluded after the collapse. "The company reached the end of the line, held in thrall to the old mode of Japanese corporate management."[9]

While the only speed Japan seemed to know was doddering and incremental, South Korea's pace was so frantic and fierce that the Korean sociologist Chang Kyung-sup labeled it "compressed modernization." The unprecedented pace of industrialization and urbanization, combined with historical chance and Korea's dependency on outside forces, created what Chang has termed "accidental pluralism,"[10] to describe an ethnically homogeneous society churned by clashing economic trends, political struggle, and competing social values.

In only thirty-five years, Koreans had accomplished what had taken most Western societies three centuries, Chang told me. Between 1960, when South Korea's rapid modernization program really began, and 1995, before the economic crash, the nation's gross national product had increased 238-fold, from $1.9 billion to $451.7 billion, and its yearly national income had risen from $79 per person to $10,076, a 128-fold jump. In a nation crossed by jagged mountain ranges and bereft of gentle, alluvial plains, gritty subsistence agriculture had accounted for more than one-third of the economy in 1960, and 72 percent of the population lived in the countryside. Yet by 1995, after the great migration of its population to major cities, 80 percent of the population was urban, and agriculture was just 6.6 percent of the national economy. Not only were Koreans more prosperous, they were also living longer. The average Korean's lifespan, 52.4 years in 1960, had reached 74 years by 2000.

All these statistics demonstrate that the South Koreans have acquired the survival skills needed to adjust to rapid change, Chang said, and that the youngest generations are especially eager to embrace globalization and its new technologies. In 2002, *BusinessWeek* declared that South Korea "has become a model for developing nations everywhere . . . Korea has already made the transition from authoritarianism to democracy and from a low-end, exporting economy sealed off from the world into one that is plugged in, dynamic and increasingly high-tech. Dare we say it? Korea is cool."[11]

As it embraces the cool, South Korea favors the fast, not the slow; the young, not the old. Risk-takers, not the risk-averse. Its people are optimists, not pessimists. In all these characteristics, vital for modern life and the economic challenges ahead, Japan and South Korea differ markedly. Why, I wondered, does life in Korea today always seem so *balli-balli*, as the Koreans put it? So headlong and, at times, reckless. Why is it so rapid, so innovative, so bold, if sometimes so contentious, and why are its people so unruly and upbeat?

Why—to return to the start of this discussion—did South Korea and Japan behave so differently when calamity struck? I found some obvious explanations, one being their enormous difference in size. For, despite a continuous period of stagnation and decline, Japan still remains the world's second largest economy, as well as the largest supplier of surplus capital to the United States, while South Korea's economy is the world's tenth largest, and highly leveraged—that is, with a far higher ratio of debt to equity, with far smaller reserves of foreign currency stored in its central bank, and with a population only one-third of Japan's. Thus, when hit by an economic tsunami, Japan acted like a supertanker barely budged by high seas, while the South Korean skiff tossed unsteadily in the giant waves. Lacking both Japan's vast storehouse of accumulated wealth and the foreign reserves to outlast a sustained attack against its own currency, Korea had little choice when assailed. It had to immediately repair to the costly emergency room of international finance in order to survive.

As I wrestled with this puzzle, I thought of how in its crisis everyone in South Korea, no matter how wealthy, seemed to feel as though they shared a common struggle they were determined to face together (though history would later prove that the wealthy had profited neatly from the Korean crisis). I thought also of the deeply committed Catholic President Kim Dae-jung who had led the way out of that crisis. Those thoughts, in turn, brought to mind something that always startled me when I arrived in Seoul after a long stay in Japan: the symbols of Christian influence. As conspicuous as the billboards hawking credit cards and Coke are the red neon crucifixes cutting through the night fog. Then there are the dozens of slender storefront churches elbowing their way into crowded neighborhoods, tucked in between the convenience stores and barber shops. Where in Japan a Christian chapel mainly serves as background for a fashionable Japanese wedding, in Seoul a single Pentecostal congregation—the Central Full Gospel Church—claims more than 500,000 members.

South Korea has, I soon came to realize, a very active tradition of Christianity, one that started in the late 1880s, under the sway of Protestant missionaries, not long after Japan had pushed itself into the Hermit Kingdom and opened it to Western influence. As a secular Jew living in Asia, I had never considered how Christianity might have influenced Korea's modernization, or the notion that a religious sensibility might profoundly affect a nation's political and economic architecture. Yet how to explain the vital differences in outlook toward globalization, self-empowerment, entrepreneurship, and civil society visible in South Korea—progressive, liberal attitudes you could not unearth among the Japanese, their more prosperous neighbor? In groping with the challenges of mastering modernization, whether in the late nineteenth century or the late twentieth, did the influence of Western religion offer Koreans a path of self-discovery and individual empowerment that Japanese, in their worship of nature, the Emperor, and Shinto ritual, could never find for themselves? On some deep level, Korea embraced Western ideals as well as Western implements, while Japan appropriated the tools of the West but renounced the culture that had helped create them.

It seemed natural, then, to investigate both how mainstream Western religions affected the essential character of Korea's modernization and whether that influence retains its relevance even today.

13.

A COMPLETELY NEW VALUE SYSTEM

Modernization first sailed into Asia in the holds of merchant trading ships, guided by rovers impatient for profits. By the end of the sixteenth century, the Japanese, already fearful of the upheaval foreign elements might instigate in their cloistered nation, had imposed draconian regulations to limit the access of traders and Catholic missionaries alike. They confined foreigners to the treaty port of Nagasaki, where Portuguese and, then, Dutch traders were required to live in quarantine on Deshima, an artificial island built offshore. These restrictions allowed the shogunate to limit commercial relations and choke off any unsettling foreign influences, like Christianity, that might threaten sovereignty. In similar fashion, the Chinese emperor restricted foreign commerce to the port of Canton, and specified that foreign barbarians could dwell there only during the "trading season," lasting from October to May, before returning home or to the Portuguese colony of Macau, at the mouth of the Pearl River.

Nonetheless, however gamely the xenophobic rulers of nineteenth-century China and Japan tried to ward off intrusions from the strange and foul-smelling barbarians from the West, the exigencies of commerce— and the superiority of Western weaponry—eventually prevailed. A first, unyielding round of "globalization" was under way. By mid-century, impatient with their marginal status in Asia, the Western powers sought to expand their trade and geopolitical influence, especially with China. Now the heavily armed warship replaced the merchant vessel as the dominant instrument battering down doors. Imperial China succumbed first, after Britain used the influence of its global drug cartel and the persuasiveness of its advanced cannonry to force the Qing dynasty to give it "most favored" trading status. The Opium War (1839–1842) and the unequal Treaty of Nanjing in 1842 gave sanction to the rapid expansion of more benign commercial influences. Two years later, France and the United States demanded and won similar concessions.

If Imperial China—Asia's mightiest and most influential nation—proved no match for Western military might, the isolated island of Japan could expect that it would soon be similarly confronted—as it was on July 8, 1853, when a thunderous cannon shot heralded the arrival in Tokyo Bay of Commodore Matthew Perry and his four warships. It took some years to unfold, but Perry's arrival eventually triggered the overthrow of the existing warlords, the enthronement of a new Meiji Emperor, and the disingenuously named Restoration of 1868,[1] as Japan rushed to acquire Western technology, master Western weaponry, and appropriate Western clothes, Western-style schools, and a Western bureaucracy. The Japanese proved exceptionally quick studies, however. By 1876, after skillfully absorbing the lessons of gunboat diplomacy they had taken from the American intruders, Japan imposed a commercial treaty on the neighboring Korean peninsula nearly as inequitable as the pact the Americans had imposed on Japan.[2]

The Japanese justified their imperialist ambitions over the Korean peninsula by arguing—to themselves as much as to the Koreans—that only they could protect the independence of the "Hermit Kingdom" still utterly secluded from foreign influence, while at the same time leading "backward" Korea down the road toward the sort of progressive, Western-style modernization Tokyo itself now seemed bent on pursuing. Since within Asia Japan became the "early adopter" that first—ahead of both China and Korea—demonstrated a commitment to modernizing, naturally it should seize the broadest mantle, become the "center of civilization," and "be ready to take responsibility for the protection of the rest of Asia," as advocated by Yukichi Fukuzawa—a translator, writer, and educator and the leading exemplar of a Japanese-style modernism that would meld West with East.³ Certainly, the Japanese felt, the Koreans were incapable of doing it themselves.

The Japanese had another motive for their ambitions. They believed that a weak Korea would be a dagger aimed at Japan's own heart: without adequate security, the peninsula would become an inviting target for Russian territorial expansion (and, indeed, Russia and Japan would wage war over Korea in 1905, and, rather surprisingly, Japan would prevail). The historian Peter Duus described Japan's rationale in seeking control over the Chosun Empire: "If Korea were truly independent, it posed no strategic problem, but if Korea remained 'backward' and 'uncivilized,' it would remain weak, and if it remained weak, it would be inviting prey for foreign predators. The 'maintenance of Korean independence,' a litany invoked by popular rights activists as well as by the Meiji leaders, required a program of Korean self-strengthening similar to the post-Restoration reforms breaking forth across Japan."⁴

The Japanese also sensed that, by following the same tactics Western colonial powers employed to achieve domination through trade and military force, they might effectively propel themselves into the first rank of nations, ahead and above other Eastern peoples. Convinced of their uniqueness, the Japanese would assert their innate superiority over other Asians, and Koreans would bear the indignity of being colonized and considered inferior—attitudes that even today cloud the complex blend of admiration, rivalry, and hatred Koreans feel toward Japanese. As the decades progressed, however, it became increasingly difficult for Japan to justify its contention that only Tokyo's soldiers could protect Korea's true independence.⁵

Korea's sudden confrontation with the modern world set off—as had Japan's a few decades before—intense political competition and friction among the nation's elite. Beginning in the 1880s, as Japanese soldiers arrived in their ports, Korean traditionalists insisted on maintaining sovereignty as well as isolation. They feared a breakdown of morality and Confucian religious sentiment, distrusted Western technology, and feared cultural contamination if they opened their gates. A small band of reformers, by contrast, argued that emulating the West could actually strengthen the nation and protect Korean sovereignty. To them, Japan's Meiji reforms offered a useful template for the sort of modernization Koreans should now rapidly embrace to dissolve their feudal backwardness and gain the scientific knowledge and technology required to guarantee the future autonomy of the Korean peninsula. This faction championed "civilization and enlightenment" and urged the Korean people—much as Fukuzawa did—to retain the "Eastern way" as they adopted "Western implements," whether steamships, locomotives, telegraphs, or firearms. These advocates, who saw in modernism a way to supplant a narrow, traditional, and oligarchic society, also hoped to create a more egalitarian one. One such proponent was Yu Kil-chun, whose unplanned voyage into the Western orbit epitomizes Korea's early, unsteady passage from insular Hermit Kingdom to eventual full-fledged membership in the modern world. It was a journey marred by four decades of Japanese colonization and three wars, the last being the Korean War, which in 1954 left the peninsula divided arbitrarily at the 38th parallel. Today, there is an unsteady armistice, but no formal peace, between South Korea and North Korea, and the world still seeks a durable solution to the isolation of the world's last Stalinist regime, based in Pyongyang.

Yu was born in 1856 into Korean nobility. As Confucian orthodoxy across Asia began to shatter under the fusillade of modern Western thinking, he was one of a number of inquisitive young Koreans who sought to learn directly from the Japanese experience of coping with and channeling modernism. In 1881, a mere five years after the Korean treaty with Japan was signed, Yu became part of the first contingent of Korean students who ventured off to Tokyo to study with Fukuzawa, who was the central intellectual influence of the Meiji modernization effort. His systematic cultivation of "barbarian" knowledge and doctrine of "strong army, rich country" helped guide Japan's swift leap into the rank of industrial powers. Fukuzawa's *Seiyo Jijo* (*Conditions in the West*) concisely described everyday Western institutions like hospitals, schools, museums, and insane asylums and became a runaway best seller in Japan after its publication in 1866. Today, Fukuzawa's graceful, kimono-clad figure still

graces Japan's ¥10,000 banknote, demonstrating his enduring significance within Japanese society.

Selected by the Korean court to examine the course of Westernization
in Meiji Japan, Yu stayed in Tokyo for nearly eighteen months. For almost
six months, he was Fukuzawa's houseguest while attending Keio Gijuku,
which would later become Keio University, the institution Fukuzawa
himself founded. Yu and a colleague were the first foreign students to enroll in Keio in June 1881.[6]

Although twenty-seven-year-old Yu considered himself an avid disciple
of the charismatic Fukuzawa, he was not satisfied to learn only from the
Japanese example. America itself beckoned. In 1883, having returned to
Seoul and joined the Foreign Ministry, he eagerly accepted an offer to accompany Korea's first diplomatic envoy to Washington, D.C. The official
delegation landed in San Francisco on September 2, under the supervision of Percival Lowell, the Japanophile and later astronomer, who served
as the group's counselor.[7] Two months later, in November 1883, Yu arrived in Salem, Massachusetts, where he lived for a time with Edward
Sylvester Morse, the prominent marine biologist and director of the
Peabody Museum, whom Yu had doubtless met during his studies in
Tokyo. Morse, a Boston socialite and one of New England's first influential experts on Japan, made three trips to Japan to gather seashells, give
lectures on social Darwinism, collect art treasures for Boston museums,
and prepare a landmark study on the architecture of the Japanese home.[8]
On his 1882 voyage to Japan, Morse had become intrigued with the
newly opened territory of Corea, as it was then spelled in the West, and,
having never met Koreans before, set out to interview a number of those
like Yu who had suddenly appeared to study at Keio.

Now, through Morse's friendship and aid, Yu became the first Korean
student ever to enroll in an American school. In May 1884, after completing his mission with the Korean delegation to Washington, Yu began
his studies at America's oldest boarding school, the Governor Dummer
Academy on the outskirts of Salem, Massachusetts, which today bears a
plaque commemorating his stay.

Yu's letters to Morse and his subsequent book—*Things I Learned While in the West*, an intellectual offspring of Fukuzawa's seminal work—demonstrate how he integrated what he had learned of modernization and Western ideals into a vision of a future modern Korean society. One can discover leafing through this correspondence how American ideas of universal liberalism, individual independence, freedom, popular rights, and pragmatism, as well as of Christian thought, thoroughly permeated his emerging worldview. "The people of the United States has [*sic*] a higher discernment, public spirit, and the independent judgment than the human race of any other nation on the globe," Yu wrote in one typically bold and slightly naive letter, believed to have been composed in October 1884. He described how members of his school class took a democratic vote to decide on a leader. "I was astonished by it, and learn [*sic*] something myself by it, because they were so intelligent, conscientious and independent. Are the boys here the best in the United States then?"[9]

Yu's stay in America was cut short by insurrection at home; by early 1885, he had already embarked on the long journey back to Seoul. In a letter to Morse, probably written aboard ship, Yu outlined how exposure to religious sentiment had already stirred his thinking. "There are no remidies [*sic*] in any religion but activity, and activity is to take an earnest thought in preparing for future. So I will propose to our people as what I have recently concluded to be good for nations when I go back to my native land, and I am on my way home now." He continued:

> I said to you that the Christianity was best, as a religion, and I would like to propose to our people to introduce that religion to our country, for the sake of our country, although I was not a believer of any religion in the world, because I thought the people of Christendom were never revolt to their [*sic*] government and always lived in a peaceful life.[10]

Although Yu's relatively short period of study in both Japan and the United States could not have entirely rinsed away his Confucian values of filial piety nor given him a comprehensive view of Western universalism, his letters show how quickly he grasped the link between Christianity, individual empowerment, and liberal, progressive thought. Christianity, he suggested in one note, is "synonymous with Western civilization as a whole"; Yu himself did not actually convert until the end of the 1880s.[11] As a crucial figure of reform in early modern Korea, he articulated a vision of individual freedom vastly different from the traditional Asian norms of duty, obedience, and filial piety. In defining freedom, for instance, he wrote, "It means freely doing what one pleases. Except for what one chooses to do or not do in accordance with right principles of the universe, one must not be bound by anything whatsoever." He went on to cite as innate freedoms those of speech, assembly, enterprise, and property.[12]

Yu was not alone. Other reformers already active in Korea envisioned an open society that would permit individuals to luxuriate in intellectual freedom and material abundance while the nation grew strong, wealthy, and independent. Deeply influenced by their faith in the "survival of the fittest," which Morse had articulated, these reformers saw free competition as the means for Korea both to become strong and to modernize, and argued that opening and reform inevitably meant incorporating some aspects of Western culture and institutions. Yu posited that what distinguished the wealth and power of the West from the weakness and poverty of the East was the character of its interactions with the outside world, and asked, "[H]as it been wide or narrow, frequent or infrequent, and whether competition has been extensive or restricted, high or low? . . . A country's rise or fall and strength or weakness depends on the scale and quality of competition." He added:

> With the nation secluded and traffic with foreign countries banned for a long time, Korea has only competed with compatriots. Should we gradually initiate interactions with other countries in line with the currents of the world, many of our people would have daily access to foreign things, be surprised at differences in customs, and impressed by advanced technologies. But it would also open the way

for our people to expand the arena of competition and build a civilized, rich, and strong country. Accordingly we must invigorate ourselves, challenge ourselves to higher and bigger competition and reinforce the spirit of competition in unison regardless of class . . . We must compare our culture and institutions with theirs, and accommodate them so as not to supplement our shortcomings. If our culture and institutions are found to be conversely superior to theirs, we must preserve them for good and further develop their merits.[13]

How markedly different was this attitude from those expressed in Japan, where interactions with the West were so closely managed and manipulated!

*   *   *

Yu's return to Seoul nearly coincided with the arrival of the first Methodist and Presbyterian missionaries. Undoubtedly, they were inspired to depart a Japan that was not prepared to receive their Gospel, and seek new and untrammeled territory after encountering the first crop of promising young Korean students like Yu while in Tokyo. In September 1884, while Yu was still studying abroad in Salem, Dr. Horace Allen, whom the Presbyterian Church had appointed to be the first Presbyterian missionary to Korea, arrived in Seoul. He was joined a few months later by Methodists, including Dr. and Mrs. W. B. Scranton; the former's mother, Mrs. Mary Scranton; and the Reverend and Mrs. Henry Appenzeller. These two groups started their work simultaneously, operated missions side by side, and to some extent cooperated with one another. Many of these evangelical fundamentalists had been inspired by the Second Great Awakening in the United States to travel across the treacherous seas to save Korean souls. They were also animated by the same spirit of Manifest Destiny—that it had become America's duty to save the world for Christendom—that would, a decade later, lead to the American conquest of the Philippines during the Spanish-American War of 1898. Since freedom of worship and missionary labor were still banned in the Chosun Kingdom, the evangelists made a strategic choice to focus their first efforts on building hospitals and schools. This tactic not only circumvented the prohibition on religious freedom, it also allowed them to gain good standing within society before attempting to propagate their faith. Indeed, just months after his arrival, a quirk of fate and his medical expertise would give Dr. Allen his first chance to influence the royal court.

Power struggles and intrigue swirled within the king's court. The Japanese, aiming to gain a foothold for themselves, worked to boost the stock of reformist elements intent on opening the society to foreigners. Qing loyalists, in turn, supported traditional conservatives who favored China's influence. This battle—pitting reformers against traditionalists, Japanese versus Chinese alliances—led to a dizzying series of attempted coups and conspiracies throughout the 1880s, and eventually to the Sino-Japanese War of 1894.

In one attempted insurrection—the same one that would force Yu's hurried return from New England—Japanese soldiers working with pro-modernization elements attempted to oust the pro-Chinese royal family during a banquet reception. An assassination attempt on December 4, 1884, severely wounded Prince Min Young-ik, a powerful conservative leader. As the crown prince lingered near death, traditional Chinese herbal remedies proved ineffective, so the court in desperation summoned the strange American doctor who practiced an unknown form of medicine. Owing to Dr. Allen's meticulous care over the next three months, Prince Min fully recovered. As a result, the royal court began to trust Western medicine and technology, as well as Americans in general. This experience confirmed the perception of late-nineteenth-century elites in both Korea and Japan that, as one Korean thinker put it, "Christianity is synonymous with Western civilization as a whole," and that modern rationalist thought and the progress of capitalism was inextricably linked to Protestantism. Indeed, this sentiment may have been responsible for many Koreans' ultimate acceptance of Christianity.

When, not long after his success, Dr. Allen petitioned the court to permit the opening of a Western-style hospital, the government readily approved. The facility opened on April 10, 1885. Dr. Allen was also appointed physician to the royal court, a position that gave him special access to power and eventually led to his deeper involvement in both business deals and diplomatic missions to cement alliances between Korea and the United States. In the early 1900s, Allen was named U.S. Minister to Korea and helped orchestrate the first emigration of Korean workers to Hawaii's pineapple plantations. Through Allen's personal relationships within the court, American corporations profited from Korea's modernization, as he helped them win concessions to build the nation's first streetcars and electrical generating plants.[14]

Although Protestant missionary work started much later in Korea than in other parts of Asia, Korea ultimately proved far more receptive to Christianity than any other Asian outpost. Indeed, no other Asian nation has so radically transformed its social values to accommodate a foreign system of beliefs. While the Spanish conquerors of the Philippines, Asia's most Catholic country, forced their religious views on their colonial subjects, the Koreans themselves took up Christianity against the wishes of their colonial masters and used the support they found in it to oppose Japanese rule. As Christianity became indigenous, it served as spiritual balm to soothe the stresses modernization imposed.

The emphasis on good works, as much as on the Good Book, seems to have been most influential. Not only did missionaries demonstrate the efficacy of Western medicine in a society that, according to the missionaries' own contemporary diaries, was far more squalid and unhygienic than feudal Japan, where the daily bath was already a common ritual, but these missionaries also used literacy campaigns, especially among women, to spread the Gospel. The Scranton family's practice of inviting women into their home for study eventually led to the creation of Ewha Women's College. The church also advocated the use of hangul, Korea's simplified alphabet, rather than Chinese kanji to increase literacy and spread knowledge of the Bible. Though invented in the fifteenth century, this twenty-four-character alphabet had been rejected by Confucian literati as a system so easily learned that even women and dogs could use it. As early as October 1889, however, several Protestant missionaries met at the home of Horace G. Underwood, scion of the famous typewriter fortune, to organize the Korean Religious Tract Society. As one missionary recounted, "This common, easy-to-learn, written language became the vehicle for popularizing the Christian message among all classes. Before schools giving a modern education were extensively established in Korea, the women, children and ignorant men in the church who never had the advantage of even an elementary education were soon learning the Korean alphabet and reading the Word of God . . ."[15] As new missionaries were taught this simple alphabet, it led to a surge of Christian literature produced in hangul. Underwood would go on, in 1915, to help found the Chosun Christian College as Korea's first modern institution of higher education, and served as its first president. The college later merged with the medical center Dr. Allen had opened, and became Yonsei University, today one of Seoul's most prestigious institutions of higher education. A statue of Underwood still stands in a place of honor at the university's formal entrance.

Their insistence on developing self-reliance was another reason for the success of Protestant missionaries in Korea. They followed the so-called Nevius method of missionary work, whose goal was to establish self-supporting, self-propagating, and self-governing national churches that did not have to depend either on foreign missionaries or on their agencies for financial or administrative support. This policy allowed the missions and their religious teachers to maneuver themselves deftly into the rising stream of nationalism and independence that was swelling throughout Korea against Japanese occupation and repression. This model of self-reliance "appealed tremendously to the Korean mind. The emphasis on self-support and self-government around the Korean spirit of independence had been long repressed under the influence of Confucian thought."[16] Instead of foreigners teaching Koreans about new religious practice, Koreans began to teach one another, thus further empowering themselves.

Protestantism's very spirit also offered a profoundly different message to a profoundly hierarchical society. In stark contrast to doctrines of filial piety, which justified ethical elitism and the concentration of welfare only on one's own family, these new thinkers, including Yun Ch'iho, advocated universality and the objective existence of moral law. Moral behavior should be inspired from within, they said, not imposed by external rules and the fear of violating them. "A completely new value system and world came into being," one Korean scholar wrote. "A subject observing religious practices as the basic unit of religious life was an individual no longer determined by a network of social relationships, but [one] who acts according to free judgment independent from the outside world . . . A new model of religiosity was established, in which the individual is the basic unit."[17]

The Roman Catholic Church, having survived numerous persecutions in the early nineteenth century, also expanded in Korea. By the time Japan formally annexed Korea in 1910, Catholics had established sixty-nine churches, installed fifteen indigenous priests among its total of seventy-one, and claimed more than seventy-three thousand believers. But the influence of the Protestant missionaries, especially those of American background, proved the more powerful. Asserting that the separation of church and state was a unique aspect of their religious doctrine, they used this distinction to argue that politics and religion, like the public and private spheres, must be kept separate. Their belief in individual conscience, in inner faith rather than outward ritual, and in self-empowerment through hard work and frugality, also helped evoke sentiments of nationalism and independence that became crucial during four decades of struggle against the Japanese. As one Korean scholar has put it, "It is widely accepted that the Protestant Church is the father of Korean society's modernization or civilization."[18]

During this same period, Japan's interactions with foreign faiths effectively marginalized Christianity. The Meiji government no longer killed Christians, as the Tokugawa had, but Japanese Protestants, many of them elites from the former samurai class, found themselves caught in the intellectual crosshairs, inviting targets to be sniped at from all sides. Though eager to master this fascinating new discourse on "civilization," they wanted both to promote Japanese independence and national development in the face of Western imperialism and to remain faithful to the ethos of service to an emperor-centered state. The Meiji court, meanwhile, seized upon the cloudy legacy of antiquity to assert its new-found legitimacy. The Imperial Rescript on Education issued in October 1890 demanded that all schooling be grounded in Confucian ethics. This proclamation asserted both that filial piety and loyalty were "the fundamental glory of Our Empire" and that a "national essence," whose values had been manifest in Japan's distant, primordial past should be the foundation for its future actions and beliefs. Thus, within Japan, social conformity, strong state intervention in daily life, and state-sponsored Shinto eroded Christian beliefs in individual autonomy, altruism, and universalism.[19]

The Russo-Japanese War of 1904, in creating political and economic chaos across the Korean peninsula, undoubtedly hastened Korean adoption of Christian principles. By the time Tokyo formally annexed the Korean peninsula in 1910, Christian-inspired nationalists were leading anti-Japanese insurrections, and an estimated 200,000 people had been identified as Protestant adherents.[20] The Korean independence movement of 1919 was notable for the number of Christians, especially Protestants, who acted as key organizers and leaders: nearly half of those who endorsed the Declaration of Independence of March First—fifteen of thirty-three signers—were Christians, as were the more than two thousand of those imprisoned for participating in demonstrations. Subsequently, churches became particular targets for Japanese military reprisals. Forty-seven churches were burned down, hundreds of Christians perished in the demonstrations, and the brutal suppression campaign, as well as the prominence of Christians among those persecuted, produced a strong—and persistent—link between Christianity and Korean nationalism.

Christian churches helped bring international pressure to bear on behalf of the Korean people against their colonial occupiers. The repression of 1919, and the international condemnation it provoked, forced the Japanese to be more hospitable to church institutions during the 1920s. In the 1930s, the colonial government's demand that all Koreans worship at Shinto shrines triggered more protest and repression, since Christians viewed such rituals as akin to idol worship. In the aftermath of World War Two, when Japanese colonial rule ended and the Korean peninsula was suddenly divided between Soviet and American spheres of influence, U.S. occupation forces quietly aided Christian missionaries in the South, giving them access to the military exchanges where, amid rampant material shortages, they could easily procure hard-to-obtain goods. The U.S. military also helped churches distribute relief supplies. For even as they cast a wary eye on South Korea's growing labor movement and feared its Communist sympathies, arriving U.S. forces naturally sought out English speakers in the postwar chaos. Korean Christians who had studied in mission schools before the war were the most likely to remember their language lessons, as well as their lectures on Western history and ideals. It soon became obvious to the population at large that affiliation with Americans, and knowledge of their culture, including Christianity, offered significant material advantages in this world, no matter what might take place in the next.

After the armistice of 1953—signed by China, North Korea, and the United States, but not by South Korea—ended the Korean War, Catholic and Protestant mission–related agencies brought millions of dollars in humanitarian supplies into the ravaged South, much as Protestant schools and hospitals had first brought Koreans into contact with Christian beliefs in the 1880s. These humanitarian groups distributed food, clothing, and medicines to needy families and acted as one of the most effective relief agencies in the poverty-wracked nation. Many Koreans reciprocated by professing a Christian faith, and Korea's first president, Syngman Rhee, who was flown into Seoul aboard a U.S. military aircraft and installed in office by the U.S. military occupation, was both a devout Methodist and a staunch anti-Communist who had studied at the Princeton Theological Seminary. His stiff and authoritarian leadership, however, would eventually lead to his downfall.

As North Korea settled into isolated and tyrannical rule, the next two volatile decades of South Korean history were marked by coup attempts, street marches, and political protest against military dictatorship. During this period, church and state were in considerable tension. Since, on the one hand, South Korean Christians tended to be fiercely anti-Communist as well as politically conservative, they tended to support the government's fierce military mobilization and autocratic rule against the threat of North Korean Communism. On the other hand, however, the churches tended to resist political pressure and demanded the right to set their own moral and social agenda as institutions of civil society separated from politics. By the mid-1960s, the "liberation theology" that opposed dictatorship in Latin America also influenced many Korean church leaders, both Catholic and Protestant, to pursue progressive social agendas.

Even as the brutal dictatorship of Park Chung-hee in the 1960s suppressed labor unions, monitored student groups, and controlled almost all opposition elements within civil society, Park's regime dared not shutter the nation's churches. Striking out against religious opponents would have stirred strong condemnation from the United States, Park's chief economic ally and Cold War patron.[21] Throughout the next two decades, as civil protest raged against the military strongmen Chun Doo-hwan and Roh Tae-woo, the churches served as both refuge for prodemocracy organizers and locus of antigovernment activities. Church leaders were sometimes seized as political prisoners for their vocal opposition to dictatorship. Compared with student or labor organizers, however, Korean clerics enjoyed far more freedom of movement, and churches themselves often served as sanctuaries for labor and student activists hiding from the political repression of the state. The nation's long march toward popular democracy finally succeeded in toppling the military dictatorship in the late 1980s.[22]

Politics aside, the social upheaval and dislocation stirred by "compressed modernization" also helps account for the rapid rise of Christian belief in Korea. In a society wracked by turmoil and hurried adaptation to a new urban lifestyle, churches offered solace and peace to an anxious population and in so doing supplanted both Confucian and shamanistic traditions. In rural villages, where a patriarchal society had long been held in place, the cleric substituted for the power of the father figure or village chief. As one religious historian wrote, "The search for religion after the war reflected the accumulated spiritual crisis: the loss of the Confucian state, successive ordeals of colonialism and liberation followed by national division and civil war; a changing basis of wealth from agriculture to commerce, rapid industrialization and the loss of property."[23]

Whatever its cause, the spread of the Christian faith within modern South Korea has proven remarkable. With its Protestant population almost doubling every decade, South Korea has today an estimated eleven million Protestants and three million Catholics—meaning that nearly one-third of the nation's 45 million people today profess a Christian faith. Indeed, Protestant Christianity is growing faster in South Korea than anywhere else on earth.

*   *   *

Korean society's embrace of Christianity—especially that of its educated elites—helped transform the political culture of the nation. The church helped social movements organize across economic classes and regional lines, allowing committed activists to build communities larger than the boundaries of family or school connections. The passion it aroused for its causes helped energize supporters—true believers; and the moral fervor it generated helped bind together students and workers, groups that might otherwise have become antagonistic in their fight against dictatorship.

"In many ways, Korea's Christian communities act as models of civil society," one political scientist noted. The church created a remarkable number and variety of cells that "meet, recruit, and induct new members, train leaders, follow rituals, share beliefs and strive toward common organizational goals cooperatively, and without interference from outside. Taken as a whole, Korea's Christian churches include representatives of all social strata and all walks of life, all ages, and as individuals, all shades of the political spectrum."[24] Today, political scholars agree that Korea's democratic transition was driven principally not by elite decision makers, but by the mass of people, the civil society, the "realm of organized social life that is voluntary, self-generating, [largely] self-supporting and autonomous from the state and bound by a legal order of set rules."[25]

The rapid growth of Korea's middle class also spurred demands for greater democracy in the 1970s, and early civil society organizations consistently promoted it. Christianity became crucial in South Korea's political evolution. In the struggle for democracy, church groups offered distinct advantages. Military generals could not easily dismiss Catholic nuns and Protestant clerics as "godless Communists" who sympathized with North Korea and sought to destabilize the South, as they could labor and student groups. And church leaders could readily tap into nationalist sentiments that had been present in their pews since the decades of Japanese occupation, as well as command access to resources from abroad. They published their own newspapers and magazines to communicate directly with the Korean people.

The churches reached out to the underprivileged, to unemployed farmers and factory workers, and especially to women—a legacy of the missionaries' earliest literacy campaigns of nearly a century before. "Realizing justice on the earth"—a slogan the churches used—suggested that vast social change was in fact God's plan. The Korean Student Christian Federation and Korean Ecumenical Youth were among the organizations that created the "people's movement camp," which wrested electoral democracy in the 1980s from the military generals who had ruled the country.

Even in the 1990s, a relatively high number of participants in civil society movements were Protestants, an indisputable legacy of the struggle for democracy in the 1970s and 1980s. The sociologist Yee Jaeyeol has described a dense network of cooperation, exchange of information, and sharing of resources among new social movements in South Korea in the 1980s and 1990s.[26] Another sociologist, Song Ho-keun, speculates that, because many of Korea's civil protest movements were formed during a period of political repression and surveillance, social movements had no choice but to rely on "personal trust" among activists to counteract the potential risks of meeting and working together.[27]

The churches, along with the ethical teachings they preached, were able to cut through the rigid relationships and traditional hierarchies that had characterized established Korean society, to help create new and more fluid networks of social trust that transcended the narrow bonds of family, region, or school. Western ethical teachings offered Koreans new perspectives on the concepts of universalism—that all are equal in God's eyes—and of individualism, that God has given each person a unique gift that he or she is duty-bound to express in some positive fashion. Moreover, the emphasis that even impoverished Korean families placed on educating their children helped spread this message.

Koreans did not renounce their strong family and regional loyalties: in Korean schools and *chaebol*, Korea's largest corporate conglomerates, hierarchical obligations remained strong. But over time many South Koreans, especially the younger generations, began to rethink these inflexible obligations as they became more comfortable with the sort of self-expression and self-determination common in the West. That many Koreans went to the United States to obtain advanced degrees also contributed to this trend. The U.S. government encouraged young Koreans to study in America, and many of those who did returned imbued with American notions of personal liberty and risk-taking.

As they developed a sense of a tangible, independent self, new generations of Koreans were able to link up with like-minded "strangers" from outside their restrictive social networks. Indeed, it isn't the worship service or the theology that primarily attracts Koreans to church today, but the personal and civic connections it fosters: rummage sales, potluck dinners, and choir rehearsals. Today many Koreans say they attend church not out of religious fervor, or to pray for God's mercy, but simply to hang out with friends, to meet people, and, especially among males, to make new business contacts. Church has become an active, joyful social space between home and office. "We use the church as a sort of social club," Han Seung-mi, who teaches at the graduate school of international studies at Yonsei University, told me. Religious sentiment seems secondary. "You don't even have to be a believer to be a member. You just go there to meet up with others and to network."

Today, the movements for corporate responsibility and a more fully participatory democracy that are roiling politics in South Korea are closely linked to the social reform that churches preach. Korea's domestic politics have radically changed as young Koreans demand more accountability of their government. Large Korean firms have been forced to become more transparent and give even small shareholders some influence. "There is a powerful dynamic now at work within our society, that somehow we overturned an established social system," Professor Jang, the corporate governance activist, told me.

Jang himself experienced culture shock when he returned to Seoul after spending a decade studying and teaching in the United States. "I came back to a completely different country," he said. The democratic revolution of 1987 had so transformed society that "I couldn't adjust myself to the new generation and new society." For a while he was so perplexed and confused he even considered returning to the United States.

While the political system had become significantly more open, however, the economic system he encountered remained under the tight control of the giant, insular, family-led *chaebol*. The 1997 financial crisis, however, forced South Korea to adapt to a new world of more open borders and more volatile financial flows. "The crisis of '97 allowed us to cleanse the country," Jang reflected. "We moved a few steps closer to a modern capitalist system."

The crisis also transformed the national psyche. "We've become a less xenophobic society," Jang said. "We Koreans stepped away from our old values and decided to accept change rather than hold on to what we already had. People's aspirations turned the crisis into opportunity."

*   *   *

While leaders of citizen activist and corporate reform movements in South Korea today seldom dwell on their Christian roots, the influence of religious thought on their lives seems palpable. Consider Kim Jungtae, the unprepossessing former chairman of Kookmin Bank and a leader of the nation's corporate reform movement, who insisted that his corporate board operate in transparent fashion, that small shareholders deserved the same rights as large shareholders, and that the bank should operate for the benefit of shareholders and employees alike, not just for corporate managers. He talks easily about taking personal responsibility for corporate decisions, and emphasizes that he is not interested in feathering the nest for fat cats. "I didn't come here to focus only on helping to increase the income of a small number of large shareholders, but to protect the interests of all shareholders, big and small," he explained one day in his large office, only a few blocks from the South Korean parliament building.

Once the head of an independent securities firm, Kim was recruited to run Kookmin, now Korea's largest commercial bank, after it merged with Housing & Commercial Bank, precisely because he had not been part of the cozy banking scene before the 1997 crisis. He became a lightning rod for protest from Seoul's wealthy elite when he reduced his bank's exposure to troubled Daewoo Motor Co. before the car maker went bankrupt, and then refused to roll over delinquent loans from Hynix Semiconductor, a troubled manufacturer of DRAM memory chips. In the past, Korean banks had, like their Japanese counterparts, tended to prop up such failing firms, fearing that bankruptcy would trigger social or political instability. But Kim had refused to go along.

"What I realized is that many firms failed to conduct the proper corporate evaluation of large companies," he explained to me. "We all know the myth of 'too large to fail' in connection with Korea's *chaebol* conglomerates. I simply decided not to deal with them at all. It only shows that I went faster than others to make the right decisions." Kim's insistence on good governance had also attracted foreign investment in his bank from the likes of Goldman Sachs and the ING Group. Ironically, financial regulators barred Kim from a second term in 2004 as Kookmin's chairman, citing financial irregularities in a corporate tax statement. Many analysts believed he was punished for stirring upheaval in the "old boys network" of Korean banking.

Did religion help Kim form his worldview? "Yes, I'm a Catholic," he said. "If it hadn't been that I was the oldest in the family," and therefore responsible for finding a job to feed his siblings, "I would have become a priest." Kim acknowledged that his religious training "had a significant effect on my consciousness . . . such that I practice on a daily basis a sense of righteousness and responsibility. That's why I feel strongly, for instance, that all shareholders should have equal rights in a firm."

Jooyoung Kim, the University of Chicago–trained lawyer who runs the Center for Good Corporate Governance, an NGO centered on corporate reform, offers another example. His group emerged as an offshoot of the struggle for democratization led by church and student movements. Many of the professionals working in or supporting his own organization, he says, cut their teeth as activists associated with the People's Solidarity for Participatory Democracy, which was founded in 1994 as "a civil organization dedicated to promoting justice and human rights in Korean society through the participation of the people."[28]

PSPD helped file the nation's first shareholder suit in June 1997 after the collapse of Hanbo Steel, whose estimated debt was $5.8 billion. On behalf of sixty-one minority shareholders, PSPD alleged that former officers of Korea First Bank took bribes to extend credit to Hanbo, and demanded reimbursement. On July 24, 1998, the Seoul District Court ruled in favor of these minority shareholders and issued a historic award of 40 billion *won* against the directors and former officers of the bank. Flush from this success, Kim's group pressured big firms such as Samsung Electronics and SK Telecom to do more to protect minority shareholders.

This activist spirit was visible in the 2000 parliamentary election, when PSPD and a coalition of other activists helped create a "blacklist" of incumbent politicians it believed should not be reelected, and succeeded in getting almost 70 percent of these candidates defeated. The transition was, in a sense, now complete. The activists were taking over the system, becoming a part of it. This grassroots movement led by civil society groups, whose initial goal was to topple military rule and bring about democracy, had evolved into a broader effort to improve democratic governance.

Encouraged by its electoral success, this same loose affiliation of civil society activists worked again in the 2002 presidential campaign and helped seal Roh Moo-hyun's narrow victory. Again in 2004, activists helped the fledgling Uri Party, formed to defend the new president against old-line conservatives, capture a majority of seats in the National Assembly. For the first time in South Korea's short democratic life, the conservative stranglehold on parliament was broken. Roh now had a real chance to pursue the independent, progressive agenda that had been denied Kim Dae-jung, and the "386 generation" of activists played the decisive role in this transformation.

Civil activism in South Korea and its growing power in national politics does not come without a price. South Korea is never as tranquil as Japan. Often lacking are the niceties of civility, cooperation, and constructive dialogue that might be expected among those trying to formulate public policy. Political parties often resemble cults of personality created to support individual politicians, rather than advocates of coherent ideological agendas, and are riddled with corruption. Almost continuous conflict between an energized, vigorous civil society and the state tend to make Korean democracy highly unstable, fractious, and fragile. A young democracy, as America's once was, is ideally served by a balanced system—with an energetic civil society monitoring traditional political institutions and keeping them honest. In Korea, such balance isn't always visible.[29] In striving to overcome decades of repression and dictatorship, at times Koreans have seemed to overreach and overcompensate—as in the fistfights that seem to break out regularly on the floor of the parliament. And South Korea has not yet completely abandoned its xenophobic past. Many South Koreans still distrust foreigners and resist the integration globalization offers.

Yet the healthy tension between civil society and the state in Korea promotes vigorous political debate, whereas in contemporary Japan any debate is more like an empty stage play of meaningless kabuki. Where even a century ago Korean Protestants and Catholic institutions were encouraging individualism and independence, Japanese institutions still insist that all Japanese are essentially the same, that relationships are informed by one's standing within a defined group, and that conformity to hierarchical controls is the prime responsibility of the citizen. As Korean church groups resisted Japanese occupation and built private, political spaces beyond state control, such a concept of civil society in prewar

Japan would have directly challenged imperial sovereignty. "Put simply," the historian Sheldon Garon notes, "there were no 'citizens' in pre-war Japan—only 'subjects' of the Emperor."[30]

Despite Japan's educated elite, its growing middle class, and its dense urban society exposed to Western culture and political ideals, civil society there has never gained the traction it has achieved in Korea, and Japanese have failed to create alternative networks for building social trust. While Koreans battled "hard" authoritarianism, political absolutism, and a military dictatorship ruling from above, Japanese remained enmeshed in a "softer," if no less harsh, group-oriented authoritarianism— where basic civil liberties are ostensibly guaranteed, but real choice is absent. As Garon describes, the U.S. occupation could never eliminate the prewar block clubs and neighborhood associations that often compelled household membership and constrained individual choice, not unlike the *gonin-gumi* of the feudal period in which members of every five family groups were obliged to monitor the behavior of the other four. Many of the most active popular organizations in postwar Japan, like the Society of Bereaved Families, advocated forms of right-wing nationalism that sought greater, not less, state intervention in everyday life. In the early 1950s, the state used the influence of the U.S. military occupation to repress Communists and militant labor unions, deracinating the political left. Later on, as Japan focused single-mindedly on economic growth, the state could, with the help of its burgeoning exports to the United States, afford to buy off social movements and absorb meek forms of civil protests.

Progressive forces in Japan have not been averse to using state power or subsidy to help mobilize and socialize the populace. Thus, they have encouraged "private" groups to work arm in arm with the state to promote household savings, hard work, and social education, but these affiliations and financial support cast doubt on the very independence these groups might have asserted. Over time, the Japanese state, which intervened in all forms of daily life, also found ingenious new ways to harness populist activism to achieve national goals, whether to reduce consumption of energy or to encourage recycling.

While Koreans organized themselves to fight "the state," against whom or what exactly are the Japanese supposed to fight? The state is a part of them, and they are part of the national collective: even if only one party ever triumphs at the polls, elections are held regularly, and all citizens are eligible to cast ballots. As one political scientist observed of the Japanese nonprofit sector, "It is very hard to conceive of voluntary action in independence of, or indeed in counter-position to, the state. Rather it is dependent on the state for its legitimacy . . . A cultural paradigm . . . emphasizes the importance of mutual aid as an essential component of society," while local and central governments lead and sanction social service groups.[31]

This link helps explain why Japanese seem neither to appreciate or fully understand what is missing from their meager civic discourse nor to accept a certain amount of friction, dialogue, and debate as healthy aspects of political life, as a necessary mechanism allowing for balance and self-correction. Democracy was imposed on Japan from the outside and weighed down by bureaucratic controls, patronage payoffs, and one-party rule. Dissent disturbs group harmony. Deviance from the mainstream endangers social relations with others; without the proper social relations, a man's livelihood or a child's education could be severely jeopardized. And despite the hardships of its abject defeat in war, the Japanese were never conquered or colonized, as the Koreans were.

Their disparate paths toward modernization help explain the stark differences today visible in the behavior of modern Koreans and Japanese. Events and geography forced South Koreans, the upstarts, to adapt and change, while Japan, increasingly isolated and defensive, has yet to recognize any deep need to relax its excessive insularity. Today, huge numbers of Koreans seek wider exposure to the outside world through foreign study or language courses, and view globalization as a two-way process of mutual benefit. In the digital economy, they have been prepared to accept and exploit global standards and adapt to open networks, so that Samsung and Hyundai have recently emerged as respected consumer brands.

As Korea moves fast, sometimes too fast, to catch up with the world,

Japan grows arthritic and domestically focused. Japanese seem eager to close themselves off from the world beyond their shores. In high tech they have frequently chosen to design new products that rely on proprietary hardware and Japan-only software protocols, so that neither Sony nor Panasonic have emerged as significant players in the U.S. cell phone market, in digital television, or in sales of new MP3 music players.

In my somewhat conventional coverage of the political and economic character of these two competing societies while working as a journalist, it had never dawned on me that the role religion played could prove so decisive in altering a people's attitudes toward self-esteem, individuation, or communal responsibility. Nothing in my background or disposition as an American Jew prepared me to accept that the rise of Western religion—and especially the Protestant Church—had served as a vital force crucial in transforming South Korean society. It may be too simple to argue that exposure to Christianity alone has changed Korean consciousness. Yet the churches have coached the Korean people in forming social networks, building trust among strangers, and accepting universal ethics and individualism in ways that served as powerful antidotes to the autocratic worldview their grandparents—and, indeed, the Japanese—had been taught.

14.

HIKIKOMORI NATION AND SHELTERING UNCLE

In the last years of the twentieth century, an acid joke began circulating among Japan's intelligentsia; how, after years of being hectored by foreign competitors, most notably the United States, over its mercantilist trade policies and insular structure, "Japan bashing" had evolved into "Japan passing" and then into "Japan nothing." The joke insinuated that, while the attention of the Western world was turned elsewhere, especially toward China, the Persian Gulf, and the Middle East, Japan's prestige and global influence continued to wither away. (In Japanese, the rhyming of the words *bashingu*, *pashingu*, and *noshingu* only enhances the humor.) To me it seemed telling that the Japanese themselves were now describing their own once-prideful and glorious nation as one that might choose to stifle itself in seclusion, rather than seek to commingle more closely with the other cultures and economies of a shrinking globe.

Though today we seem to live in an era of rapid-fire global integration, no people seem destined to be as isolated and lonely as the Japanese. No other nation shares its unique culture. Its peculiar form of economic nationalism, neither open and truly capitalist nor explicitly socialist, has never become firmly embedded anyplace else. Relatively few Japanese permanently emigrate to foreign lands, and those who do abandon the mother islands choose to assimilate relatively rapidly into the culture of their new-found lands—far more than say, Taiwanese- or Korean-Americans, for instance, who closely monitor events back home long after they have moved far away, and who choose, despite the great distance, to take an active role in home-country politics. Japanese-Americans quickly adopt an American lifestyle and sever almost all ties to the motherland, as if they immediately sense that, once departed, they may never be able to go home again. In addition, Japanese possess no universal religion or ideology to which citizens in other nations might easily relate.[1]

A nation that cannot define itself clearly cannot hope to act in its rational self-interest. In periods marked by rapid social change, traditional identities dissolve and new ones must be forged. Yet for decades Japan was able to avoid this struggle for identity by immersing itself compulsively in its drive to catch up to the West, to make its country, as opposed to its people, wealthy, to acquire products and an advanced lifestyle, and to mimic the consumption patterns it witnessed in foreign lands; to build the suburban towns, golf courses, and strip malls that seemed to bespeak a sense of prosperity. When its economic miracle finally broke apart in the early 1990s, however, Japan found it could not settle the most fundamental questions regarding its own character. What should it hope to be? Beyond the allure of designer purses and the sheen of luxury automobiles, how should its people find satisfaction? What are its peoples' dreams? In a society dominated by collectivist thinking, where individual instincts have been routinely suppressed to meet group demands and whose geopolitical strategy has for the last six decades been thoroughly dictated by the United States, what does it really mean to be Japanese in the twenty-first century? "What is the Japanese soul, what is the Japanese heart?" a member of Japan's ruling Liberal Democratic Party, Koichi Kato, asked in an April 2005 speech, acknowledging the despair running deep among his constituents. "It's not a question we can answer in five or ten minutes."[2]

In the summer of 2000, I found the identical question proposed far more provocatively by Hitoshi Saeki, the thirty-two-year-old designer of display windows for one of the chic women's boutiques crowded into Tokyo's trendy Aoyama neighborhood. Along the long glass wall in front of the shop, not a single slinky skirt or silk camisole was visible. Instead, eight blood-red boxing gloves hung suspended from the ceiling, like carcasses passing through a slaughterhouse. Each glove hovered above a plastic petri dish proffering a tiny icon.

The first contained a toy red Ferrari.

Another, the token from a Monopoly set resembling a suburban split-level home. Still another overflowed with British pounds. A hypodermic syringe beckoned from a fourth. The fifth displayed a condom. Another offered a minibar bottle of Stolichnaya vodka. The next a business card embossed with the title "president." The last dish contained only a beaker of sand with a large red question mark painted on it.

Underneath the display, the caption read: "What is your goal?"

When I eventually tracked down Saeki to ask what he was up to, the designer told me, "It's more of a generational thing than a national thing but I think young people all over the world ask, 'What is our fundamental reason for being alive? What is our objective in living?' " He continued, "I wanted to use that shop window to say, 'What are we living for?' I really wanted to throw that question out there for people to think about."

Posing the question was so remarkable because it demonstrates how difficult Japanese find it is to answer—at both the panoramic and the microscopic levels. They have been raised since the end of World War Two without an autonomous military, or an independent foreign policy, and lack a honed and bounded sense of nationalism or national interest with which to establish identity and national goals. Japan's most influential contemporary visual artist, Takashi Murakami, the creator of *anime*, grotesque, cartoonlike sculpture, and more recently, handbags for Louis Vuitton, sees his nation as having been traumatized by the atomic bombings it endured in silence in 1945, and also by its subsequent immature embrace of Western consumerism that demonstrated "that the true meaning of life is meaninglessness" and that his people could easily "live without thought."

"The bottom line," Murakami notes,

is that for the past sixty years Japan has been a testing ground for an American style capitalist economy, protected in a greenhouse, nurtured and bloated to the point of explosion. The results are so bizarre, they're perfect. Whatever true intentions underlie "Little

Boy," the nickname for Hiroshima's atomic bomb, we Japanese are truly, deeply, pampered children . . . We throw constant tantrums while enthralled with our own cuteness.[3]

To simply blame American intervention for Japanese modern disaffection and disengagement, however, is to let the Japanese themselves rather lightly off the hook. Murakami fails to acknowledge how the defects so deeply embedded within Japan's own cultural fabric make its people unable to articulate for themselves a new vision and new goals—even spiritual ones—after their tradition-bound culture began to give way and the American occupation ended. For even at the most granular and personal levels, Japanese have been schooled to look outside themselves—at group and contextual norms, rather than at inner conscience—as a means to define moral purpose. Without really understanding themselves, of course, the Japanese cannot hope to understand others. Yet rather than recognize and work to counteract their innate loneliness, Japanese seem to relish their singular inwardness—or seem, at least, resigned to their solipsistic fate, unable to imagine a different future in which they might interact and share comfortably with outsiders. After all, a treacherous sea separates them from the rest of the world's people, so, as in Nagasaki harbor in the seventeenth century, they still get to choose when to call off the harbor patrols and allow strange foreign ships to dock in their ports.

Confronted by a world of increased uncertainty and risk, conscious that its natural ability to integrate with others will always appear awkward and feeble, Japan seems most likely to pattern its future coping behavior after the young *hikikomori* lurking in its midst—those who flee to the protective womb of their rooms rather than stake out an independent path that would eventually lead to self-awareness. In fact, a whole series of Japanese behaviors can be attributed to the deepest desires of this island fortress just to be "left alone."

* * *

Whenever Japanese are asked to describe their country, they often use the word *semai*, a term that suggests "cramped," "narrow," or "crowded." Usually, they are referring to the population density of their rugged archipelago of 126 million, about the size of California, where sharply etched mountains limit both suburban sprawl and agricultural cultivation. But the term *semai* encompasses more than mere physical constraint; the populations of other small nations like South Korea and the Netherlands are actually denser than Japan's, yet these two nations have proved to be far more open to the outside world and less fearful of contact with foreigners. Perhaps that is because the Koreans and the Dutch have no recourse to physical separation from those living around them, as the Japanese do. (Asked to explain why the Dutch were so cosmopolitan and international, Han, a friend in Amsterdam explained, "If we accidentally fall asleep on the train, we wake up in another country.")

In fact, *semai* denotes not simply topology, but also the constraints of the heart, attitudes imposed by narrow-minded or conventional thinking and constricted, exclusive human relationships. Close contact and tight social networks crimp both personal space and individual freedom, and such narrowness can be better understood as the creation of the Japanese mind, the "emotional consequence of Japan's rigid systems which bind individuals and keep out the fresh air of new ideas from abroad," as the writer Alex Kerr has noted.[4] The modern nuclear household also remains *semai*, especially when compared with the expansive multigenerational household of earlier periods.

Such detachment represents another way Japan chooses to shut out the sunshine of pluralism, as the Japanese "system," an overpowering and idiosyncratic mechanism of social control—the "crass group," as the psychiatrist Hisako Watanabe once characterized it to me—proves ruthlessly efficient at insulating its people from those pernicious influences that seem to invade from beyond the oceans. In fact, the nation can be seen as employing an array of cunning tactics—bullying being the most pronounced—to preserve its unusual sense of collective self, security, and well-being.

As it subconsciously adopts *hikikomori* withdrawal behavior—in rejecting global integration when it cannot dictate the terms—Japan seems to mirror its own seventeenth-century policy of systematic seclusion known as *sakoku*, or "closed country," so successfully employed for more than two hundred years during the Tokugawa shogunate. Any Japanese who wandered from the islands during this period was killed on his return, and foreign ships accidentally straying into Japanese waters were sacked and burned. Dutch merchants were permitted to trade with the Japanese, but their presence was strictly limited to Deshima, that tiny artificial island erected in Nagasaki harbor. Only those with special passes could travel the causeway linking Deshima to the mainland; at night the traders had to return to their island compound, where guards isolated them behind locked gates and designated geisha entertained them.

Today, despite the collapse of so many physical barriers in the "virtual" and "borderless" world, the cruel reality is that no external force short of military invasion can radically alter Japanese national conduct as Commodore Perry did in 1853—or as, in 1945, when the atomic attacks on Hiroshima and Nagasaki forced the abrupt conclusion to the Pacific War. Today, no one has leverage over a Japan that possesses enormous national wealth, a robust military capable of mounting a vigorous self-defense, and defensible borders. Its giant and ever-expanding trade surplus, as well as its constant purchase of foreign debts give it, in turn, outsized influence over an American economy chronically plagued with twin budget and trade deficits. If Japan wants to be "left alone," free to pursue policies that continue to leave its people trapped and oppressed and disconsolate, no one—not the International Monetary Fund or the United Nations or the OECD or the Pentagon—can readily interfere.

There is also the question of why you would choose to. Even today, after fifteen years of recession, there remains much to admire in the Japanese system, and many elements that its people naturally seek to protect. The nation is stable and calm, its streets are safe and seem nearly crime-free, its transportation system functions with punctilious efficiency, and its schools provide high levels of basic skills to the vast majority of students, who go on to score relatively well on standardized tests, even if they no longer perform quite as well as they once did. In global terms, national incomes remain high. A manufacturing ethic that demands quality and precision endures. Japanese rightly want to preserve their aesthetics, the safety and order of their collectivist social architecture, and the modesty and industriousness that have enriched them. After all, they did transform their small island nation into a great industrial power.

When other great powers like imperial Spain or the British Empire collapsed, the culprit was usually what the historian Paul Kennedy has labeled "imperial overstretch." As these empires sought hegemony over ever-larger and more far-flung territories, they began to exhaust the resources and manpower necessary to maintain their grip. Some believe this may prove America's ultimate destiny, as our reach exceeds our grasp—as the Iraq adventure has demonstrated the limits of our power. Japan, however, confronts no such similar concerns. Unique among great nations, it emerged an economic superpower in the 1970s without accumulating either the political responsibilities or the territorial dependencies of empire. It has no military installations from which it need withdraw, no nations it must prop up, thanks entirely to the military protection the United States offered its defeated adversary at the end of World War Two.[5] The doctrine first articulated by Prime Minister Shigeru Yoshida in the early 1950s—that Japan would focus only on economics, while Washington took care of everything else—has worked spectacularly well.

Today, however, as it gets older, grayer, and less prosperous, a shrinking and more anxious Japan may take up the McDonald's hamburgers and Nike sneakers the world puts at its doorstep, even as it resists many deeper aspects of international integration, whether this assimilation be expressed through global accounting rules or technology standards it cannot control, or as a consequence of free markets and open trade. Suspicious of radical change, determined to preserve its homogeneous traditions and ancient culture, uncomfortable in communicating with the outside world, Japan erects intractable social, economic, and legal barriers that keep foreigners at bay, as it doggedly blocks foreign immigrants and deters foreign investors.

Many Japanese honestly recognize the challenges their nation faces. In April 2005, the government issued a new white paper, reminiscent of the old, neglected Maekawa Report, which outlined a "21st Century Vision" of a new Japan. It accurately diagnosed a Japan that, if it failed to reform and rejuvenate itself, would be saddled with "an increasing number of people [who] lose hope" and a "Japan that will be left behind in globalization." It described this path as a "gradual but steady pathway to decline."[6]

As an alternative strategy, the panel advocated turning Japan into a "bridging country" by making it a "country without walls," one which would promote intellectual and cultural exchange "on a foundation of trust and confidence," reduce the power of government by encouraging decentralization, and create a "virtuous cycle" of enhanced productivity and rising incomes—a world in which resources are allocated competitively and innovation is promoted. Unfortunately, there is precious little evidence that any of these spectacularly worthy goals would ever be implemented.

An important distinction remains, however, between this Japan that systematically keeps at bay the powerful forces of global integration that demand adaptation, and the sympathetic young *hikikomori* who seeks refuge in the isolation of his room. Most of the *hikikomori* I spoke with actually want to break down the system of collective consciousness and control that immobilizes them, but find themselves powerless to do so. Each genuinely seeks the freedom to express his true character. He wants more of the openness and relative disorder the West has come to accept; he hopes to communicate his genuine feelings to others, but finds no means to compel the collectivist constraints of the Japanese "system"—a system no single entity or group actually controls—to yield. Japan's power centers, however, continue to propagate and prop up their pilotless "system"—the same now failing bulwarks that for decades allowed them to act as gatekeepers, controlling economic outcomes, managing political stability, and containing social influences that might destabilize, none more dangerous than the virus of individualism itself. While a *hikikomori* wants to "break out" of the enforced discipline of collectivism and seeks emancipation from these faceless jailers locking him in, these same gatekeepers shut out as much of the outside world's influence as they can in order to keep their systems functioning and their authority unchallenged. Ultimately, more than mercantilism alone explains Japanese insularity.

As Japan embraces its own *hikikomori* behavior as the most comfortable means to cope with its bounded future, this stratagem can succeed only if the United States plays along and continues to embrace its role as the enabling, codependent parent. For just as an isolated child needs a parent's protection, Japan can survive in its course of renewed isolation only if we Americans agree to act as the guardian who gallantly commands Japan's national defense while allowing Japan's export industries unfettered access to U.S. markets.

*   *   *

Both the economic and the security dimensions of this Japanese-American codependency remain profound. In 2004 alone, Japan's trade surplus routinely exceeded $9 billion a month, bulked up not only by sales of consumer electronics and automobiles to the United States and Europe, but also by expanding exports of capital equipment and semiconductors to China. Toyota, Nissan, Sony, and Matsushita Electronics are among the well-known Japanese exporters who have used superior production methods, precise cost-control techniques, and technological sophistication to make the giant leaps required to compete in the global marketplace. These firms employ thousands of workers at home and generate billions of yen in profits each year, even as they build dozens of their newest factories overseas. As these, Japan's most productive firms, put nutrients at the nation's door—as expressed through Japan's massive and continuous trade surpluses—this enormous reservoir of hard cash permits its leaders to maintain national autonomy, fulfill the need to purchase foreign oil and import food, and influence less-developed nations through donations of technical and in-kind assistance.

These efficient exporters make an enormous contribution to Japan's economy, yet represent only 10 percent of Japan's annual GDP. In effect, they subsidize the vast majority of a Japanese economy that remains remarkably lame and unproductive. Japan should be striving to boost its overall efficiency as its population declines, yet the OECD estimates that Japan's overall labor productivity remains 30 percent below that of the United States and is the lowest among the world's seven largest economies.[7] In Japan, just the food-processing sector alone employs more workers than the combined total of those making steel and building cars, machine tools, and computers; they comprise nearly 11 percent of all manufacturing jobs. Needless to say, this sector was only 39 percent as productive as the U.S. industry.[8] No wonder Japan's trade barriers remain high, and that consumers are gouged by relatively high prices and meager choices.

Japan effectively mounts its own "manic defense" against the porous networks, generalized trust, and ethical universalism that could readily undermine Japan's traditional way of life by being hyperaggressive in foreign markets as it shields its home soil against the penetration of outsiders, including potential business competitors. For Japanese leaders know that choice is an enemy. If they give their people too much choice and autonomy, whether in the marketplace or in the workplace, their closed and inflexible system might just crumble away.

While America keeps its market wide open to Japanese goods, because our consumers relish low prices, Japan (and now China) in turn keeps America from being forced to bear the costs of its own profligacy. America's financial system is propped up by its consumers, whose spending constitutes two-thirds of our economic activity. The only way for the nation to continue to run up mammoth and persistent trade deficits, spending far more than it earns, is for someone to play banker and loan us the difference. Japan's phenomenal savings allows it to fill the gap and to keep plowing funds into U.S. Treasury notes and other instruments. These massive purchases of dollar assets by the Bank of Japan, as well as similar ones in recent years by the Bank of China, help America maintain artificially low interest rates, sustain its remarkable housing boom, and continue on a path of what seems to be unsustainable levels of consumption. Should Japan stop funding these debts, the U.S. government would have to raise interest rates sharply—a measure that would in turn boost what American consumers pay for home mortgages and credit card debt and slow the domestic economy.

This economic *amae*, or codependency, inures to Japan's benefit as well. As the Bank of Japan buys up American debt, it artificially depresses the value of its own currency, ensuring that Japanese manufactures stay competitive in U.S. markets. In 2003 alone, Japanese purchased an estimated $200 billion of U.S. Treasury securities in order to weaken the yen and make its exports more attractive to American consumers. Of course a cheaper yen makes Sony TVs and Toyota trucks more affordable to American consumers, who pay in stronger dollars. Akio Mikuni and R. Taggart Murphy argue that it is Japan's deep dependency on its massive stock of U.S. dollar reserves—a product of its traditional mercantilist policy of blocking imports and subsidizing exports—that set off Japan's deflationary spiral of falling prices and declining wages in the 1990s and exacerbated economic stagnation. By accumulating so much productive capability like factories, machine tools, and robots, and so many claims on the assets of foreign countries through its massive dollar-denominated portfolio, the Japanese have deliberately undertaken policies that reduce the uncertainty and danger of dealing with outsiders. This giant portfolio of "rainy day" funds makes it easier for Japan to cut its ties with the rest of the world, should it choose to. Since the late nineteenth century, they argue, the implied goal of Japanese economic policy has been "the building of an industrial structure that would reduce reliance on foreigners to the bare minimum."[9] Just as a *hikikomori* might horde food to keep from having to leave his room, Japan hordes the cash it might need to sustain itself through a long, dark winter.

In its international affairs, likewise, Japanese themselves wonder whether theirs will ever become a truly adult and "normal nation," after following its unusual path of dependency since defeat in World War Two. Japan has been encouraged to carry on Yoshida's doctrine and resist developing its own, truly independent foreign policy by a United States that wanted dominance in the region. Today Japan still lurks in the large shadows cast by its giant American patron.

The historian John Dower has documented what he has termed

Japan's "almost sensual embrace" of the United States so quickly after being devastated by the war.[10] The conquered people of Japan almost immediately accepted the Americans not as mere occupiers, but as a revolutionary army that would both free the citizenry from the yoke of militarism and treat a defeated people far more benignly than they might rightly have expected. The Americans, in turn, felt a need to immunize this vital Asian nation against the viral threat of Communism.

When a brash utopian group of New Deal reformers, under the command of General Douglas MacArthur, descended on Tokyo to administer a defeated nation, a complete transformation of society was uppermost in its mind. These reformers were determined to use the authority of the U.S. occupation to create a vibrant liberal democracy, an open, market-based economy, and a social system that would eradicate any vestiges of prewar feudalism. They sought to create independent labor unions and carried out agricultural land reform, for instance, in an attempt to loosen feudal bonds.

But as Dower recounts in *Embracing Defeat*, the American occupiers also had to consider how best to prosecute the unfolding Cold War in Asia and prepare for the likelihood of military confrontation on the Korean peninsula, even as they tried to put a war-ravaged nation back on its feet. As conflict loomed in Korea, the priorities of the United States shifted radically as it realized what an important asset an orderly, pliant, and reindustrialized Japan could prove both for basing soldiers to fight in that war and for keeping Communism at bay. Thus, Japan's American occupiers encouraged Japanese society to rebuild swiftly, and in ways that repressed open networks of trust and subverted genuine democracy. Indeed, in its utterly pragmatic approach to postwar governance, our government became thoroughly complicit in short-circuiting the market-based democratic liberalism that today prevails in so much of the industrial world. Thus, despite our original hope to establish and promote liberal democracy, we Americans unwittingly promoted the reemergence of economic bureaucratism within Japan while helping to fashion one of the most restrictive foreign trade and foreign exchange control systems ever devised by a major free nation.[11]

This political and ideological rationale for "reversing course" not only made for Japan's rapid emergence as a strong, pro-American bastion in an Asia under threat, but also demonstrated to the Japanese that collaboration and cooperation with the conquerors from the United States could prove mutually beneficial. In rehabilitating the most conservative and corporatist elements of Japanese society, Dower notes, under the aegis of "continued American *parenting* of this 'abnormal' market economy" [emphasis added], even former war criminals were restored to positions of power to run the vast *keiretsu* networks of industry. This is just the opposite of our current policy in vanquished Iraq, where the Americans summarily fired all Sunni Baathists loyal to the regime of Saddam Hussein.[12]

By reenlisting members of the old guard to get the country up and running and by suppressing left-wing opponents, the American attempt to impose democratic governance from above inevitably helped create a weirdly misshapen and defective political system. Essentially, a single political party, the Liberal Democrats, has governed for the past fifty years. Like the old political machine operated by Richard Daley in Chicago in the 1960s, it is a party ruled by bagmen rather than by statesmen, and one where patronage, not policy or ideology, frames most debate. The domination of this single party has permitted a conservative corporate coalition to coopt interest groups, redistribute wealth to those needing support, and blunt the "battle of ideas" that usually shapes politics in normal democratic societies. Such single party domination, and its unpalatable heredity, also helps explain why Japan today remains unable to come to terms through honest reflection with its brutal colonial and militarist past. Unlike postwar West Germany, in which opposition parties ultimately gained control of government, incumbent right-wing leaders readily regained power in Japan and were never compelled to look back seriously and judiciously or take responsibility for their past deeds. Forcing Japan to shelter under America's protective umbrella also gave the Japanese time and space to defer resolving those basic questions of national identity and self-interest, issues that linger uncomfortably in the twenty-first century.

The Japanese were also compelled to accept a pacifist constitution, written by the U.S. occupation, that declared that "the Japanese people forever renounce war as a sovereign right of the nation and the threat or use of force as means of settling international disputes." The postwar Japan promised to never maintain "land, sea and air forces." Yet as U.S. fears of surging Communist expansion across Asia grew more pronounced, the Americans reversed course here, too, and backed the quiet rebuilding of Japan's military, now duly labeled Self-Defense Forces to distinguish them from their Imperial forebears. Tokyo and Washington also signed a Security Treaty in 1952, revised in 1960, which gave American forces control over key naval and air bases on the island of Okinawa. Today, these bases for Marine, Army, and Air Force units serve as crucial elements in Pentagon strategies for projecting military power throughout the Pacific region while the SDF has over the years outfitted itself with advanced jet fighters, naval warships, and high-tech missile batteries. Theatre Missile Defense, a system which would allow Japanese rockets to intercept incoming missiles from space, looms on the horizon.

Though the Cold War is now over, this Faustian bargain remains in full force. As a direct result of the Security Alliance, Japan has found itself with little choice in recent years but to wholeheartedly support U.S. foreign policy, even if it might actually work against longer-term Japanese interests. No better example was the Iraq war in 2003, when Prime Minister Junichiro Koizumi felt he had both to publicly support his friend George W. Bush during the invasion to topple Saddam Hussein and to dispatch Japanese troops afterward to conduct humanitarian aid as an expression of symbolic support. The deployment of a Japanese unit to Iraq took place in obvious contravention of Japan's own pacifist constitution, but Japanese politicians worried that if they defied American wishes in the Middle East, who could they expect to rise up and protect them if North Korea decided to launch a nuclear strike against Japanese territory? This deployment also undermined Japan's long-held aspiration to acquire a permanent seat on the U.N. Security Council, since the Iraq war was launched unilaterally and without U.N. sanction. Only now, sixty years after World War Two, are the Japanese seriously discussing plans to revise their constitution to drop the pledge never again to wage war. But a Japa-

nese military suddenly liberated from its old constraints and able to operate freely around the world might set off a destructive and destabilizing
arms race in capitals like Beijing, Seoul, and Taipei, while triggering alarm
in other Asian nations where painful memories of Japanese occupation remain vivid.

Washington's utter domination of Japan's security policy has had other
pernicious effects, too. It has permitted Japan's political and business
elites to avoid, until recently, any tough calculations or even vigorous
public debate over crucial issues that could help Japan calibrate its rational self-interest: What sort of nation should Japan become in the
twenty-first century? How should an old, inflexible system navigate a
more complex globe? What sort of influence should Japan seek to exert
beyond its borders? How should it react to the rise of China? And what
would Japan look like if it steered a security course independent of the
United States? Most Japanese are unable to answer these questions; the
nation has sought to accommodate, rather than actively influence events;
until recently, open public debate over important issues like the U.S. Security Treaty itself was considered taboo. It is a healthy sign that the debate within Japan is finally beginning, though Tokyo and Washington are
so strongly wedded to their codependency that it is difficult to imagine
any quick change on either the security or the economic fronts. Ultimately, Tokyo and Washington are stuck with each other. For although
Westerners might advocate rapid deregulation, greater foreign investment, and the development of risk-based capital investment to spur entrepreneurship, outsiders cannot readily force Japan's Iron Triangle to
unbend unless Tokyo also demands to free itself from America's military
subjugation and become truly independent. As was demonstrated during
the U.S-Japan "trade wars" of the late 1980s and early 1990s, the threat
of sanctions or punitive tariffs against Japanese industries will always ring
hollow as long as U.S. jet fighter squadrons and naval warships need to
be based on Japanese soil. By the same token, Japan can never expect to
mature politically and stand on its own if it remains forever locked within
the stifling American embrace.

*   *   *

To resist global integration and deflect the dangerous influences of out-siders, Japan employs an insidious array of tactics. Among these are a bottomless fear of immigration, an unwelcoming attitude toward foreign direct investment, and half-baked methods to get its people to master foreign languages.

By most measures, Japan remains among the world's least open economies, certainly the least open in Asia, despite a new policy of open-ness proclaimed by Prime Minister Junichiro Koizumi.[13] Foreign direct investment has surged, but only from a minuscule base. Today imports and exports account for only 18 percent of Japan's economic output, compared to 73 percent for South Korea or 202 percent for Malaysia. Only 1.36 percent of Japanese workers are employed in foreign-affiliated firms, while some 11 percent of America's workforce is employed by for-eign capital. As a percentage of GDP, Japan's stock of foreign direct in-vestment is one eleventh of the United States' and one twenty-second of Germany's, according to a report commissioned by the American Cham-ber of Commerce in Japan in 2003.[14] In a single year, more foreign money poured into mainland China, an estimated $52 billion, than has been cu-mulatively invested in Japan. Both China and South Korea have created explicit government policies that give foreign companies incentives to build factories or invest in the domestic economy. Japan has none.

Japan's neighbors and economic competitors have systematically opened their corporate and production networks to foreign firms—apparently on the theory that they can learn new skills and benefit fundamentally from greater interaction with foreign investors. China, for one, has become a giant magnet for foreign capital and advanced high technology, despite the nation's lack of protection for intellectual property and the arbitrary manner in which its commercial laws are often enforced. Yet Japan's rel-atively high costs and utter lack of incentives help put a lid on foreign participation in the giant domestic economy, even after the success that

French investors wrested from troubled Nissan Motor Co. under the bold leadership of Carlos Ghosn, who put the debt-ridden automotive behemoth back on its feet; or that U.S.-owned Ripplewood Holdings achieved with its purchase of the failed Long-Term Credit Bank in 1999, which it transformed into the profitable Shinsei Bank. Though Shinsei has operated more along the lines of a Western-style bank, it has not altered fundamental Japanese resistance to corporate reform nor has it broken into the clubby networks of Japanese finance. The bank remains an outsider, looking in.

Using regulatory as well as informal barriers, the government has maintained hallowed sanctuaries in sectors ranging from agriculture services and transportation to health care and education. And since shareholders have few legal rights, the hostile takeover strategies often employed in the West to force mergers of inefficient or debt-laden firms seldom succeed.

With its birthrate plummeting, Japan will inevitably face a shortage of workers, especially in the service economy, since young Japanese continue to refuse to do the dirty and dangerous unskilled labor and service work their parents once performed. Such shortages might be averted, however, were Japan to move radically away from its own inward-looking, xenophobic past and open its doors wide to foreign workers who might settle, raise families, and become Japanese citizens.

Within the past half decade, a surprising number of government officials and business leaders have broached the formerly untouchable subject of altering government policies to encourage foreign workers to relocate to Japan. Taiichi Sakaiya, the former Economic Planning Agency minister, is among those who frequently argue that Japan must open its borders and encourage immigrant workers. In response, the government has opened the doors a tiny crack. In its latest revision of the immigration law, it granted special access to descendants of Japanese who migrated to Brazil, Peru, and other South American countries early in the twentieth century, a "reform" designed to maintain racial purity.

Yet a broader transformation hardly seems likely. Opening the migratory spigots for those foreigners without a drop of Japanese blood apparently stirs deep national anxiety, and the government steadfastly refuses to alter restrictive policies that make it difficult for such foreigners to win work permits or gain citizenship. Japan fears that a swell of unruly foreign-born workers might taint the gene pool by marrying the locals, and subvert Japan's unique and unusually homogeneous society. Such a multicultural society might permanently taint national values, they believe. Still today, Japan denies citizenship rights to third-generation residents of Korean ancestry, and courts have upheld the rights of a government ministry to block the promotion of a second-generation Japanese of Korean descent because she was not a citizen. Chong Hyang-gyun, a public health nurse born and raised in Japan, who speaks Japanese as her first language, was barred from taking a civil service exam by the Tokyo metropolitan government in 1994 because she did not hold Japanese nationality. She sued; in May 1996, the Tokyo District Court ruled that the Constitution did not extend to foreigners the right to work in public posts related to "state decision-making"—in this case, as a nursing supervisor. In January 2005, more than a decade after the incident, the Supreme Court affirmed the decision to bar her from promotion, saying: "Japanese nationality is necessary for positions which are linked to the exercise of public power." The landmark decision, which effectively ruled that even mid-level civil service jobs could be filled only by Japanese, was greeted with dismay by antidiscrimination campaigners.[15]

Technically, it is not impossible for a foreigner to gain full Japanese citizenship, but winning permanent status is, in reality, exceedingly difficult.[16] Very few foreigners choose this route, typically 15,000 per year, of which two-thirds are resident Koreans. In 2002, by contrast, a total of 700,000 low-wage foreign workers were living as "guests" in Japan, though it was estimated the country would require an estimated 610,000 immigrants each year over the next fifty just to maintain a stable working population.[17]

Japan also remains very hostile to political refugees. In January 2005, it deported a Turkish Kurd and his adult son in direct defiance of a finding by the United Nations High Commissioner for Refugees that the two faced imminent danger if returned to their homeland. Earlier, Japan had deported Afghan refugees similarly endangered. The behavior, the UN-HCR noted, was "unprecedented" and "contrasts with Japan's humanitarian assistance towards refugees and disaster victims abroad."[18]

DNA, not equity, sets immigration policy in Japan, as the recent case of the former Peruvian president Alberto Fujimori proves. Though wanted on corruption charges in his homeland, Fujimori was welcomed with open arms by Japanese immigration officials when he fled to Tokyo in 2000 rather than face arrest. He was quickly granted Japanese citizenship status, and the Justice Ministry refused to extradite him because, when he was born in Lima in 1938, both his parents were Japanese citizens who registered his birth at the Japanese embassy.

While blue-collar laborers confront towering barriers, even high-wage foreign professionals who today are permitted to work in Japan often feel like those Dutch traders, living in an artificial world separated by an invisible causeway from the genuine Japanese mainstream. Foreign employees in Japanese firms find a "rice paper ceiling" blocks their advancement into senior ranks. Few are given management responsibility. One American friend who spoke perfect Japanese and had lived in Tokyo for thirty years told me the clearest sign of a crisis brewing inside his own company was when senior management held meetings and excluded him. "My loyalty and my knowledge are never questioned," he said, "but I'm always outside the tent looking in."

It is true that a few foreign firms have gradually built up sizable portfolio investments in Japanese companies or even come to manage certain troubled Japanese firms like Nissan. But mostly they remain marginal actors with little opportunity to rewrite the broader rules by which Japanese conduct business. Japanese almost always prefer to merge with other Japanese; "global standards," a term used to connote transparent accounting and corporate governance practices in Western economies, remains an essentially "foreign" concept in Japan.

Not surprisingly, many ambitious young Japanese find themselves as suffocated by the system as their American counterparts, so thousands of the best and most talented flee to the breathing room more open societies offer. Just as *hikikomori* who venture off to Thailand, India, or the

United States suddenly gain confidence and self-esteem, these expatriates experience emancipation abroad, where rules of generalized trust and transparency are more accepted. Whether fashion photographers in Paris or software programmers in Silicon Valley, these Japanese find that, after living outside Japan for just three or four years, it is nearly impossible for them to return and readjust to Japan's narrow strictures. Altruistic Japanese often choose to work in government-sponsored development programs or in humanitarian assistance in foreign lands because they can prove themselves more effective overseas than at home. The Japanese government, in fact, is a major donor to such aid programs, and its generous contributions to foreign projects help divert attention from its extreme insularity and basic hostility to foreign interlopers and international standards at home.

Many of those Japanese who do choose to return home after years overseas say they censor their own thoughts and monitor their own behavior in order not to "stick out." They often report having trouble fitting back into the rigid systems of their traditional companies, which insist that they "wipe clean" their memories of being abroad so as not to differentiate themselves excessively from, and cause friction within, the workgroup. Many end up leaving their former employers to work for foreign-owned firms within Japan. If their children have learned a foreign language or adopted the nonverbal behavior or facial expressions of a non-Japanese culture, they, in turn, often are subjected to vicious bullying and abuse at school.

Some Japanese expatriates conclude they simply can't go home again; the chasm is just too wide. American law and CPA firms are today full of talented Japanese who came to the West to study and realized they could never go back. The organizations they abandoned tend to remain impermeable, uninterested in profiting from the skills and knowledge their former employees have acquired.

Beyond its group-dominated culture and stifling hierarchies, language remains another conspicuous barrier keeping Japanese apart. Even though a majority of Japanese frequently tells polltakers that learning and speaking English is essential in the twenty-first century, and Japan spends an estimated $20 billion per year on English language study, the language skills of Japanese consistently test among the lowest in Asia. Year after year, the average score of Japanese students taking the Test of English for International Communication is the lowest—tied with students from North Korea—among seventeen nations in both listening and reading. Chinese, South Korean, and Southeast Asian students regularly outperform their Japanese counterparts, though Japanese are required to study English for six years in junior high and high school.

In 2003, Japan's Ministry of Education declared that "cultivating 'Japanese with English Abilities' is an extremely important issue for the future of our children and for the further development of our country," and pledged to formulate a "concrete action plan" by 2008 to improve the English ability of Japanese students.[19] But many Japanese observers doubt whether this *tatemae* will lead to fundamental reform.

* * *

So as Japan's wealth, population, and prestige slowly wither in this new century, the nation confronts a competing set of painful choices. It can undertake fundamental reforms and social adjustments to rejuvenate the economy, create a more vibrant and pluralistic society, empower the individual, encourage more risk-taking, flatten hierarchies, and induce its people to integrate more effectively with the outside world. Alternatively, Japan can resist all but the most cosmetic responses to globalization, as it slowly and steadily withdraws from the world. While not necessarily uncomfortable, such a slide would inevitably force Japan to accept the distasteful prospect of China's replacing it as Asia's strategic center and of Tokyo's being relegated to secondary status. This process of slow marginalization—of "Japan nothing"—may already be under way as China continues to signal its desire to insinuate itself more quickly into the global economy and to integrate more effectively with the other nations of Asia. In November 2004, Beijing signed an agreement with ten Southeast Asian nations to create the world's largest free trade area by 2010—a region that would encompass 1.7 billion people and trade valued at $1.2 trillion. Rather pointedly, Japan was kept out of the proposed deal. Such a free trade zone would further expose the competitive weaknesses of Japan as a high-cost country within a low-cost region; yet Japan has few strategic cards to play if it hopes to counter China's momentum.

Although China's inevitable rise will dramatically transform the political map of Asia, it will not in itself necessarily lead to domestic upheaval or displacement within Japan. Japan could well bury any lingering dreams of global, or even regional, superiority and choose instead to turn itself into an Asian model of Switzerland, a peaceful, relatively prosperous, insulated, and increasingly irrelevant nation, a quiet and stable second-rank power. Could the Japanese vote on it, I have little doubt that a majority would choose such gradual decline over any radical, destabilizing change.

Or, Japan could seek to change the rules—and find ways to create a solid and peaceful relationship with Beijing independent of Washington's firm guidance. Such a dramatic transformation would require nuanced and sophisticated leadership and the realization of several taxing prerequisites. Japan would have to revise its pacifist constitution to permit full-fledged military deployments abroad and create greater distance from Washington. Its prime ministers would have to stop making ceremonial visits to the Yasukuni Shrine in Tokyo, which venerates war criminals. At the same time, Tokyo would have to rein in Japan's radical nationalists who seek confrontation with China, while signaling to Beijing that Asia's two great powers can actually work together to build cooperation within a fractious Asian region that lacks much of the international infrastructure that has stabilized Europe. Such a balanced, forward-looking integrative strategy may, however, lie beyond the capabilities of Japan's current political leaders, who can nurture the perceived "China threat" to help the U.S. military, which now wants to redeploy its troops throughout Japan to help contain China's rise. As the violent anti-Japanese demonstrations that sprang up across China in the spring of 2005 clearly demonstrated, however, many Chinese have not forgotten the bitter history of the Japanese occupation and may not be willing to accept any form of cooperative relations with Japan. Nor has Japan signaled a ready willingness to address its current stalemate. Foreign policy is seldom even debated among the public at large, and many young Japanese students are still not accurately taught in their textbooks about Japan's colonial expansion in the early twentieth century or about what led their nation to war.

Besides, psychological constraint, as much as cultural friction, may also limit this course. For bound as they are in Japan's "cultlike" web of obligations, discipline, loyalty, and denial, its citizens tend to adjust themselves to social reality rather than rouse themselves to influence or change it; faced with adversity, they tend to grow passive. "The more you struggle [in this web], the more you get entangled," the child psychiatrist Hisako Watanabe told me. "So the best way to succumb is through helplessness." To really change Japan's social structure, to destroy its stifling hierarchies and create open lines of communication, would require the sort of revolution in values and self-assertion that has seemed beyond the nation's abilities in recent decades.

* * *

Japan's ability to retool will affect America, too. For while American leaders are tempted to assert that their global influence and military power guarantees Tokyo will always and inevitably follow U.S. dictates, they fail to recognize how nagging domestic preoccupations and growing pessimism could someday trigger a fierce nationalistic response and cause a serious rupture in U.S.-Japan relations, despite Tokyo's official support for the war in Iraq. Someday America may discover it has pushed Japan too far.

U.S. policy makers may be blinded by their own hubris. They have long assumed that a vigorous Japan will continue to form the vibrant center of an Asian region in which American military forces help integrate its diverse elements, keep the peace, promote Western interests, and contain China. In these American eyes, Japan serves both as the "unsinkable aircraft carrier" on which the United States bases its warplanes and security policies, and as our pivot point for defense against China's military ambitions.

But what if Japan is no longer quite so vibrant? As it grows increasingly pessimistic and self-absorbed, Japan might—like the *hikikomori* who lashes out and beats his father—turn to a fierce new form of nationalism, including a new strain of anti-Americanism, to create at least the illusion of positive momentum. Today, one of Japan's most popular politicians is Shintaro Ishihara, the governor of metropolitan Tokyo and co-author of the famous book *The Japan That Can Say No*. The governor frequently lashes out at mainland China, disparages the presence of Asian immigrants in his city, and believes an assertive Japan should emerge from behind the shadows of the American flag. Meanwhile, within the ruling Liberal Democratic Party, a sizable number continue to distrust the United States, to worship at Yasukuni Shrine, the massive Shinto shrine in Tokyo which commemorates Japanese war criminals, and to support controversial textbooks that gloss over Japan's war record and colonial past. Many seek not just to revise the pacifist constitution, but to strengthen the nation's military posture across the region. There also remains a sizable bloc of voters opposed to increased Japanese militarism or any revision of Article Nine.

Regardless of its ultimate course, as Japan's ambitions and economic influence diminish, the balance of power across Pacific Asia will dramatically pivot, profoundly affecting America's future prospects within Asia. For decades, the United States has maintained strong alliances with South Korea as well as Japan as a means to guarantee a strong presence in the region and contain Chinese military aspirations. Good relations with Seoul and Tokyo, the thinking has been, make it easier to address the rise of China. As Japan struggles with its own malaise, however, U.S. relations with South Korea have also become seriously strained during the administration of George W. Bush. As a result, America might soon confront an unanticipated crisis in Asia for which it is woefully short of allies and ill-prepared.

Once the strongest of American allies, South Korea is close to abandoning its historic ties to the United States. In South Korea today, a majority of young adults believe that George W. Bush poses a greater danger to world peace than North Korean dictator Kim Jong-il, and that China, not America, represents the best hope for the future. More South Korean students today are studying Mandarin Chinese than English, and there is more Korean foreign investment taking place in mainland China than in the United States. At the same time, a growing number of American conservatives believe that Seoul and Washington no longer share strategic objectives, and that America's presence in South Korea should be sharply curtailed.

The once vital relationship between Seoul and Washington began to unravel during Bush's first term, as South Korean society was moving to the left while Washington was making a sharp turn to the political right. In Seoul, the successive administrations of Kim Dae-jung and Roh Moo-hyun sought to increase economic ties with North Korea—a so-called sunshine policy—as a way to get Pyongyang to curb its dangerous development of nuclear missiles, while the Bush administration resolutely refused to negotiate, saying it would not submit to such nuclear "blackmail." The South Koreans support direct talks between Washington and Pyongyang to resolve the impasse, while the Americans insist the conversation should bring Russia, Japan, and China to the table as well. In addition, the Bush team has been far more preoccupied with its military campaign in Baghdad than with Pyongyang's brinksmanship, while young Koreans are convinced that even a nuclear-armed North Korea would never attack the South. "With North Koreans, we share blood," a South Korean dentist once told me. "With Americans, we only shed blood."

These sharp differences have caused some Americans to question whether the presence of the U.S. military along the Demilitarized Zone separating North and South is sufficiently "appreciated" by the South Koreans, while South Koreans increasingly wonder why U.S. troops still hold on to giant bases in downtown Seoul, fifty years after the fighting stopped. As Korean leftists view these troops as vestiges of occupation, a chorus of American conservatives believe that the United States no longer has real interests to protect in the South, and that the South Koreans have sufficient military troops and resources to defend themselves. Once close allies, Seoul and Washington now talk past each other, and when Japan sought a U.N. Security Council seat in 2005, South Korea joined Beijing in opposing Tokyo's bid.

Yet the day may come when the isolated dictatorship in Pyongyang finally does fall, and the Korean peninsula is again unified. South Korean political leaders already are developing blueprints of how to merge the high-technology capabilities of Southern industries with the cheap labor of the famine-plagued and underdeveloped North, so as to compete more effectively against Japan in global markets. Thousands of North Koreans already work in South Korean–owned factories built in a special industrial zone in Kaesong, five miles north of the Demilitarized Zone.

With relations between Seoul and Washington on increasingly shaky ground, as the American government seems increasingly remote and hostile, it seems likely that someday soon American troops will be forced to abandon Korean soil, and that South Korea will seek instead to broaden its cooperative and strategic alliances with Beijing, returning to its historic status as a tributary state. The net result would be that China— which is already rebuilding close ties with such vital nations of Southeast Asia as Thailand, Indonesia, and Malaysia, with which it shares cultural affinities as well as economic and linguistic ties—would reclaim its influence over the entire Korean peninsula as well. Fifty years after sending its troops south in an effort to conquer Seoul, China will finally prevail. This eventuality would divide Asia along two axes. One will link Tokyo and Washington with other peripheral powers, including the Philippines, Australia, and New Zealand. All other nations on the Asian continent will array themselves on the other side, under Beijing's considerable sway. This is a schism that—in strategic, security, and political terms—would radically rearrange the regional balance in East Asia and prove detrimental to U.S. interests.[20]

These trends suggest that, if Washington continues to prop up a declining Japan—a Japan the rest of Asia still manifestly distrusts—the other dynamic nations of Asia may well return to the Chinese sphere of influence in which they were once enfolded centuries before the Americans arrived. At that point, with only a fading Tokyo as our chief Asian ally, we in America would find ourselves in the disturbing—and uncomfortable—position of being on the outside, looking in.

15.

"A SINGLE RAY OF LIGHT"

In March 2003, the Japanese film director Hayao Miyazaki captured the first Academy Award ever presented to a work of Japanese *anime* for his feature-length cartoon adventure *Spirited Away*. The award recognized Miyazaki's grand and creative vision while it tacitly acknowledged that the fantasy world of wide-eyed girls, urban mayhem, racing spacecraft, and violent samurai swordplay his genre so vividly captures has mesmerized young adults throughout the Western world, much as it has in Asia. Cartoon animation books of *manga* have become such important new components of Japanese export consciousness, rivaling camcorders, cars, and TV sets, that some observers argue that cartoon culture—along with Japan's fashion industry and J-pop music, which has already attracted large audiences in South Korea and Thailand—demonstrates Japan's potential to emerge as a cultural superpower in the twenty-first century, an arbiter of "gross national cool."[1]

Undoubtedly, this *anime* aesthetic reverberates powerfully with young people in the postmodern affluence of today's Japan where, as Takashi Murakami, the authority on *anime*, has suggested, nearly all things seem flat, colorful and rootless, devoid of texture, and without historical context, much like the jumble of products available under the harsh fluorescent lights at the typical Japanese 7-Eleven *combini*, or convenience store. Yet two powerful images embedded within Miyazaki's own film echoed the experiences I, too, found while exploring the *hikikomori* and their nation's "adjustment disorder." In one crucial scene, a character named "No Face," a masked spirit who is hooded in black, who moans but cannot speak, offers nuggets of gold to lure strangers within reach, and then gobbles them up to appropriate their ability to communicate. Miyazaki also reveals that the domineering proprietress of the fabulous bathhouse, where ghosts and spirits come to soak away their worldly troubles, nurtures an oversized infant, still swathed in diapers, who is hidden away to live in the shadows, beneath a protective mound of pillows and bolsters. This giant baby seems unable to abandon the safety of his refuge. Sometimes he attacks his mother in a violent rage. (This being only a cartoon fantasy, the mother is never injured.) After the infant is "spirited away" on an adventure in the world outside, however, he comes back standing on his own two feet and speaking like an intelligent adult.

Through these vignettes, Miyazaki seems to suggest that hope still remains for such social recluses to emerge from their stifling hiding places. Within the film, both the enormous infant and the masked spirit are transformed as a result of the trusting friendship and warm embrace offered them by Chihiro, the child heroine, who expresses neither wariness nor criticism, but only enthusiastic encouragement. And clearly, picking up and abandoning the isolated refuge of Japan has proven, for some of its young, to be one successful response to their own "adjustment disorder."

Is there real hope, then, for the *hikikomori*? What about Kenji, the thirty-four-year-old waif who emerged from his home suddenly one day after twenty years of isolation to speak to me about his pain and his life as a *hikikomori*? This man is now desperately searching for a way to rejoin society—seeking, as he acknowledged in one letter to Masahisa Okuyama, the head of the parents' group for *hikikomori*—"a single ray of light" to help him open his door.

Kenji's goal, he said to me the second and final time we met, is simple. "I need to easily say '*Ittekimasu*' ["I'm going and coming"] and '*Tadaima*' ["I'm back"]"—the common refrains one uses when leaving and returning to the Japanese home. Kenji's ambition is simply to go out into the world and be "normal." Later, over lunch, he told me of how he longs to abandon the social isolation of the past two decades, when he was "frozen out" of his junior high school environment, but wondered whether he has sufficient courage and strength. "People try to tell you that you are free, free to do anything. But before you become a part of the society, you have already given up a part of yourself. That makes me feel helpless about society.

"Unless adults show examples to young people, and raise kids in a way to allow them to be free, it's very difficult"—to emerge from one's hiding place and to find channels that might ultimately lead to genuine self-expression. This is the modern paradox of Japanese life. Society cannot change until the culture changes; the culture is unlikely to change unless society does.

"There was a story about a boy who was raised by a wolf," Kenji told me, tapping his fingers nervously on the table. "He was raised by wolf parents and eventually finds that even though he tries, he can't go back into society. A child raised by a wolf becomes a wolf. You can't go back into normal society," he said, tugging at his thinning black hair, a scowl slowly creeping onto his face, his eyebrows tensing once again. "That's how I feel. Teachers tell you, 'You are free to grow up and become what you want.' But adults can't show us any example where that's true. Maybe that's because being adult simply is not attractive."

Listening to Kenji, I thought of Masako, the imprisoned princess, a woman bursting with potential to break molds, who now seemed an emblem of her nation's distress. When in 2003 her husband, Crown Prince Naruhito, told the nation in the oblique language typical of the imperial family that "there were developments that denied Masako's career as a diplomat as well as her personality," many Japanese, especially young adults, applauded his candor. Nearly a year later, however, the Crown Prince apologized publicly for his previous criticism, apparently having been forced to recant. "I made the remark out of hope that people would be made aware of the situation Masako was in," the prince said at a press conference to mark his forty-fifth birthday in February 2005. "Nonetheless, I feel sorry for causing trouble for both the Emperor and Empress over the remark." The prince's contrition did nothing to alter the reality, however. As of early 2006, the princess remains—much like a *hikikomori*—in nearly complete seclusion, unable to speak for herself in public.

*   *   *

Many Japanese believe that as individuals they possess virtually no power to alter their nation's faltering course. "It can't be helped," they tell one another. "*Shikata ga nai.*" In a world forged by consensus, as a Japanese journalist once explained to me, it is terribly difficult to get everyone to agree. Besides, he added, if you demonstrate "reason" or "logic" that differs from the group's, "it is very dangerous. You could be killed for it."

Such attitudes were clearly on display when three Japanese humanitarian workers who had been held hostage by Iraqi insurgents returned home in April 2004, after nearly three weeks in captivity. On their safe return, the three were greeted not with prayers of thanksgiving, but with the cold stares of a disapproving nation. "You got what you deserve!" one Japanese wrote on a sign posted at the airport when they landed. The government billed them $6,000 for airfare, and a government spokesman denounced their decision to ignore government warnings that humanitarian relief work in the war-torn country was dangerous. "They may have gone on their own," Yasuo Fukuda, the government's chief spokesman, said, "but they must consider how many people they caused trouble to, because of their action." It was left for the American secretary of state, Colin Powell, to praise the three for being "willing to put themselves at risk for a greater good, for a better purpose."

The three were taken for counseling to the psychiatrist Satoru Saito, who told the *New York Times* that the stress they were enduring was "much heavier" than what they suffered during their captivity in Iraq. Asked to name their three most stressful moments, the ex-hostages told him, in ascending order: the moment of their kidnapping on the way to Baghdad; the day when the three were displayed on television with knives at their throats; and "the moment they watched a television show, on the morning after their return here, and realized Japan's anger with them."

Instantly, the hostages found themselves under crushing pressure, Saito said. "Let's say the knife incident, which lasted about ten minutes, ranks ten on a stress level," Saito went on. "After they came back to Japan and saw the morning news show, their stress level ranked twelve."[2]

The danger in appearing to be contrary—or in "causing trouble," as the Japanese call it—suggests Japan's ultimate "adjustment disorder": its system, expertly engineered for one era, has no responsive mechanisms to force adaptation to this new one. In its constant need to accommodate, it has lost its ability to dig deep and find its own essence. And the system itself has become so all-encompassing and self-referential that most of those living inside the bubble are unable to see or judge its flaws, since they know nothing else with which to compare it. Insulated from most of the outside forces that might create the pressure for change, it just keeps plowing ahead on its old path because it is determined to maintain "harmony" and social cohesion—even though it is, in fact, alienating a people no longer quite so unified and homogeneous. This system seems unable to recognize how much its own young adults have already been awakened to new possibilities, and how they now grasp—however tentatively and, at times, inarticulately—for new goals.

Among the growing number of Japanese who, like Dr. Saito, deplore the rigid demands of this system—and, as a result, perceive a grim future for Japan—is a mechanical engineer named Yotaro Hatamura. A professor at Tokyo's Kogakuin University, Hatamura is a dispassionate scientist and keen observer. He is the sort of old-school analyst who for decades helped drive Japan's industrial prosperity by wresting ever-greater precision from standard mechanical processes and by finding ways to build appliances and cars with more energy efficiency.

In a nation all too frequently paralyzed by silence and denial, Hatamura is the odd Japanese who actually revels in failure, who laps up examples of industrial mishaps, train wrecks, and airplane disasters to dissect their causes. Hatamura established the Mistake Society, a nonprofit organization, precisely because he believes that looking squarely at blunders and understanding why they have occurred teaches lessons essential for achieving any enduring success.

When I asked him to turn his analytical lens on his own country, he told me that, despite the deep pessimism infecting much of the nation, "nobody really wants to change. Maybe seventy percent of the Japanese people think life will be okay without any change at all. They still have lots of food on the table and roofs over their heads. And you know, unless you sense that you really need to change, then you probably can't change at all.

"If," he continued, "things keep going this way for another fifty years, Japan will simply disappear from the map. Since we don't teach our people to challenge, they will just go on accepting" the status quo of gradual deterioration and decline.

When we met, I was captivated both by his easy smile and his devastating candor. Hatamura was closely monitoring American officials' response to the disaster of the space shuttle Columbia, which had blown up over the big blue Texas skies in February 2003, killing its seven-member astronaut crew and littering debris from Arizona to Florida. He was impressed with the way American forensic scientists were systematically determining the precise cause of the mishap, gathering as many pieces of the doomed vessel as possible in order to reconstruct the fuselage. They were sifting through telemetry data and compiling hundreds of eyewitness accounts. The American system demanded such strict accountability, he marveled. There would be lawsuits and independent inquiries, and even newspapers and TV networks would conduct their own analyses of what went wrong. A diverse group of players with competing interests would struggle to establish the truth.

In similar circumstances in Japan, however, officials "would simply apologize to the country and that would be it," he said. "We don't search for deeper causes and therefore we don't go out and look for design flaws. This doesn't lead us anywhere, of course, so we tend to make the same mistakes again and again." (This absence of spirited inquiry helps explain how Japan fell so far behind in the past few years in its effort to design booster rockets reliable enough to launch commercial satellites into space.)

Hatamura's analysis of Japan's failures offers little real basis for hope.

"There isn't much transparency in Japan," he said to me. "People aren't accountable. Nobody really tries to learn what happened. So our system doesn't gather or receive feedback."

This absence of repercussion when things go wrong is the nation's single biggest failing, Hatamura told me. Japanese—especially the older generation, with its heavy investment in the status quo—"don't *like* feedback. If people just accept what is happening around them," rather than oppose it, "then they are assured of maintaining a place for themselves" within the traditional bounds of Japanese society where, ultimately, they can be assured of being cared for. "In the old days, we could just follow skillfully what was already established," he said. "We didn't have to take risks, and we could be happy. But now we are standing still. People ask, 'How long can this stagnation go on?' and I myself assume it will continue for another ten or fifteen years," or until a new crisis arises.

The white paper issued by the government in April 2005 once again offered a series of policy options intended to open up the Japanese system, embrace globalization, decentralize government, and create new centers of innovation. These stratagems all sounded so good. But like many earlier white papers and reports that preceded this one, there is little reason to hope that any of its laudatory goals will be implemented, because, as Hatamura suggested, in Japan "nobody [in power] really wants to change." Who will take the role of Chihiro, that young *anime* heroine from another world who persuades the closed networks of commercial and political life that they must open up? A nation that cuts out the feedback receptors, that diffuses the power of the individual inside collective systems, that puts harmony over friction and stability over competition eventually loses its dynamism and its capacity to adapt. In a nation without trust, and without a transcendent system of fixed values, on what anvil can fundamental change be hammered? And how might Japan reconcile its modern form with its premodern essence? This is not a new struggle for Japan, only one that is now more relevant than ever. For as the writer Natsume Soseki noted in 1911, the enlightenment force that swept the West "was internally generated, while Japan's was externally generated. By internally generated I mean natural emergence and development from within, just as a flower strains outward through a parted bud. By externally generated, I mean the reluctant assumption of an outward form under pressure from outside."[3]

Might it just be the fear of loss that keeps Japan from embracing its need for fundamental change? Of being forced to abandon many important aspects of its economic and cultural life—characteristics the rest of the world prizes as well? Among these are the patience and discipline of the Japanese craftsman, the reverence for detail, and the obligation to honor the customer. So, too, is the pursuit of perfection a very Japanese quality. The gentle, minimalist character of traditional Japan, that which seeks harmony with nature instead of trying to tame it, and finds beauty in the sparse rather than in the abundant, has much to teach a contemporary world now confronted by physical and resource limits. Japan's recent commitment to energy conservation, to finding new ways to reduce emission of greenhouse gases, and to developing alternatives to the conventional gasoline engine, even demonstrate that a nation can seek profits while also helping to create a more sustainable environment. I suspect that the innate conservatism of Japan goes much deeper, however, than a simple desire to protect its "beautiful traditions." It also reflects the rigid emphasis on stability and harmony in a society that has not learned how to apportion social trust. A nation unwilling to acknowledge—or adapt to—its internal dislocations ends up closing like a clamshell to preserve what it has.

*   *   *

Today, the truth is that globalization—with its radical compression of time and space—has brought new challenges and pressure points to all the world's developed nations, not least my own, the United States. Indeed, in this book, I have tried to avoid assuming a superior position, of seeming to raise America onto a pedestal while attacking Japan, as might well have been tempting half a decade ago, when the United States was still a leader in encouraging open trade, environmental protection, multilateral confidence building, nuclear disarmament, and a global effort to fight rogue states and terrorist organizations.

Since September 11, 2001, however, when America plunged into a global "war on terror," we have insisted on trying to reorder the world according to our own unilateralist blueprint and policies. We have often ditched pragmatism and compromise for the sake of moral absolutism, and manufactured evidence to justify war-making, while sealing off our borders to potential foreign visitors, lest they be "terrorists." Like Japan, we seem to want to become safe, secure, and hysterical.

Now, we in America run the risk of becoming over time as insular and isolated as modern Japan, as our two nations are apparently turning out to be enablers of one another's social pathology. We have encouraged Japan to withdraw and retreat and to loyally follow our commands, while Japan has quietly bankrolled our own overstretched global ambitions. Like an overprotective mother of a *hikikomori*, we promise food and protection as long as the child agrees not to become too disruptive.

For while Japan envisions a world of defensive, unilateral withdrawal as a means of national protection and preservation, many Americans seem to believe unilateral intervention—visiting war on other nations—can make our own homeland safe. Where Japan is impaired in its quest for renewal by its lack of universal moral values, America's government increasingly imagines itself as being the proud possessor of those values and on a crusade to impose its own idea of those values onto others.[4] If Japan has yet to acknowledge the crucial role of the individual in creating social responsibility, then we in America have failed to articulate the sense of community and community obligation needed to mitigate the excesses of individualism. Where Japan would rather withdraw from the world than be forced to transform its own character, America seems bent on transforming the character of the world to make it more like our own—no matter what others' history or culture might demand. In a global era that demands flexibility, invention, and pragmatism, both worldviews are rigid and ultimately doomed. Neither fundamentalist doctrine can succeed in an era in which our borders have become less relevant, in which physical space no longer protects and need not separate us, and in which the pace of change unfolds ever faster.

With American resources now stretched thin, the Bush administration has become more eager for Japan to send troops to Iraq, to revise its pacifist constitution, to reestablish itself as a military power with ballistic missiles and a blue-water Navy, and to serve as a proxy for American military power in the Pacific against a rising China. Giving Japan such license would certainly trigger an arms race throughout Asia and cause consternation among other Asian nations, who wonder if Japan has actually learned the lessons of World War Two and is prepared to act responsibly as a "normal nation."

Ultimately, neither withdrawal from the changing world nor a hegemonic quest to run it can lead any nation to peace, stability, and prosperity. And, ultimately, the only truly practical coping mechanisms are those that embody tolerance, inclusion, diversity, and, yes, trust and the mechanisms to enforce trust—along with the fundamental humanistic values of equality and the right to self-expression.

* * *

So is there a single ray of light for Kenji and his fellows in hiding? Can they be like that giant baby who is "spirited away" to return as a functional adult? Or will they, as Kenji fears, remain lone wolves?

His sharp observation—that he could point to no adults who had grown up to be "free," to become what they wanted—troubled me deeply. I can think of no more gloomy diagnosis of a modern people. Having coaxed Kenji out of his house, I felt it was my duty to find him some sort of professional help; otherwise I would feel as if I were only exploiting his dreadful situation. I had hoped that bringing him out and into the light of day might help him. I thought of putting him in contact with Yuichi Hattori, the sympathetic counselor I had watched treat dozens of men like him and whom I had grown to trust. When I asked Kenji if he was interested in pursuing therapy, his face tensed and his eyes narrowed.

"I have a feeling of what one form of therapy might be like," he said quietly, "but I'm not sure that I am feeling that way yet. On the one hand, I feel like I have to do something, but before I left, on my way here, I felt like I didn't want to come." Coming out of his house, he added, made him feel tremendously anxious.

A few weeks after this talk and not having heard from Kenji, I asked my assistant, Emi, to call his house again to see how he was doing. His mother, who answered the phone, sounded distraught and angry. She complained that leaving his room for lunch with me had proven "too stimulating" for her son: he was now suffering frightful dreams of people chasing him, of strangers deceiving him, of being hurt. She had taken him to the hospital, she said, in order to get a prescription for some powerful sedatives.

"Sometimes he overdoes it," she went on. "He puts too much stress on his own shoulders. He has a good heart, but . . ."

Kenji's mother was annoyed that outsiders had tried to intervene. "Do not call us for a while. We don't want to be disturbed." There's little an outsider can do anyway, she suggested. "I will call you again when it's appropriate," she snapped finally, before hanging up.

Her phone call never came.

Acknowledgments

For an American who chooses to live in Japan, a foreign correspondent's assignment offers a most privileged perch from which to gain access to a relatively opaque society. It may surprise Americans to learn that in the Japanese culture even today, a journalist is still held in surprisingly high esteem—something I first learned when an innkeeper in a small village on the Sea of Japan bowed humbly before me when she learned of my profession. Yet as a foreigner in Japan you are also permitted to bend, if not defy, many of the unwritten rules that constrain most members of the Japanese domestic media.

Despite receiving many indirect benefits from my privileged status, this book could not have been completed without the support and encouragement of many others.

The first nudge I received to collect my thoughts on Japan's social dysfunction into a full-length book came from Richard Samuels, professor of political science at MIT, who, when I first described my interviews with *hikikomori* over coffee one afternoon in Tokyo, nearly pulled me by the lapels of my jacket with enthusiasm, urging me to press ahead. "Damn it, you've got to turn this into a book," he told me, and now—for better or worse—I have.

A second nudge came from Henri Claude de Bettignies, with whom I first studied Japanese culture and corporate management while attending Stanford University's Graduate School of Business. I'm grateful for his encouragement and support during the trying phases of mastering this manuscript, and for his friendship through the years.

Other important mentors, colleagues, and friends who have helped me refine my thinking on Japan include Edward Lincoln, who was advising U.S. Ambassador Walter F. Mondale when I first arrived in Tokyo in 1996; Richard Katz, Peter Ennis, and Takao Toshikawa of the *Oriental Economist*; Karel van Wolferen, Naoko Abe, Paul Addison, Bob and Fumiko Neff, Ron Bevacqua, Brian Kushnir, Becky Schimpff, John Neuffer, Robert Dohner, Kathy Tolbert, Michael Lev, Sonni Efron, Mark Magnier, Ulrike Schaede, Eric Gower, Karen Reilly, Liz First, Dan Raddoch, Norihiko and Stacy Shirozu, Robert "Skipp" Orr, Takeshi Yamawaki, Todd and Rachel Walzer, Marshall and Nobuko Gittler, David and Naomi Sneider, Taisuke and Katherine Susanuma, Toshiko Morikawa, Kazuko Kawachi, Takashi Inoguchi, Yuichi Hattori, Hiroshige Hanabusa, Mitsuya Goto, Marla Fujimoto, Takashi Fujimoto, Bernard and Deborah Krisher, Gerald Curtis, Ignacio Cronin, and Richard Christenson. Toshiko Oguchi, my Japanese tutor, was also a patient and forgiving guide. James Raymo reviewed some of my research on demographic work and corrected some errors. My work on Korea was also benefited by conversations with Moon Chung-il, Kim Jon-wan, Scott Snyder, Hahm Chaibong, Han Seung-soo, Richard Samuelson, David Steinberg, Paul Eckert, and Scott Talkington.

My predecessor as Knight Ridder's Tokyo bureau chief, Lewis M. Simons, and his wife, Carol, could not have been more supportive of my wife and me when we arrived in Japan, or more helpful through the transition. I am also deeply indebted to support received from others at Knight Ridder and at the *San Jose Mercury News*, including Paul van Slambrouck, Francine Kiefer, David Yarnold, Jerry Ceppos, Jay T. Harris, Jonathan Krim, and Michael Winter, as well as John Walcott and Clark Hoyt in Knight Ridder's Washington bureau.

Emiko Doi became my assistant about six months after my arrival in Japan, and she proved herself a patient, loyal, and incredibly dedicated translator, interpreter, troubleshooter, and negotiator. A great many of the interviews conducted for this book simply could not have been arranged without her sympathetic concern and good judgment. She was a great treasure to work with and I remain always in her debt.

After returning from Japan, I was privileged to be able to conduct my follow-up research at the University of California-Berkeley. I am grateful for the assistance and hospitality offered me by T.J. Pempel, director of the Institute of East Asian Studies, as well as Joan Kask, Martin Bergstrom, Kaja Sehrt, Jumi Hadler, and Rochelle Halperin of the Institute staff, and Keiko Hjersman of the Center for Japanese Studies. For my research into the work of Yu Kil-chun, I am also grateful for the assistance I received from the Peabody Essex Museum in Salem, Massachusetts, especially from Susan S. Bean and Irene V. Axelrod, and from the Governor Dummer Academy in Byfield, Massachusetts.

Research for this book was assisted by a grant from the Abe Fellowship Program of the Social Science Research Council and the American Council of Learned Societies, with funds provided by the Japan Foundation Center for Global Partnership. Tony Judge helped nurture my confidence in this project, and my agent, Marly Rusoff, helped find the necessary support. Nan Talese believed in this book from the moment it was first brought to her attention, and I remain indebted to her and her staff at Doubleday, for their unstinting support. Phoebe Hoss' keen eye and sense of structure contributed enormously in helping prepare this manuscript for publication.

Diane Abt was as forgiving a partner as any author could dare expect during our long period of life abroad and during the trying period in which I was completing this book. I owe her a debt of gratitude and my enduring love.

Naturally, all errors of insight, omission, and misunderstanding are mine alone to bear.

Notes

Introduction

1. The wedding of Masako Owada was covered as widely, and with as much fanfare, as the wedding of Princess Diana to Prince Charles. One sign of the secrecy that is commonplace within the Imperial Household Agency, however, is that news of the engagement was first disclosed by the *Washington Post*.

2. See Takashi Murakami, "Earth in My Window," from *Little Boy: The Arts of Japan's Exploding Subculture* (New Haven: Yale University Press, 2005), p. 100, for one Japanese view of the nation's deep sense of dislocation.

3. Perry kept careful accounts of his Japanese foray. See especially *Narrative of the expedition of an American squadron to the China seas and Japan, under the command of Commodore M.C. Perry, United States Navy*, compiled at his request and under his supervision by Francis L. Hawks; abridged and edited by Sidney Wallach (New York: Coward-McCann, 1952). Also Ian Buruma, *Inventing Japan, 1853–1964* (New York: Modern Library, 2003).

4. The emergence of a unique, and superior, Japan was best summarized in Ezra Vogel's *Japan as Number One: Lessons for America* (Cambridge, Mass.: Harvard University Press, 1979), which became an instant bestseller.

5. A senior and very powerful Japanese politician once complained to me privately—and bitterly—that in its quest for economic wealth, Japan had become a nation blessed with massive arms, but an underdeveloped brain.

6. See Murakami, "Earth in My Window."

7. In 2004, about 1.111 million babies were born in Japan, the lowest number recorded since statistics were first compiled in 1899. Births exceeded the num-

ber of deaths by a mere 82,000. *Japan Times*, July 17, 2005. In 2005, deaths exceeded births by 10,000.

Chapter One

1. See Dr. Tamaki Saito, "Hikikomori in Korea and Japan," *Chuo Kouron*, December 2004.

2. By the end of 2004, there had been no comprehensive evaluation by independent psychiatrists within Japan to clearly determine that *hikikomori* patients fail to show up in DSM IV evaluations. In the course of researching this book, I have tried to get Japanese and Western experts to collaborate in a research study to confirm this finding.

3. Shigei said the fact that the bus departed when it was nearly full, and not according to a predetermined schedule, allowed him to set himself at ease.

Chapter Two

1. Global Entrepreneurship Monitor, 2004 Executive Report, http://www.gemcon sortium.org/download/1133643045765/GEM_2004_Exec_Report.pdf, first cited in Paolo Hjelt, "Here's a Surprise," in *Fortune*, February 9, 2004. Other rankings of the availability of venture capital, development of independent business, and start-ups and incubation of new business also consistently place Japan near the bottom.

Chapter Three

1. Masaru Tamamoto applies the same formula to Japan's ability to think strategically about its place in the world: "U.S. military protection and Japanese willful subordination to American political leadership have allowed Japan to live in a state of cultivated ignorance about the harshness of international politics." See "After the Tsunami: How Japan Can Lead," *Far Eastern Economic Review*, February 2005.

2. Laws against domestic violence have only been recently introduced in Japan, and, as in the United States, record-keeping is suspect. But a consensus among psychiatrists who deal with *hikikomori* suggests that more than half attack or abuse their parents.

3. "Shut-in Says He Killed Family Because They Took His Space," *Japan Times*, November 27, 2004.

4. Interviews with Kosuke Yamazaki and Susanne Vogel. It sometimes takes American therapists a number of hours to realize that the term "domestic violence" has a different meaning in Japan.

5. See, for instance, Emily Ohnuki-Tierney, *Illness and Culture in Contemporary Japan: An Anthropological View* (Cambridge, UK: Cambridge University Press, 1984), for a discussion of the reluctance of the medical community in Japan to embrace Western psychiatric standards.

6. KHJ represents the acronym combining the Japanese translations of three psychological conditions. K stands for *kyohakusei shogai*, or obsessive-compulsive disorder; H is for *higaimooso*, or paranoia; and J represents *jinkaku sei shogai*, or personality disorder.

7. Yoshiharu Kin, Survey on the Prevalence Rate of *Hikikomori* (Department of Adult Mental Health, National Center of Neurology and Psychiatry, National Institute of Mental Health), with the assistance of Itsuko Horiguchi and Chika Yokoyama (Department of Public Health, School of Medicine, Juntendo University, Tokyo).

8. Kosuke Yamazaki, "Child and Adolescent Mental Health in Modern-Day Japan," in *Recent Progress in Child and Adolescent Psychiatry,* ed. Masanori Hanada (Tokyo: Springer-Verlag, 1999), pp. 231–45. See also Hideki Hara, "Justification for Bullying among Japanese Schoolchildren," *Asian Journal of Sociology* 5 (2002): 197–204.

9. Masao Miyamoto, *Straitjacket Society: An Insider's Irreverent View of Bureaucratic Japan* (Tokyo: Kodansha International, 1995), pp. 148–49.

10. Beth Morling, Shinobu Kitayama, and Yuri Miyamoto, "Cultural Practices Emphasize Influence in the United States and Adjustment in Japan," *Personality and Social Psychology Bulletin* 28, no. 3 (March 2002): 311–23.

11. Steven J. Heine, Darrin R. Lehman, Hazel Rose Markus, and Shinobu Kityama, "Is There a Universal Need for Positive Self-Regard?" *Psychological Review* 106, no. 4 (1999).

12. George DeVos, *Socialization for Achievement: Essays on the Cultural Psychology of the Japanese* (Berkeley: University of California Press, 1973), p. 35.

Chapter Four

1. For an engaging discussion of this, see Robert N. Bellah, *Imagining Japan: The Japanese Tradition and Its Modern Interpretation* (Berkeley: University of California Press, 2003).

2. Chie Kanagawa, Susan Cross, and Hazel Rose Markus, " 'Who am I?' The Cultural Psychology of the Conceptual Self," *Personality and Social Psychology Bulletin* 27, no. 1 (2001): 90–103.

3. Takeo Doi, *Anatomy of Dependence*, translated by John Bester (Tokyo: Kodansha International, 1973), p. 13.

4. Ibid.

5. National census, Management and Coordination Agency, as reproduced in Emiko Ochiai, *The Japanese Family System in Transition: A Sociological Analysis of Family Change in Postwar Japan* (Tokyo: LTCB International Library Foundation, 1997).

Chapter Five

1. See Norimitsu Onishi, "An Aging Island Embraces Japan's Young Dropouts," *New York Times*, June 6, 2004.

2. Shintaro Tominaga, a Japanese business consultant, has described in an online forum how, as a young boy of thirteen or fourteen he heard his father and other veterans of the Imperial Japanese Army describe the wartime atrocities they carried out against Chinese civilians. "This conversation still remains in my memory, and it never leaves me," he wrote. See National Bureau of Asian Research Forum, July 29, 2005, www.nbr.org.

Chapter Six

1. See the writings of political scientist Masao Maruyama, especially *Nihon No Shisho Shi Kenkyu*, translated as *Studies in the Intellectual History of Tokugawa Japan*, translated by Mikiso Hane (Princeton: Princeton University Press, 1974).

2. Political scientist Yukio Noguchi of Tokyo University refers to this as the "1940s system," to suggest that the wartime mobilization orchestrated during a fascist era continued with little change during postwar reconstruction. Economic conquest replaced territorial imperialism as the object of the battle.

3. Masatoshi Koshiba, awarded the Nobel Prize in physics in 2002, proudly told reporters he had barely graduated from Tokyo University. Koichi Tanaka, of Shimadzu Corporation, who won the chemistry prize the same year, told reporters that even his wife thought there was a mistake when she heard on the radio that a man named Tanaka had won a Nobel Prize.

4. See James Fallows, *Looking at the Sun: The Rise of the New East Asian Economic and Political System* (New York: Pantheon Books, 1994), and Alice H. Amsden, *Asia's Next Giant: South Korea and Late Industrialization* (New York: Oxford University Press, 1989).

5. Edward J. Lincoln, *Arthritic Japan: The Slow Pace of Economic Reform* (Washington, D.C.: Brookings Institution Press, 2001), p. 20.

6. To drive the point home, more than half of Japan's largest corporations usually hold their shareholder meetings on precisely the same day each year to thwart shareholder activists, some of whom are actually *yakuza,* gangsters, looking for hush money while masquerading as muckrakers.

7. See "Report of the Economic Structure Adjustment Study Group for Integrating the Economy into the World" white paper, known popularly as the Maekawa Report of 1986, reprinted in Ministry of Foreign Affairs, Documents on Japan's Economic Structural Adjustment, June 1987, pp. 19–30.

8. See the Maekawa Report of 1986.

9. Even today, Japan's consumption as a percentage of economic output significantly lags behind that of other major industrial nations. See, for instance, Ross Harvey, Comparison of Household Savings Ratios: Euro area/United States/Japan, OECD Statistics Brief, no. 8, June 2004, compiled by the Organization of Economic Cooperation and Development. Available at http://www.oecd.org/dataoecd/53/48/32023442.pdf.

10. See Gillian Tett, *Saving the Sun: A Wall Street Gamble to Rescue Japan from Its Trillion-Dollar Meltdown* (New York: HarperCollins, 2003), for details on the collapse of Long-Term Credit Bank.

11. For data, see *The Economist*, April 20, 2002.

12. Richard Katz, *Japan, the System That Soured: The Rise and Fall of the Japanese Economic Miracle* (Armonk, N.Y.: M.E. Sharpe, 1998), p. 6.

13. See "The Coming Demographic Deficit: How Aging Populations Will Reduce Global Savings," McKinsey Global Institute, January 2005, available at http://www.mckinsey.com/mgi/publications/demographics/index.asp.

14. The Japan Post's Savings Bank held an estimated $3 trillion in assets on its books and was frequently used by politicians as a piggy bank to fund pet projects off the national balance sheet. Prime Minister Junichiro Koizumi, long an opponent of the postal savings institution, won a landslide victory in a special election held in September 2005 when he failed to win his own party's approval

for a measure to privatize the post service. But privatization of the bank won't be fully completed until 2017.

15. "Japan's Spending Habit Roils Plan to Sell Big Bank," *New York Times*, August 23, 2005.

16. For deeper academic analysis, see Laurie Anne Freeman, *Closing the Shop: Information Cartels and Japan's Mass Media* (Princeton: Princeton University Press, 2000), p. 21.

17. Miyamoto, *Straitjacket Society*, pp. 133–51.

18. See Karel van Wolferen, *The Enigma of Japanese Power: People and Politics in a Stateless Nation* (New York: Knopf, 1989), pp. 35–49.

Chapter Seven

1. See figures compiled at http://www.oecd.org/document/7/0,2340,en_2649_34447_35397703_1_1_1_1,00.html. The United States actually ranked below Japan, which reflects the nation's traditional indifference to foreign aid, and also its outsized military spending. This data does not include private or charitable contributions made by nongovernmental organizations.

2. Interview with Taiichi Sakaiya, and Sakaiya, *What Is Japan?* (Tokyo: Kodansha International, 1993).

3. See John Dower, *Embracing Defeat: Japan in the Wake of World War II* (New York: W. W. Norton, 2000), for an extensive treatment of Japan's postwar mood.

4. Sakaiya, *What Is Japan?*, pp. 123–25.

5. Marius B. Jansen, *The Making of Modern Japan* (Cambridge, Mass.: Belknap Press, 2000).

6. Robert N. Bellah, *Tokugawa Religion: The Cultural Roots of Modern Japan* (New York: Free Press, 1985), pp. 133–76.

7. Masao Maruyama, "Theory and Psychology of Ultra-Nationalism," in *Thought and Behavior of Modern Japanese Politics,* ed. Ivan Morris (London: Oxford University Press, 1963), pp. 1–24.

8. Thomas P. Kasulis, "Intimacy: A General Orientation in Japanese Religious Values," *Philosophy East and West* 4, no. 4 (October 1990): 433–49.

9. Hayao Kawai, "Pathology of Japan's Maternal-Instinct Society," in Japanese (translated by Emi Doi).

10. Morling, Kitayama, and Miyamoto, "Cultural Practices Emphasize Influence in the United States and Adjustment in Japan."

11. Hazel Rose Markus and Shinobu Kitayama, "The Cultural Construction of Self and Emotion: Implications for Social Behavior," in *Culture and Emotion,* ed. Shinobu Kitayama and Hazel Rose Markus (Washington, D.C.: American Psychological Association, 1994).

12. For details on some of these fascinating real-world experiments, see Takahiko Masuda and Richard Nisbett, "Attending Holistically Versus Analytically: Comparing the Context Sensitivity of Japanese and Americans," *Journal of Personality and Social Psychology* 81, no. 5 (2001): 922–34.

13. Robert Putnam, "The Prosperous Community," in *The American Prospect* 4, no. 13 (March 21, 1993). For a more extensive treatment of the power of social capital, see Putnam, *Bowling Alone: The Collapse and Revival of American Community* (New York: Simon and Schuster, 2000).

14. Francis Fukuyama, *Trust: The Social Virtues and the Creation of Prosperity* (New York: Free Press, 1995), p. 205.

15. Dennis Tachiki et al., "Diffusion and Impact of the Internet and E-Commerce in Japan" (The Center for Research on Information Technology, UC Irvine, 2004).

16. See Wharton School special report on Japan, http://knowledge.wharton. upenn.edu/papers/download/Japan_SpecialReport.pdf.

17. Americans consistently believe the random stranger is probably a decent person. This spirit was recently captured in massive advertising from eBay, the online auctioneer, which loudly proclaimed "People Are Good."

18. See Toshio Yamagishi, *The Structure of Trust* (Tokyo: Tokyo University Press, 1998), available online in English at http://lynx.let.hokudai.ac.jp/members/yamagishi/english.htm.

19. Daikichi Irokawa, "The Survival Struggle of the Japanese Community," in *Authority and the Individual in Japan,* ed. J. Victor Koschmann (Tokyo: University of Tokyo Press, 1978), pp. 270–71.

20. Toshio Yamagishi, Karen S. Cook, and Motoki Watabe, "Uncertainty, Trust and Commitment Formation in the United States and Japan," *American Journal of Sociology* 104, no. 1 (July 1998): 172.

21. Takashi Inoguchi also tries to bridge the gap between Fukuyama and Yamagishi. See Inoguchi, "Broadening the Basis of Social Capital in Japan," in *Democracies in Flux: The Evolution of Social Capital in Contemporary Society,* ed. Robert Putnam (New York: Oxford University Press, 2002).

22. Ibid.

23. Lynne G. Zucker, "Production of Trust: Institutional Sources of Economic Structure, 1840–1920," in *Research in Organizational Behavior* 8 (1986): 53–111.

24. Robert Cole, "Telecom Competition in World Markets: Understanding Japan's Decline," paper initially prepared for Conference on Institutional Change in East Asian Economics, Harvard University, Nov. 7–8, 2003. Provided courtesy of the author.

25. "Psychiatric Care Still Mired in Dark Ages," *Japan Times*, September 12, 2001.

26. Alex Kerr's *Dogs and Demons: Tales from the Dark Side of Modern Japan* (New York: Hill and Wang, 2002) offers a particularly rich portrayal of this controversy.

Chapter Eight

1. "Can the High End Hold Its Own?" *BusinessWeek*, June 30, 2003, http://www.businessweek.com/magazine/content/03_26/b3839107_mz033.htm.

2. "PC Animation Geeks a Market 'Maid' to Order," *Japan Times*, February 3, 2005.

3. Having purchased her Vuitton purse, one twenty-four-year-old woman told a Japanese newspaper, "Every time I carry one, I feel like I've risen a class above myself," *Mainichi Daily News*, February 1, 2003.

4. "Can the High End Hold Its Own?"

Chapter Nine

1. The population of South Korea has in the past half decade fallen below even Japan's, with a fertility rate of 1.19. But unlike Japan, South Korea's government for many years encouraged women to limit their family size to two children. "South Korea, in Turnabout, Now Calls for More Babies," *New York Times*, August 21, 2005.

2. Statistical handbook of Japan, http://www.stat.go.jp/english/data/handbook/c02cont.htm#cha2_2.

3. United Nations Population Division, World Population Prospects, 2002 Revision, http://esa.un.org./unpp, as cited in Eberstadt, "Power and Population in Asia," *Policy Review*, February 2004, http://www.policyreview.org/feb04/eberstadt.html.

4. Noriko Sakakibara, "Parents Buy Place in Elite Primary Schools," *Yomiuri Shimbun*, March 10, 2004.

5. *Japan Times*, November 13, 2004.

6. The seminar was attended by Emi Doi, my Tokyo assistant.

7. The survey was conducted by the Japan Youth Research Institute. Cited in *Japan Times*, August 1, 2001.

8. Masahiro Yamada, "The Expectation Gap: Winners and Losers in the New Economy," *Chuo Kouron*, December 2004.

9. Comparable figures from Monthly Labor Review, September 2003.

10. Miho Iwasawa, "Partnership Transition in Contemporary Japan," presented at International Union for the Scientific Study of Population (IUSSP) Conference, March 2001.

11. Hiromi Ono, "Women's Economic Standing, Marriage Timing, and Cross-National Contexts of Gender," *Journal of Marriage and the Family* 65, no. 2 (2003): 275–86.

12. Quoted in Yuri Kageyama, "Why Women Won't Embrace the Pill Soon," Associated Press, published in *San Jose Mercury News*, September 1, 1999, p. 21A.

13. Miho Iwasawa, "The Transformation of Partnerships of Japanese Women in the 1990s," National Institute of Population and Social Security Research, March 2000 (NIPSSR Working Paper Series (E), no. 9).

Chapter Ten

1. Human Rights Watch has documented cases where Japanese authorities "failed to enforce even the minimal available legal protections" to protect Thai sex workers from abuse. See http://www.hrw.org/wr2k1/women/women5.html.

2. Most of the data which follows comes from surveys conducted by the National Institute of Population and Social Security Research, Japanese Ministry of Health, Labor and Welfare.

3. Ibid.

4. Some 28 percent of married men and 34 percent of married women said they had not had sex with their spouse for at least one month, the period determined to be the defining point of sexlessness, in a survey conducted by the Health Ministry. *Mainichi Shimbun*, April 26, 2005. In addition, a survey of more than 1,600 married women across Japan conducted by Mayumi Futamatsu—author of *Tonari no Shinshitsu* (The Bedroom Next Door), a book on marital sex— found that 45.1 percent had sexless marriages. "Until Death Do We Part," *Japan Times*, December 12, 2004. Viagra data courtesy of Pfizer, e-mail communication.

5. Quoted in *Yomiuri Weekly*, October 17, 2004.

6. See Thomas P. Rohlen, *For Harmony and Strength: Japanese White-Collar Organization in Anthropological Perspective* (Berkeley: University of California Press, 1974), pp. 93–120; 237–42.

7. Andrew Gordon, *The Wages of Affluence: Labor and Management Practices in Postwar Japan* (Cambridge, Mass.: Harvard University Press, 1998), p. 200.

8. Other signs of rising virtuousness in America include a decline in domestic violence, drunk-driver fatalities, alcohol consumption, and teen pregnancy. See, for instance, David Brooks, "The Virtues of Virtue," *New York Times*, August 7, 2005.

Chapter Eleven

1. Quoted in Anthony Faiola, "Internet Suicides Plague Japan," *Washington Post*, August 24, 2003, p. A1.

2. Figures compiled by National Police Agency; data reported by the Associated Press, July 10, 2004. In calendar year 2004, a total 32,325 committed suicide, the agency reported. *Japan Times*, June 3, 2005.

3. See World Health Organization data, available at http://www.who.int/mental_health/prevention/suicide/suiciderates/en/.

4. Hiroyuki Itsuki, quoted in *Asahi Shimbun*, July 19–20, 2003, p. 28, from a speech delivered at the Foreign Correspondents' Club of Japan.

5. Ibid.

6. "Insurers Must Pay Benefit in Suicide Case, Top Court Rules," Kyodo News Service, March 25, 2004.

7. The Mizuho story was a source of serious corporate embarrassment and was covered for weeks in the Japanese press.

8. H. Aihara and M. Iki, "An Ecological Study of the Relations between Recent High Suicide Rates and Economic and Demographic Factors in Japan," *Journal of Epidemiology*, no. 13 (January 2003): 56–61.

9. "Psychiatric Care Still Mired in Dark Ages," *Japan Times*, September 12, 2001.

10. "Most Suicide Victims Didn't Seek Prior Help," *Daily Yomiuri*, July 4, 2004.

11. "Until Death Do We Part," *Japan Times*, December 12, 2004.

12. Hayao Kawai, *The Japanese Psyche: Major Motifs in Fairy Tales of Japan*, trans. Hayao Kawai and Sachiko Reece (Woodstock, Conn.: Spring Publications, 1996).

13. GlaxoSmithKline reports.

14. *Japan Times*, May 4, 2002, p. 4.

15. *Japan Times*, July 31, 2003; *Asahi Shimbun*, June 24, 2004.

16. OECD Health Data, 2003, 3rd ed., www.oecd.org.

Chapter Twelve

1. Associated Press, January 7, 1998; Bloomberg News, January 9, 1998.

2. See Tamaki Saito, "*Hikikomori* in Korea and Japan," *Chuo Koron*, January 31, 2004.

3. See Rudiger Frank, "Information and Communications in South Korea and Japan: Reforms and Visions Compared," http://www.koreanstudies.de/London_4_2004/Frank_Paper.pdf. The "386 generation" has been the subject of great political discussion among sociologists and journalists.

4. The irony was not lost on elderly South Koreans that the young soccer fans were waving flags long associated with the Communist North.

5. *Korea Herald*, April 16, 2004.

6. William Pesek Jr., "Despite Setbacks South Korea Inc. Seems On Track," Bloomberg News, March 31, 2003.

7. Even Prime Minister Junichiro Koizumi, elected as a rump reformer, was forced to call snap elections in September 2005 after failing to convince his own party to support privatization of Japan's postal service, the world's largest financial institution. His landslide victory helped boost a stock market recovery.

8. James Brooke, "A Quiet Invasion of Korea's Giants," *New York Times*, May 20, 2004.

9. *Nikkei Shimbun*, March 12, 2004.

10. Chang Kyung-sup, "Compressed Modernity and Its Discontents: South Korea in Transition," *Economy and Society* 28, no. 1 (February 1999).

11. "Cool Korea," *BusinessWeek*, June 10, 2002.

Chapter Thirteen

1. The term Meiji Restoration is a fictive one, since the new throne was a modern creation, and since the new leaders of Japan sought to jettison most vestiges of the feudal past.

2. Jansen, *The Making of Modern Japan*, p. 424.

3. I am grateful to Yosuke Nirei of Sophia University and the University of California, Berkeley, for sharing his doctoral thesis, "Ethics of Empire," which quotes Fukuzawa at some length.

4. Peter Duus, *The Abacus and the Sword: The Japanese Penetration of Korea, 1895–1910* (Berkeley: University of California Press, 1995), p. 21.

5. Ibid.

6. Frederic A. Sharf, "Yu Kil-chun, A Korean Abroad," *The Korean Collection of Peabody Essex Museum.*

7. See A. Lawrence Lowell, *Biography of Percival Lowell* (New York: MacMillan, 1935).

8. See Christopher Benfey, *The Great Wave: Gilded Age Misfits, Japanese Eccentrics, and the Opening of Old Japan* (New York: Random House, 2003).

9. Letters of Yu Kil-chun, Peabody Essex Museum.

10. Lee Kwang-rin, "Letters of Yu Kil-chun," *Korean Studies* 14 (1990).

11. Dong-hyun Huh, "Forms of Acceptance of Social Darwinism by the Korean Progressives of the 1880–1890s," *International Journal of Korean History* 2 (2001): 41–63.

12. Yu quoted in Lee Sang-ik, "On the Concepts of 'New Korea' Envisioned by Enlightenment Reformers," *Korea Journal* 40, no. 2 (Summer 2000): 34–64.

13. Yu quoted ibid., p. 53.

14. A number of scholarly essays have detailed the early days of missionaries in Korea. See Wi Jo Kang, *Christ and Caesar in Modern Korea: A History of Christianity and Politics* (Albany, N.Y.: State University of New York Press, 1997).

15. Ibid.

16. Ibid.

17. Hyeon Beom Cho, "A Study on the Protestant Discourse of Civilization in Early Modern Korea," *Korea Journal* 41, no. 1 (Spring 2001): 18–43.

18. Ibid., p. 38.

19. Jansen, *The Making of Modern Japan.*

20. Kenneth M. Wells, *New God, New Nation: Protestants and Self-Reconstruction Nationalism in Korea, 1896–1937* (Honolulu: University of Hawaii Press, 1990), p. 33.

21. Donald Clark, "History and Religion in Modern Korea: The Case of Protestant Christianity," in *Religion and Society in Contemporary Korea,* ed. Lewis R. Lancaster, Richard Karl Payne, and Karen M. Andrews (Center for Korean

Studies, Institute of East Asian Studies, University of California, Berkeley, 1997).

22. Donald N. Clark, "Protestant Christianity and the State," in *Korean Society: Civil Society, Democracy, and the State,* ed. Charles K. Armstrong (London: Routledge, 2002), pp. 187–206.

23. Clark, "History and Religion in Modern Korea: The Case of Protestant Christianity."

24. Clark, "Protestant Christianity and the State."

25. Larry Diamond, "Towards Democratic Consolidation," as quoted in Armstrong, *Korean Society.*

26. Ho-keun Song, "Analysis of Participants in the New Social Movements in Korea," *Korea Journal* 40, no. 3 (Autumn 2000); Jaeyeol Yee, "Network Analysis of Solidarity Ties among Social Movement Organizations," *Korea Journal* 40, no. 3 (Autumn 2000).

27. Ibid.

28. See PSPD literature and PSPD Web site, http://eng.peoplepower21.org/contents/actionbody_transparent.html. It is notable that PSPD's English Web site is readily accessible.

29. Sunhyuk Kim, "Civil Society and Democratization," in Armstrong, *Korean Society*, pp. 92–108.

30. Sheldon Garon, "From Meiji to Hesei: The State and Civil Society in Japan," in *The State of Civil Society in Japan,* ed. Frank J. Schwartz and Susan J. Pharr (Cambridge, UK: Cambridge University Press, 2003), p. 43.

31. Stephen P. Osborne, ed., *The Voluntary and Non-Profit Sector in Japan: The Challenge of Change* (London: RoutledgeCurzon, 2003).

Chapter Fourteen

1. For a discussion of how Japan fits into the hierarchy of global cultures, see Samuel P. Huntington, *The Clash of Civilizations and the Remaking of World Order* (New York: Simon & Schuster, 1996), pp. 134–35, 137.

2. Koichi Kato, speech to the Foreign Correspondents' Club of Japan, April 15, 2005.

3. Murakami, "Earth in My Window," p. 141.

4. Kerr, *Dogs and Demons*, pp. 351–57.

5. Kennedy's thesis is examined at length in Paul Kennedy, *The Rise and Fall of Great Powers: Economic Change and Military Conflict from 1500 to 2000* (New York, Random House, 1987).

6. http://www.keizai-shimon.go.jp/english/publication/pdf/050419visionsummary_overview.pdf.

7. OECD Japan economic survey, January 2005.

8. "Why do Certain Countries Prosper?" by Virginia Postrel, *New York Times*, July 15, 2004.

9. Akio Mikuni and R. Taggart Murphy, *Japan's Policy Trap: Dollars, Deflation, and the Crisis of Japanese Finance* (Washington, D.C.: Brookings Institution Press, 2002), p. 30.

10. Dower, *Embracing Defeat*, p. 23.

11. Ibid., pp. 544–46.

12. Ibid., p. 546; see also Leon Hollerman, "International Economic Controls in Occupied Japan," *Journal of Asian Studies* 38 (August 4, 1979).

13. Edward J. Lincoln, *East Asian Economic Regionalism* (Washington, D.C.: Brookings Institution Press, 2004), pp. 30–36.

14. "Foreign Direct Investment and the Japanese Economy," American Chamber of Commerce in Japan, http://www.accj.or.jp/document_library/FDI/106842 4402.pdf.

15. *Japan Times*, February 1, 2005.

16. One American-born English teacher, David Aldwinkle, has taken up the cudgel against discrimination in Japan. Married to a Japanese woman, he has changed his legal name to Arudou Debito, has won Japanese citizenship, and campaigns against Japanese hot spring resorts, or *onsen*, who bar access to foreigners. His Web site is http://www.debito.org.

17. *Daily Yomiuri*, June 13, 2004.

18. UNHCR press release, January 18, 2005, http://www.unhcr.org.

19. http://www.mext.go.jp/english/topics/03072801.htm.

20. "Chinese Move to Eclipse U.S. Appeal in South Asia," *New York Times*, November 18, 2004.

Chapter Fifteen

1. See, especially, Douglas McGray, "Japan's Gross National Cool," *Foreign Policy*, May/June 2002.

2. Norimitsu Onishi, "Japanese Are Cold to Freed Hostages," *New York Times*, April 23, 2004.

3. Soseki quoted in Matsumoto Sannosuke, "The Roots of Political Disillusionment: 'Public' and 'Private' in Japan," in *Authority and the Individual in Japan*, ed. J. Victor Koschmann (Tokyo: University of Tokyo Press, 1978), p. 32.

4. For an admirable explication of the moral aims of the Bush administration, see James Mann, *The Rise of the Vulcans: The History of Bush's War Cabinet* (New York: Viking, 2004).

Dictionary of Japanese Terms

akuru-hara—alcohol harassment

amae—a close dependency, as between a mother and her son

anime—Japanese cartoon animation

boosozoku—a motorcycle gang or "tribe" of juvenile delinquents

combini—a convenience store such as 7-Eleven or Family Mart

enjo kosai—literally, "compensated dating," a euphemism for schoolgirl prostitution

furusato—the rural "hometown," often a quiet village, mythically rendered in Japanese stories and songs. Long after moving to the big city, many Japanese maintain some form of emotional or psychological longing for their hometown.

futoko—a young person who refuses to go to school

gaiatsu—pressure from outside, that is, from foreigners or foreign governments

gaman—endurance. Japanese often encourage each other with the phrases *Gambaro* and *Gambatte* (Persevere!).

geta—traditional raised clogs with soles made of wood

go-kon—a matchmaking party involving five couples

gonin-gumi—a surveillance organization first established during the Tokugawa period. Groups of five families were made responsible for the conduct of every other member of the group. If one family failed to follow regulations, all five were punished.

hanko—a Japanese seal, used for stamping business documents

hansei—self-criticism

haragei—literally, "abdomen sensitivity" or "belly talk," heart-to-heart communication in which words are not needed

hikikomori—social isolation; one who suffers from social isolation, never leaving his bedroom or home.

Hinomaru—the Japanese national flag, a red circle, representing the sun, on a white field

hito—a person

honne—honest feelings, seldom expressed, as opposed to superficial sentiments, or "face." See *tatemae.*

ie—the traditional kinship household

ijime—bullying

ikebana—the Japanese art of flower arranging

jiyu—freedom or independence

juku—Japanese cram school

kami—a spirit, usually found in nature

kanji—Japanese-style ideographs, or characters used for writing, imported from China

karoshi—death from overwork

kawaii—cute, or cuteness, a highly desirable quality among Japanese women; the Hello Kitty doll personifies *kawaii*

kimono—traditional Japanese robe, usually made of silk

kireru—to "snap," as in a sudden burst of violent rage

kokoro—the heart or spirit of something

kuro fune—black ships, a reference to Commodore Matthew Perry's voyage which ended Japan's two centuries of seclusion

mai homu shugi—period in Japan in which adults sought to emulate the American suburban lifestyle, purchasing such things as color TV sets and home air conditioners and many moved to new suburbs

Makudonarudo—McDonald's, the hamburger restaurant

manga—thick Japanese comic books

matsuri—a local festival, where residents don *happi* coats, dance traditional dances, and parade with portable shrines known as *omikoshi* in the streets to please the gods

meishi—the business cards that Japanese exchange at first introduction

mizu shobai—the "water world" of Japanese massage parlors, "Turkish" baths, and other venues for entertainment, prostitution, and illicit sex

mushi—to ignore someone

nihonjinron—an ideology that celebrates the unique, special quality of "being Japanese"

nomikai—the conjunction of *nomu*, to drink, and *kaigi*, meeting; literally, a drinking meeting, essential for conducting business in Japan

obi—the embroidered sash that binds a Japanese kimono

omamori—a colorful good-luck amulet purchased at a Shinto shrine

omiai—an arranged marriage

omikoshi—a portable Japanese shrine, carried on long poles during a *matsuri*

onigiri—a rice ball, Japan's most popular snack food

O-shogatsu—Japan's New Year celebration, its most important annual holiday; sometimes called *shogatsu*

otaku—literally, the honorific form of "home," but also a term used to describe someone who becomes such an obsessive fan of some cultural icon or cartoon character that he seldom leaves the house. Can also mean a "nerd" or "geek." Many fans of *anime* are said to be *otaku*.

pachinko—a form of gambling involving a pinball-like game

parasaito—"parasite single," a young adult, usually a woman, who works but chooses to live at home with her parents rather than marry or set up an independent household

saké—an alcoholic beverage fermented from rice which is usually clear and often tastes like a dry wine. The best saké is drunk cold.

samurai—a member of the Japanese warrior class

sarariman—a salaryman, a corporate worker

sembei—Japanese rice crackers

sensei—an honorific term meaning teacher

seppuku—ritual disembowelment with a short sword; a form of suicide *shabu shabu*—a Japanese dish of boiled beef dipped in sauce

shigarami—the "tangling vines" of corporate and social obligation, like the entangled vines of a Japanese wisteria

shikata ga nai—literally, "it can't be helped"

shinjinrui—literally, a "new human species"; a term used in Japan to define the seeming difference in behavior being expressed by the younger generation. Japanese commentators have noted various waves of such *shinjinrui*, who usually revert back to convention after their young adulthood passes.

shochu—a clear, distilled alcoholic beverage, like vodka, usually made from rice or buckwheat

shoji—translucent screens used to divide rooms or to obscure windows

soto—outside; see *uchi*

sushi—raw fish thinly sliced and embedded over a handful of rice. Raw fish served without the rice is known as *sashimi*.

tanin—a stranger; someone unrelated to you

tansu—a Japanese set of wooden dresser drawers

tatemae—superficial feelings, or "face," as opposed to honest feelings, or *honne*

torii—the large, ceremonial wooden entrance gate to a Shinto shrine, usually made of three pieces

uchi—inside; also the home. See *soto*.

utsubyo—depression

wa—harmony; also things "Japanese." *Wa-shoku* connotes Japanese food.

yakimono—Japanese ceramics; literally, "fired things"

zaibatsu—prewar Japanese industrial conglomerate. In postwar Japan, such conglomerates became known as *keiretsu*.

zoku—a tribe

Selected Bibliography

Anchordoguy, Marie, "Grappling with Globalization: The Case of Japan's Software Industry," in *Responding to Globalization,* ed. Aseem Prakash and Jeffrey A. Hart (London: Routledge, 2002).

Armstrong, Charles K., ed., *Korean Society: Civil Society, Democracy, and the State* (London: Routledge, 2002).

Barshay, Andrew E., *The Social Sciences in Modern Japan: The Marxian and Modernist Traditions* (Berkeley: University of California Press, 2004).

Bellah, Robert, *Habits of the Heart: Individualism and Commitment in American Life* (Berkeley: University of California Press, 1985).

———— *Imagining Japan* (Berkeley: University of California Press, 2003).

———— *Tokugawa Religion: The Cultural Roots of Modern Japan* (New York: Free Press, 1985).

Benedict, Ruth, *The Chrysanthemum and the Sword* (Boston: Houghton Mifflin, 1946).

Benfey, Christopher, *The Great Wave: Gilded Age Misfits, Japanese Eccentrics, and the Opening of Old Japan* (New York: Random House, 2003).

Burt, Ronald S., "The Network Structure of Social Capital," in *Research in Organizational Behavior,* volume 22, ed. Barry M. Staw and Robert I. Sutton (Greenwich, Conn.: JAI Press, 2000), http://gsbwww.uchicago.edu/fac/ronald.burt/research/NSSC.pdf.

————, "Structural Holes and Good Ideas," *American Journal of Sociology,* http://gsbwww.uchicago.edu/fac/ronald.burt/research/SHGI.pdf.

Chang, Kyung-sup, "Compressed Modernity and Its Discontents: South Korea in Transition," *Economy and Society* 28, no. 1 (February 1999).

————, "The State and Families in South Korea's Compressed Fertility Transition," unpublished.

Cho, Hyeon Beom, "A Study on the Protestant Discourse of Civilization in Early Modern Korea," *Korea Journal* 41, no. 1 (Spring 2001).

Ch'oe, Yong-ho, Peter H. Lee, and Wm. Theodore de Bary, *Sources of Korean Tradition from the Sixteenth to the Twentieth Century* (vol. 2) (New York: Columbia University Press, 2001).

Chung, Chai-sik, "Changing Perceptions of Japan," *Korean Studies* 19 (1995).

Clark, Donald, "History and Religion in Modern Korea: The Case of Protestant Christianity," in *Religion and Society in Contemporary Korea*, ed. Lewis R. Lancaster and Richard Karl Payne, Center for Korean Studies, Institute of East Asian Studies, University of California, Berkeley, 1997.

Coleman, Samuel, *Japanese Science from the Inside* (London: Routledge, 1999).

DeVos, George, *Socialization for Achievement: Essays on the Cultural Psychology of the Japanese* (Berkeley: University of California Press, 1973).

Diamond, Larry, and Byung-Kook Kim, ed., *Consolidating Democracy in South Korea* (Boulder, Colo.: Lynne Rienner Publishers, 2000).

Doi, Takeo, *The Anatomy of Dependence*, trans. John Bester (Tokyo: Kodansha International, 1973).

———— *The Anatomy of Self*, trans. Mark A. Harbison (Tokyo: Kodansha International, 1986).

Duus, Peter, *The Abacus and the Sword: The Japanese Penetration of Korea, 1895–1910* (Berkeley: University of California Press, 1995).

Einsenstadt, S.N., "Trust and Institutional Dynamics in Japan: The Construction of Generalized Particularized Trust," *Japan Journal of Political Science* 1 (2000): 53–72.

Fallows, James, *Looking at the Sun: The Rise of the New East Asian Economic and Political System* (New York: Pantheon Books, 1994).

Feldman, Ofer, ed., *Political Psychology in Japan: Behind the Nails That Sometimes Stick Out (and Get Hammered Down)* (Commack, N.Y.: Nova Science Publishers, 1998).

Freedman, Craig, "When Change Is Not Reform: Transforming the Japanese Economy," in *Economic Reform in Japan*, ed. Craig Freedman (Northampton, Mass.: Edward Elgar Publishing, 2001).

Fukuyama, Francis, *The Great Disruption: Human Nature and the Reconstitution of Social Order* (New York: Free Press, 1999).

—— *Trust: The Social Virtues and the Creation of Prosperity* (New York: Free Press, 1995).

Gordon, Andrew, *The Wages of Affluence: Labor and Management Practices in Postwar Japan* (Cambridge, Mass.: Harvard University Press, 1998).

Hara, Hideki, "Justification for Bullying among Japanese Schoolchildren," *Asian Journal of Psychiatry* 5 (2002): 197–204.

Hayashi, Chikio, and Yasumasa Kuroda, *Japanese Culture in Comparative Perspective* (Westport, Conn.: Praeger Publishers, 1997).

Huh, Dong-hyun, "Forms of Acceptance of Social Darwinism by the Korean Progressives of the 1880–1890s," *International Journal of Korean History* 2 (2001).

Inoguchi, Takashi, "Broadening the Basis of Social Capital in Japan," in *Democracies in Flux: The Evolution of Social Capital in Contemporary Society*, ed. Robert D. Putnam (New York: Oxford University Press, 2002).

Jansen, Marius B., ed., *Changing Japanese Attitudes Toward Modernization* (Princeton: Princeton University Press, 1965).

—— *The Making of Modern Japan* (Cambridge, Mass.: Belknap Press, 2000).

Kang, Wi Jo, *Christ and Caesar in Modern Korea* (Albany, N.Y.: State University of New York Press, 1997).

Katz, Richard, *Japanese Phoenix: The Long Road to Economic Revival* (Armonk, N.Y.: M.E. Sharpe, 2003).

—— *Japan, the System That Soured: The Rise and Fall of the Japanese Economic Miracle* (Armonk, N.Y.: M.E. Sharpe, 1998).

Kawai, Hayao, *The Japanese Psyche: Major Motifs in Fairy Tales of Japan*, trans. Hayao Kawai and Sachiko Reece (Woodstock, Conn.: Spring Publications, 1996).

Kim, Sunhyuk, *The Politics of Democratization in Korea: The Role of Civil Society* (Pittsburgh: University of Pittsburgh Press, 2000).

Kirmayer, Laurence J., "Psychopharmacology in a Globalizing World: The Use of Antidepressants in Japan," *Transcultural Psychiatry* 39, no. 3 (September 2002).

Kitayama, Shinobu, and Hazel Rose Markus, ed., *Emotion and Culture: Empirical Studies of Mutual Influence* (Washington, D.C.: American Psychological Association 1994).

Koschmann, J. Victor, ed., *Authority and the Individual in Japan: Citizen Protest in Historical Perspective* (Tokyo: University of Tokyo Press, 1978).

Kuhnen, Ulrich, and Daphna Oyserman, "Thinking about the Self Influences Thinking in General: Cognitive Consequences of Salient Self-concept," *Journal of Experimental Social Psychology* 38 (2002): 492–99.

Lee, Kwang-rin, "The Letters of Yu Kil-chun," *Korean Studies* 14 (1990).

Lee, Sang-ik, "On the Concepts of 'New Korea' Envisioned by Enlightenment Reformers," *Korea Journal* 40, no. 2 (Summer 2000).

Lim, Hy-Sop, "Historical Development of Civil Society Movements in Korea: Trajectories and Issues," *Korea Journal* 40, no. 3 (Autumn 2000).

Lincoln, Edward J., *Arthritic Japan: The Slow Pace of Economic Reform* (Washington, D.C.: Brookings Institution Press, 2001).

Lowell, A. Lawrence, *Biography of Percival Lowell* (New York: MacMillan, 1935).

Madsen, Robert A., "What Went Wrong: Aggregate Demand, Structural Reform and the Politics of 1990 Japan," MIT working paper 04.01, Center for International Studies, MIT.

Maruyama, Masao, "Theory and Psychology of Ultra-Nationalism," in *Thought and Behavior in Modern Japanese Politics*, ed. Ivan Morris (London: Oxford University Press, 1963).

Mathews, John A., "Fashioning a New Korean Model Out of the Crisis," Japan Policy Research Institute, working paper no. 46, May 1998.

McCreery, John L., *Japanese Consumer Behavior: From Worker Bees to Wary Shoppers* (Honolulu: University of Hawaii Press, 2000).

McDaniel, Edwin R., "Japanese Negotiating Practices: Low Context Communication in a High Context Culture," San Diego State University Center for International Business Education and Research (CIBER), Working Paper Series 1–112, 2001 (http://www-rohan.sdsu.edu/dept/ciber/112McDaniel.pdf).

Mikuni, Akio, and R. Taggart Murphy, *Japan's Policy Trap: Dollars, Deflation, and the Crisis of Japanese Finance* (Washington D.C.: Brookings Institution Press, 2002).

Miyake, Kazuo, and Kosuke Yamazaki, "Self-Conscious Emotions, Child-rearing and Child Psychopathology in Japanese Culture," in *Self-Conscious Emotions: The Psychology of Shame, Guilt, Embarrassment, and Pride,* ed. J.P. Tangney and K.W. Fischer (New York: Guilford Press, 1995).

Miyamoto, Masao, *Straitjacket Society: An Insider's Irreverent View of Bureaucratic Japan* (Tokyo: Kodansha International, 1995).

Moon, Chung-in, "In the Shadow of Broken Cheers: The Dynamics of Globalization in South Korea," in *Responding to Globalization,* ed. Aseem Prakash and Jeffrey A. Hart (London: Routledge, 2002).

Moon, Chung-in, and Sang-young Rhyu, "The State, Structural Rigidity and the End of Asian Capitalism," in *Politics and Markets in the Wake of the Asian Crisis,* ed. Richard Robinson et al. (New York: Routledge, 2000).

Morishima, Micho, *Why Has Japan Succeeded?* (New York: Cambridge University Press, 1982).

Morling, Beth, Shinobu Kitayama, and Yuri Miyamoto, "Cultural Practices Emphasize Influence in the United States and Adjustment in Japan," *Personality and Social Psychology Bulletin* 28, no. 3 (March 2002): 311–23.

Nisbett, Richard, *The Geography of Thought* (New York: Free Press, 2003).

Ohnuki-Tierney, Emily, *Illness and Culture in Contemporary Japan: An Anthropological View* (Cambridge, UK: Cambridge University Press, 1984).

Osborne, Stephen P., ed., *The Voluntary and Non-Profit Sector in Japan: The Challenge of Change* (London: RoutledgeCurzon, 2003).

Oyserman, Daphna, Heather M. Coon, and Markus Kemmelemeier, "Rethinking Individualism and Collectivism: Evolution of Theoretical Assumptions and Meta-Analyses," *Psychological Bulletin* 128, no. 1 (2002).

Pempel, T.J., *Regime Shift: Comparative Dynamics of the Japanese Political Economy* (Ithaca, N.Y.: Cornell University Press, 1998).

Reed, Steven R., *Making Common Sense of Japan* (Pittsburgh: University of Pittsburgh Press, 1993).

Retherford, Robert D., and Naohiro Ogawa, *Japan's Baby Bust: Causes, Implications and Policy Responses*, Population Health Series 118, East-West Center, Honolulu, 2005.

Roland, Alan, *In Search of Self in India and Japan* (Princeton, N.J.: Princeton University Press, 1988).

Sakaiya, Taiichi, *What Is Japan?* (*Nihon to wa nani ka?* published in 1991) (English edition: Tokyo: Kodansha International, 1993).

Saxer, Carl J., *From Transition to Power Alteration: Democracy in South Korea, 1987–1997* (New York: Routledge, 2002).

Schaede, Ulrike, *Change and Continuity in Japanese Regulation*, Zeitschrift für Japanisches Recht, 1. Jahggang 1996 Heft 1.

Scharf, Frederic A., "Yu Kil-chun, A Korean Abroad, 1881–1885. A Study of Korea's Emergence from Isolation at the End of the Yi Dynasty," Salem, Mass.: Peabody Essex Museum Collections, vol. 133, 1997.

Schwartz, Frank J., and Susan J. Pharr, ed., *The State of Civil Society in Japan* (Cambridge, UK: Cambridge University Press, 2003).

Song, Ho-keun, "Analysis of Participants in the New Social Movements in Korea," *Korea Journal* 40, no. 3 (Autumn 2000).

Stiglitz, Joseph, *Globalization and Its Discontents* (New York: W.W. Norton, 2003).

Triandis, H.C., *Individualism and Collectivism* (Boulder, Colo.: Westview Press, 1995).

Vereijken, C.M., J.M. Riksen-Walraven, and C.F. Van Lieshout, "Mother-Infant Relationships in Japan: Attachment, Dependency and Amae," *Journal of Cross-Cultural Psychology* 28, no. 4 (July 1997): 442–62.

Victoria, Brian, *Zen at War* (New York: Weatherhill, 1997).

Vogel, Ezra, *Japan as Number One: Lessons for America* (Cambridge, Mass.: Harvard University Press, 1979).

Watanabe, Hisako, "The Transgenerational Transmission of Abandonment," in *Infant and Toddler Mental Health*, ed. J. Martin Maldonado-Duran (American Psychiatric Publishing, 2002).

———— "Paranoia and Persecution in Modern Japanese Life," in *Even Paranoids Have Enemies: New Perspectives on Paranoia and Persecution*, eds. Joseph H. Berke et al. (New York: Routledge, 1998).

Weber, Max, *The Protestant Ethic and the Spirit of Capitalism: and Other Writings*, edited, translated, and with an introduction by Peter Baehr and Gordon C. Wells (New York: Penguin Books, 2002.)

Wells, Kenneth M., *New God, New Nation: Protestants and Self-Reconstruction Nationalism in Korea, 1896–1937* (Honolulu: University of Hawaii Press, 1990).

Yamada, Masahiro, *Japanese Family in Transition* (Tokyo: Foreign Press Center of Japan, 1998).

Yamagishi, Toshio, *Trust and Social Intelligence: The Evolutionary Game of Mind and Society* (Tokyo University Press, 1998). (English version never published; only available on Web: http://lynx.let.hokudai.ac.jp/members/yamagishi/english.htm.)

Yamagishi, Toshio, Karen S. Cook, and Motoki Watanabe, "Uncertainty, Trust, and Commitment Formation in the United States and Japan," *American Journal of Sociology* 104, no. 1 (July 1998).

Yamazaki, Kosuke, "Child and Adolescent Mental Health in Modern-Day Japan," in *Recent Progress in Child and Adolescent Psychiatry*, ed. Masanori Hanada (Tokyo: Springer-Verlag, 1999), pp. 231–45.

Yamazaki, Kosuke, Johji Inomata, and John Alex MacKenzie, "Self-Expression, Interpersonal Relations, and Juvenile Delinquency in Japan," in *The Role of Cul-*

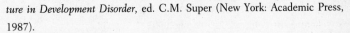

ture in Development Disorder, ed. C.M. Super (New York: Academic Press, 1987).

Yee Jaeyeol, "Network Analysis of Solidarity Ties among Social Movement Organizations," *Korea Journal* 40, no. 3 (Autumn, 2000).

Yoshikawa, Hiroshi, *Japan's Lost Decade* (Tokyo: International House of Japan, 2002).

Young, Jerome, "Morals, Suicide and Psychiatry: A View from Japan," *Bioethics* 16, no. 5 (2002): 414–24.

Yu, Chai-shin, ed., *Korea and Christianity* (Seoul: Korean Scholar Press, 1996).

Zucker, Lynne G., "Production of Trust: Institutional Sources of Economic Structure 1840–1920," in *Research in Organizational Behavior* 8 (1986): 53–111.

Index